RUPTURING ARCHITECTURE

RUPTURING ARCHITECTURE

Spatial Practices of Refuge in Response to War and Violence in Iraq, 2003–2023

Sana Murrani

BLOOMSBURY VISUAL ARTS
LONDON • NEW YORK • OXFORD • NEW DELHI • SYDNEY

BLOOMSBURY VISUAL ARTS
Bloomsbury Publishing Plc
50 Bedford Square, London, WC1B 3DP, UK
1385 Broadway, New York, NY 10018, USA
29 Earlsfort Terrace, Dublin 2, Ireland

BLOOMSBURY, BLOOMSBURY VISUAL ARTS and the Diana logo
are trademarks of Bloomsbury Publishing Plc

First published in Great Britain 2024

Cover design: Sana Murrani
Cover image: Ruptured map of Baghdad layered over an image of the blanket
Sana Murrani sought refuge in when she left Iraq in June 2003.

A catalogue record for this book is available from the British Library.

Library of Congress Cataloging-in-Publication Data
Names: Murrani, Sana, author.
Title: Rupturing architecture : spatial practices of refuge in response
to war and violence in Iraq, 2003-2023 / Sana Murrani.
Description: London ; New York : Bloomsbury, 2024. |
Includes bibliographical references and index.
Identifiers: LCCN 2024011075 (print) | LCCN 2024011076 (ebook) |
ISBN 9781350325340 (hardback) | ISBN 9781350325388 (paperback) |
ISBN 9781350325357 (pdf) | ISBN 9781350325364 (ebook)
Subjects: LCSH: Housing–Iraq. | Dwellings–Iraq. | Space–Social aspects. |
Architecture, Domestic–Iraq.
Classification: LCC HD7359.A3 M87 2024 (print) | LCC HD7359.A3 (ebook) |
DDC 307.3/3609567–dc23/eng/20240408
LC record available at https://lccn.loc.gov/2024011075
LC ebook record available at https://lccn.loc.gov/2024011076

ISBN: HB: 978-1-3503-2534-0
ePDF: 978-1-3503-2535-7
eBook: 978-1-3503-2536-4

Typeset by Integra Software Services Pvt. Ltd.
Printed and bound in Great Britain

To find out more about our authors and books visit www.bloomsbury.com
and sign up for our newsletters.

Dedicated to the enduring spirit of all Iraqis – those whose lives have been tragically lost, those who have been born into resilience and those who have grown up in the shadows of trauma. Your strength shapes this narrative.

This book is also a solemn tribute to the cherished memories of my maternal uncle, Dr Sabah Sam, a beacon of kindness and dedication. A veterinarian whose life was cruelly cut short by a roadside bomb in Baghdad, while he stood in line for fuel amidst the peak of sectarian strife. To my great aunt, Nadjia Murrani, a poet who gifted me my name and shared her profound literary talents with the world. Her legacy, a testament to the power of words, remained vibrant until her passing in Damascus as the Syrian revolution began, heralding a period of profound turmoil in 2011. And to my paternal grandmother, who found a reluctant sanctuary in Auckland, New Zealand, granted humanitarian refuge at the twilight of her life at 92. Though safety was hers at last, her heart remained with the homeland she was forced to leave during the dark days of 2006–7. Their stories, marked by displacement and loss, yet underscored by an unyielding connection to their roots, inspire every word penned in this narrative.

CONTENTS

ILLUSTRATIONS

PREFACE

As an architect with lived experience of war, trauma and loss, which I witnessed from the Iraq–Iran War until the aftermath of the 2003 invasion, I found that the concepts and conditions explored in this book gave me an understanding of the value of architecture that is beyond the usual concerns of professional standards, aesthetics and cultural sensibilities. Now, I value everyday spatial practices in violated homes and cities, and the indigenous making of architecture that stems from the volatile moments of trauma as much as it does from the history and ancestry and heritage of a place. I am captivated by the unconventional spaces that emerge or change function locally out of need, like my grandmother's outdoor clay oven that presented a potential hiding place during the sectarian violence in Baghdad between 2006 and 2008. I am inspired by the ingenious creativity and invention produced in times of difficulty by people in search of refuge, like the wayfinding skills developed by Iraqis when blast walls filled the streets of Baghdad throughout the first decade of the millennium. This is bottom-up architecture that is socially just, driven by the people and capable of change and adaptation in response to local needs. I do not, however, wish to glorify nor fetishize the impact of war and violence by focusing on such violated and traumatized spatial practices. War is ugly and the destruction and deterioration of cities that follow it have adverse effects on the quality of people's lives. Nonetheless, it is important that we examine these spatial practices in order both to recognize the scale of impact and to learn lessons so that we can be prepared for future crises. The first two chapters of this book establish a conceptual framework for understanding these volatile spatial practices. They position and contextualize trauma in spatial terms, while providing a methodological and ethical approach to the fieldwork detailed in Chapters 3 and 4. The book concludes with a call to action – a manifesto for spatial justice.

Over a span of eighteen months, I embarked on a deeply personal journey, engaging in numerous conversations and interviews with Iraqis, both within their homeland and in the diaspora. My aim was to delve into their lived and felt experiences, capturing the nuances of trauma as it manifests in place-making practices. Throughout the fieldwork part of the book, readers will encounter extensive quotations from these Iraqis, minimally edited to retain their authenticity.

These poignant narratives reveal the myriad ways in which individuals grapple with the shadows of violence, illustrating their resilience as they carve out, adapt and redefine places of refuge across various spatial scales. Through a careful analysis of their shared recollections, I discerned common threads and themes, which I have visually composed through maps. Not only do these maps serve as tangible reflections of their collective memories, but the act of mapping itself became a tool – a process to challenge and reshape new conversations in architecture.

In July 2023, I made the final touches to this book, marking two decades since I last set foot in Baghdad. A city that once embraced me in its vibrant tapestry now feels distant, not only in miles but also in memories. The mere thought of returning, even for a fleeting visit, has been a constant emotional turmoil. After militants claimed our family home in 2006, and as my loved ones dispersed, seeking refuge elsewhere, the Iraq I cherished transformed into a land of shadows and silhouettes. Venturing back seemed daunting; I feared it would be more harrowing to confront this altered reality than to cling to the nostalgic remnants of my homeland. Yet, penning this narrative has been a therapeutic journey. It was not solely a means of reconciling with my past, but a shared healing with many Iraqis who generously bared their souls, intertwining their tales of pain, hope, loss and resilience with mine. Through these pages, we collectively mourn and celebrate the Iraq that was, and envision the Iraq that might still be.

FOREWORD

In *Rupturing Architecture*, world-leading scholar and experimental architect Dr Sana Murrani expertly guides the reader through the complex legacies of the war, violence and displacement endured and resisted by the people of Iraq between 2003 and 2023. Intimacy and care are inherent within the deep listening, theorizing, mapping and writing that underpin this book, leaving us, at the forefront of our minds, with the lingering challenge of comprehending how the people of Iraq have navigated the unimaginable loss and trauma resulting from acts of genocide, urbicide and domicide, whilst embracing the intensity of the love, friendship and hope that continues to propel people to forge a more just path for the future.

As Dr Murrani – who in 2003 was living with her family in the Al-Amiriyah district of Iraq's capital city, Baghdad – and her interlocutors narrate their memories and map their journeys, so too do they carefully expound the meaning they seek to find from their varying locations and positions (whether in Iraq, in exile or the broader diaspora). In so doing, their accounts are informed by personal experiences of violence and of both seeking and making refuge, and are firmly embedded in their conceptualizations and theorizations of everyday life and imagining better futures. It is upon the foundations of the knowledge shared by men and women from across the cities, towns and mountainous regions of Iraq, including Christians, Muslims, Yazidis and Kurds, that *Rupturing Architecture* offers a powerful manifesto, a call to action to 'us', the reader, the collective, irrespective of our individual positionality, to carefully account for the multiple, often overlapping or contiguous ruptures that have punctuated Iraq's recent history, with a view to tracing the contours of a more inclusive and just world.

While the wounds of the past remain unhealed and the scars continue to be both visible and invisible, this vital book demands that we go beyond the quest for short-term 'plasters', and instead requires a deeper understanding of how violence itself does not simply destroy, but also creates. It requires a recognition that violence is productive in seemingly contradictory and paradoxical ways: just as it has the potential to destroy all tenses at the same time (past, present and future), so too is it creative in that it lays the foundations for what is both possible and imaginable. While carefully documenting the ruptures and resistances of the past, it is the continuous and the futural which is so present throughout *Rupturing Architecture*, urging us as readers to continue asking ourselves: What are we to do with this knowledge, what are the implications for us? What is the meaning of this for the way we know and respond to the world around us today and tomorrow? How does the intimate, personal and political knowledge shared with us through these pages not only enable but in fact require us to respond differently to wars and displacements around the world?

As we read this book, we are reminded of the mass-scale destruction across Iraq that the international media and politicians reported (and concealed) over the course of over two decades, but more-so, the power of this book is that the nature and impacts of violence repeatedly 'come home' to the reader. Erupting into people's lives and homes were the bullets that killed and maimed loved ones; shattering their windows and becoming embedded in their walls; splintering headboards and the possibility of rest; and penetrating the spines of books like the one in your hand right now. Just as spaces and objects associated with the domestic and the personal came to be equated with danger and risk, so too were they remade as spaces of potential refuge. The dining table where I sat to read this manuscript and to write this foreword was a hiding place and refuge for the author and her family and friends. While I myself have no tanoor (clay oven) to either bake my family bread or to hide in, Dr Murrani's grandmother's tanoor both made bread and made the future possible, just as my daughter's grandmother did in Baddawi refugee camp as she sought to nourish and protect her family in times of extreme hardship and war in North Lebanon. Throughout the research for and writing of this book, but also in our reading of it, the feminist adage that 'the personal is political' could not be more pertinent.

As the holder of two passports issued by European countries whose troops occupied Iraq, like many readers of this book, I have had the privilege of never personally having experienced war or displacement. Nonetheless, my reading of *Rupturing Architecture* is inflected both by my pre-existing – partial and mediated – knowledge of the ongoing impacts of the occupation of Iraq (based on what I have read, the documentaries and films I have watched, and the displaced people I have spoken with and listened to around the world), and also by the vicarious memories and visceral stories of my husband's time spent in a bomb shelter as a child in Baddawi camp in Lebanon, as violence shattered the world above, below and within, leaving unspeakable and often unspoken traumas that endure to this day. The bomb shelters which Yousif M. Qasmiyeh and I are continuing to write about together and separately as part of the Imagining Futures research project are now empty and 'invisible' to the untrained eye, yet, we have argued, they are simultaneously 'unarchived pasts' of the camp: they remain as the subterranean traces of the destruction to which the camp and its residents were subjected in the 1980s and 1990s, but they are also the constitutive foundations of parts of Baddawi camp itself as it has been built and rebuilt over time.

I could not but return to these vicarious memories and our ongoing research into the bomb shelters of Baddawi camp as I revisited Dr Murrani's account of Al-Amiriyah shelter, one of two near her home in Baghdad in which she and her family had previously sought sanctuary, which notoriously came to be immortalized in personal, national and international memory after all of those people seeking refuge there were killed by two American 'smart missiles' at the start of the first Gulf War. This, the single attack with the highest number of casualties in the first Gulf War, transformed Al-Amiriyah shelter from a 'symbol of refuge [into] a metaphor for trauma'. It led, as Dr Murrani's interlocutors explain, to Iraqis refusing to enter bomb shelters ever again. In the midst of the urbicidal violence – the killing of people and cities – spaces designed to preserve life and living became spaces of death. As derelict buildings, such spaces remain as indelible scars on the urban landscape. Even after demolition, the trauma of that space will always remain. It is, Dr Murrani reminds us, only through reckoning with both the visible and invisible wounds and wounding of diverse spaces and places that social and spatial justice can be achieved.

Even after closing the covers of the book, I continue to hear the echoes of Al-Amiriyah. For it is from such violent ruptures, and from the void created from and remaining in the aftermath, that echoes emerge and continue to reverberate. These are echoes that belong to the dead and the living, as spine-chillingly rendered in the searing performance of 'Happened at Al-Amiriya' by the renowned Iraqi oud player, Naseer Shamma.[1] Shamma's painful rendering reminds us that memories can and must be rearticulated and revisited to archive both the voids and their echoes. In centralizing the echo, as Shamma himself repeats to us, he not only seeks to archive the trauma and the suffering of the specific crime of Al-Amiriyah, but also to draw us to the continuity of ruptured spaces and lives across time and space, in Iraq and further afield, including the echoes of other shelters. As readers and listeners we must recall that remembering is an active process: it has to do with the will to change things. From the rupture, there is born the echo and the need to respond.

Unable to seek refuge in either their homes or the 'purpose-built shelters' which came to be equated with such intense loss, the intimate story of what Dr Murrani conceptualizes as 'ruptured domesticity' also sheds essential light on the silenced story of internal displacement, a story silenced due to the prioritization and hypervisibility of international border crossings, or at least particular border crossings (i.e. into Europe). While European and North American audiences may view Iraq as a 'producer of refugees', it is internal displacement – within and across urban and rural areas and geographies – which has numerically been most salient and yet remains so ignored and under-explored. By placing refuge-seeking

[1]Oresteia, 'Naseer Shamma - Happened at Al-Amiriya', YouTube, 2010. Available online: https://www.youtube.com/watch?v=V7a_K6kQ8p0 (accessed 29 May 2024).

and refuge-making at the core of her analysis, and with meticulous attention to the heterogeneity of the people of Iraq, *Rupturing Architecture* insists on going beyond and against the fetishization of the figure of the refugee, and challenges the epistemic violence characterizing the ongoing relative invisibility and inaudibility of internally displaced people. Contra hierarchies of suffering or worth, the author offers a space for us to learn from the fraught and incomplete quest for safety of Baghdadi ceramicist Basma Al-Azzawi and her daughter – whose claim for asylum in the UK remains outstanding – alongside the ongoing precarity experienced by Yazidi survivors such as writer Shahab Sameer and biologist Amera Ibrahim due to the domicidal violence to which they and the residents of their villages in different parts of Sinjar were subjected. Interweaving such narratives with deep-maps, photographs and beautiful if heart-rending graphics, *Rupturing Architecture* reminds us of the importance of challenging processes that both solidify existing and create new divisions and tensions, whether under the guise of 'securitization' or 'reconstruction', or through rendering refugees hypervisible (as threats or victims), while internally displaced people remain invisible and silenced.

Beyond and against the walls that divide (and constitute the very division between) 'us' and 'them', *Rupturing Architecture* most powerfully echoes the call for 'us' to pursue social and spatial justice for all. In her centralization of the 'ethics of care in the making and re-making of refuge', Dr Murrani insists on seeing – and iteratively mapping – refuge itself as resistance, but also demands collective responsibility. In her book, she not only offers the very best of auto-ethnographic analysis alongside her critical and nuanced explorations of what she rightly conceptualizes as 'the progression, rather than production, of knowledge-making' with her interlocutors, but also, I would argue, shares the kernel of what the Chicana theorist, Gloria Anzaldúa embodied as 'auto-teoría' (auto-theory). Rather than the 'auto' being an individual in isolation, Dr Murrani's *Rupturing Architecture* is an important book for us all precisely through its insistence on critically theorizing the self-in-relation, and committing to creatively co-producing and co-progressing knowledge in our quest for justice as a community of interlocutors and readers alike.

Elena Fiddian-Qasmiyeh

Professor of Migration and Refugee Studies, Director of the Refuge in a Moving World network and Co-Director of the UCL-Migration Research Unit, University College London (UCL), 6 October 2023.

ACKNOWLEDGEMENTS

It is with deep gratitude and humility that I acknowledge the contributions of all those who journeyed with me on this exploration. First, I extend my sincerest appreciation to the fifteen Iraqis who bravely shared their experiences of two decades of trauma. Their strength and openness in sharing their stories and photographs from Basra, Babylon, Mahmudiyah, Baghdad, Sinjar, Mosul, Sulaimani and Alqosh made this book possible. To Dr Nawrast Sabah, Abrar Wadi, Professor Jaafar Jotheri, Sanar Hasan, Dr Dhirgham Alobaydi, Dr Ula Merie, Dr Farah Murrani, Dr Zeinab Shuker, Basma Al-Azzawi, Shahab Sameer, Amera Ibrahim, Raad Sultan, Ali Al-Baroodi, Dr Rozhen Kamal Mohammed-Amin and Dr Rawaa Qasha, I express my deepest admiration and gratitude.

My heartfelt thanks also go to the esteemed researchers and experts around the world whose contributions significantly shaped this work. Their insights and extensive experience with spatial practices in and about the Global South provided me with invaluable direction throughout the writing of this book. My gratitude extends to Professor Nasser Rabbat, Professor Anooradha Iyer Siddiqi, Professor Ghada Alslik, Professor Camillo Boano, Murad Ismael, Dr Ammar Azzouz and Professors Sandi Hilal and Alessandro Petti. I am deeply thankful to Louise Chapman, the editor who maintained my voice while enhancing my English, as I wrote my first monograph in a second language.

I am deeply thankful for the constant guidance of my mentor, Professor Michael Punt, who encouraged me to embark on the writing of this book, and who has supported my career for the past twenty years. I am also grateful for the unwavering support of Professor Eleanor Robson, whose faith in my work and shared love for Iraq have been pivotal in this journey. My admiration for Professor Elena Fiddian-Qasmiyeh, my role model, knows no bounds. Her commitment to the field and the far-reaching impact of her work are truly awe-inspiring, and I am thankful to have been able to include her voice in the foreword of this book. I would also like to thank my research assistants, Dr Laura Hopes, Merrydith Russell and Jordan Beh, without whose valuable assistance the spatial practices outlined in this book would not have seen the light of day. This gratitude extends to my Master of Architecture and PhD students, and research and faculty colleagues at the University of Plymouth, who have provided a supportive environment for my research.

It has been an absolute pleasure to collaborate with Bloomsbury on this book. Many thanks go to my publisher James Thompson, commissioning editor Alex Highfield and editorial assistant Ros O'Cleirigh, for supporting this work. I am grateful also to the British Institute for the Study of Iraq (BISI) for the funding that supported the iterative process of map-making and the online archive, both of which were instrumental in developing the methodology of this work. A special thanks goes to the London School of Economics Middle East Centre for funding an exhibition of the work, with the help of their events coordinator extraordinaire, Nadine Almanasfi. My conversations with previous and current centre directors, Professor Toby Dodge and Dr Michael Mason, as well as deputy director Dr Robert Lowe, opened up further research collaborations and avenues, all of which have jointly influenced the writing of a policy piece on Iraq through an Arts and Humanities Research Council (AHRC) Impact Accelerator fund. This confluence of funding and support has truly brought this work to life.

I reserve my deepest thanks for my parents, Selma and Waleed. My mother, Selma, with her tenacity for learning and culinary expertise, has been a beacon of personal growth. My father, Waleed, a respected Professor of Genetics and Biostatistics, has provided the academic path I have endeavoured to emulate. My siblings, Samer, Sally and Sura, have been invaluable in this journey. Their continual encouragement, combined with memories of shared spaces and moments of levity and introspection, have provided both solace and motivation. The broader constellation of my extended family has offered unwavering support, for which I remain eternally grateful. I dedicate this work to my wonderful children, Nina and Ramsey, whose support has been my greatest motivation. I fervently hope for a peaceful future for you both. A nod to our family dog for his patience, his silent company during countless hours of writing has been a source of serene comfort. My gratitude to Tom, my husband, is boundless. Over two decades, he has been my rock, offering unwavering support, love and understanding. His dedication, especially over the past eighteen months, in managing familial responsibilities, has granted me the space and time crucial to the fruition of this work, to you I am forever grateful. Thank you.

INTRODUCTION: THE SPATIAL STRUCTURE OF *RUPTURING ARCHITECTURE*

Rupturing Architecture uncovers and examines locally negotiated, spatial approaches to the architecture of domestic, urban and border spaces in times of war, conflict and displacement. The first two chapters of this book provide the conceptual and methodological framing for the diverse spatial practices that are critically examined in the latter two chapters. The book proposes and then analyses the emergence of spaces of refuge as places of resistance, and emphasizes the significance of the multiplicity of spatial practices in response to trauma – the abundance of place-making and refuge-making forms of spatial practices and actions operating at different scales and frames of sociality and power. As people struggle with their geography (Said 2000; Soja 2010), resisting and challenging injustices generated by the trauma of war and violence, they simultaneously coexist with violence. This coexistence is marked by the different forms of spatial practices they produce along the way. A multiplicity of ruptures (place-making following 'place-wounding' [Kearney 2016]) is then conceptualized within material objects, home-places, new urban and rural connections, and forms of drifting and mobility. Using maps, memory-work and lived/felt experiences as case studies from Iraq's recent history, this book explores the interface between indigenous spatial responses of refuge, and people's dynamism, creativity and imagination within the protracted spatial struggle of trauma.

The book adopts a feminist, postcolonial and post-structuralist, research-based spatial practice as a framework for a deep mapping (Springett 2019) methodological approach. It crosses spatio-temporal disciplinary boundaries performatively (Della Dora 2009) in order to connect layers of knowledge in imaginative, ruptured and violated spatial practices. *Rupturing Architecture* is thus an examination of transient changes to the built environment that serve to yield new spatial approaches to spaces of refuge (Daiute 2017). The book utilizes a multimodal methods approach, which combines textual analysis, storytelling through interviews with Iraqis (either currently living in Iraq, in exile/diaspora or on the borders in camps) and case studies of architectural buildings and events. These are typically supported by visual material depicting ruptured spaces of refuge, counter-maps provided through multiple dialogues between the researcher and the participants. The work engages with Iraqis' constant struggle with spatial trauma, and reveals how they influence and shape new, just spatial practices for refuge-making in times of crises. This book asks:

- What possibilities do negotiated, disrupted and ruptured spaces of refuge offer for the reframing of spatial practices, particularly in post-war architectural responses to trauma?
- How can place-making practices in trauma-ridden geographies contribute to the field of spatial justice?

The use of the suffix *-ing* in the word *rupturing* in the title of this book provides a deliberate emphasis, presenting a continuous verb that signifies intent and action unfolding in the moment. *Rupturing Architecture* focuses on the acts and processes of trauma and violence, rather than merely their spatial products. The resulting spatial practices from these actions are continuously made, destroyed while being remade, and both receive and impart meaning over time. In psychological and philosophical thought, this process is referred to as 'plasticity' (Malabou 2012). It is inherent in our brain's ability to cope with and react to trauma, and is fundamental to the very nature of trauma and memory, which serve as pivotal frames for the unfolding spatial practices throughout this book. I align this concept of plasticity with the fluidity of 'map-making' (Rose-Redwood et al. 2020), especially through the counter-maps and deep maps that arise from events, history and actions interwoven with modes of resistance and the creation of spaces of refuge. I utilize a palimpsestic (Dillon 2007) approach to deep mapping that delves into ruptured events, time, place and memory performatively, further fragmenting the remembered and imagined spatial practices. This process yields a variety of spatial practices of refuge that span both time and space.

Employing practices of othering (Petrescu 2007) and thirding (Soja 1996) in place-making paves the way for a dynamic critical spatial practice where refuge surpasses mere fixed spatiality and instead encompasses movement, mobility, memory and imagination. This dynamic forms the crux of the performativity inherent in the spatial practices of refuge discussed in this work. Hence, this book critically reveals diverse spatial traumas between 2003 and 2023 in Iraq, examining them performatively across the concepts of rupturing, place-making and place-wounding, all via map-making. Such fluidity in the emergent spatial practices of refuge necessitates the use of corresponding processual and iterative multimodal research methods. Navigating the complexities of constantly shifting concepts, events and spaces in research practice poses a distinct challenge. The inconsistency and unpredictability of these elements require an approach that is not only adaptable but also transient. Traditional methods or fixed perspectives might not capture the intricacies of such fleeting phenomena adequately. Therefore, in the face of such instability, there is a pressing need for transient methods in creative research practice. Only through such flexible creative tools can we competently address, decipher and compose the multifaceted nature of these evolving geographies.

The book is a culmination of a decade's research into the uncertainty, dynamism, incompleteness and messiness of sudden changes to the built environment inflicted by war, conflict, displacement or any other major crisis. These sudden changes not only physically alter the built environment but also require the people affected to adapt and modify their way of life, creating new spatial practices dictated by the necessity to seek refuge (Murrani 2016). The book gives voice and visibility to Iraqis and their spatial practices of refuge, and reveals the informal and indigenous making and remaking at three levels of spatiality: home, urban and border spaces. The book focuses on the collective memories and the lived and felt experiences of people subjected to such events in the context of Iraq's recent history. This spans the 2003 US-led invasion, the sectarian violence between 2006 and 2008, atrocities committed by the Islamic State of Iraq and Syria (ISIS), also known as Daesh, in 2014 against the Yazidi community in Sinjar (to the northwest of Iraq) and Mosul, the 2019 Tishreen Movement (also known as the October Movement – Tishreen is the Arabic word for October), the Covid-19 pandemic and the manifestation of climate crises in Iraq, up to 2023.

The scarcity of research about the region concerning its informal refuge-making spatial practices has also made it necessary to focus on Iraq, as has Iraq's diverse range of traumas and social, political and spatial struggles across history. The book is a homage to all Iraqis; those still with us and those whose lives have been lost over decades of war and destruction. The memories, events, case studies and data collected for this book have all been borne from strenuous conditions such as trauma, violence and forced displacement. But as well as focusing on these traumas, the book also sheds light on people's creative responses to these extreme conditions in their search for refuge. These conditions pivot on the plasticity, multiplicity and dynamism of concepts, such as trauma and memory, refuge and place-making/wounding, home and domesticity, and creativity and imagination, just as much as they materialize within the incompleteness and messiness of their geographies.

Although the idea for this book has existed in my mind since I left Iraq two decades ago, I did not have the emotional strength to embark on the journey of writing it until 2021, when I was able to draw together the transdisciplinary research methods, concepts and ideas I have been working on throughout my academic life. While the context of the book focuses on Iraq in particular, its conceptual framework, methods and outcomes can be utilized within any other trauma-related contexts, especially those of war, conflict or forced displacement. What the book does not do, however, is engage deeply with the political volatility in Iraq and the multi-structural forms of power that emerge where politics and religion mix. Furthermore, although it acknowledges the efforts of reconstruction and peacebuilding by local and international architects and agencies such as the United Nations, amongst others, it does not examine or critique the success or failure of such approaches, especially concerning heritage preservation. Equally, the book does not engage with financial aspects such as the lack – or indeed surplus – of funding for these reconstruction efforts. Examples of these include the UNESCO project to revive Mosul after ISIS incursions, the controversy and competition concerning the reconstruction of the Nuri Mosque, and the Royal Institute of British Architects (RIBA)-led competition for the new Iraqi Parliament building in Baghdad, which was won by a London-based practice, Assemblage, then granted to Zaha Hadid, whose proposal was placed third in the competition.

Another important element that should be mentioned about this book is that, although it includes statistics, it does not engage in debates through numbers, for example, the number of homes destroyed during the war, or the number of people who have lost their lives or been forcibly displaced during certain events. I have chosen not to build arguments around such statistics because the data never seemed to reflect the sheer pain and agony endured by Iraqis, nor did they reflect the actual realities of certain situations (whether political, religious or social), given that these highly volatile situations do not move, change or progress linearly. One final important point to mention is the timing of the start of the events included in this book. In the lead up to the 2003 invasion of Iraq, social media was not in operation. Iraqis had no mobile phones, access to internet was restricted and search engines were censored during the oppressive political regime. Even digital cameras were a rarity at that time. This muting of voices within and the shielding of information from outside Iraq meant that the US-led offensive, 'Shock and Awe', was able further to traumatize Iraqis (inside and outside Iraq) more than any other nation (neighbouring or further afield). The resulting lack of social media coverage of the war dampened its impact internationally and diluted the extent of its trauma and violence both socially and spatially, not to mention politically. More importantly, it alienated – and continues to alienate – Iraqis from the rest of the world as they struggled for survival, for refuge and protection, and for a better future.

Rupturing Architecture concludes with a model of just and socially driven spatial practice to provide alternative responses to the destruction of homes and cities caused by war, civil unrest or natural disasters. It builds its spatial justice through amplifying the muted voices of ordinary Iraqis by documenting how they have engaged with the incessant changes to their everyday built environment. It conceptualizes and contextualizes these voices through a research-based spatial practice centred on the nuanced interplay of spatiality, encompassing the domestic, urban and border realms. At its heart lies an exploration of spaces of refuge and becoming – spaces that remain open-ended, negotiated and reimagined. Rooted in the tumultuous backdrop of Iraq between 2003 and 2023, the narrative delves into the profound complexities that arise from the protractedness of ruptures and their associated trauma. Such conditions demand recognition of the dynamic and volatile nature of spatial practices, from wartime-modified homes to the appropriation of buildings as spaces of refuge. A central theme is the intricate relationship between spatial trauma and memory which is approached by drawing on its meaning and applications across the fields of architecture, geography and psychology. The text pivots on the complex and incomplete dependency between creative spatial reactions to trauma and the ways in which these traumatic events shape collective and individual memories. By situating these spatial practices in the lived realities of Iraq, the work avoids mere theoretical musings, grounding itself in the country's locality, spatial reality and historic struggles. The book's adoption of a feminist spatial practice gives it a unique lens. It grapples with different forms of struggle over refuge-making practices, intertwining dynamic concepts such as place-making and 'place-wounding' (Kearney 2016). Furthermore, it contextualizes Edward Soja's (2010) 'spatial justice' within a Middle Eastern context.

Underpinning this exploration is the compelling notion of viewing refuge as an act of resistance always in the making. Such a perspective is innately political, reframing spatial practices as a form of political practice. Relying on a creative, multimodal methodology, the work seeks to set boundaries for a just spatial practice, considering the role of memory in shaping post-war responses. Building upon Daniele Rugo's (2023) insights on 'art practice' as a lens to understand conflict, the spatial stories conveyed through maps in this text serve a disruptive purpose. These maps, continuously evolving in their details, scales and meanings, challenge conventional representations of past traumas and emerge as spatial possibilities and tools for practices of refuge-making. In its conclusion, the book proposes a manifesto that recognizes rupture as a transformative tool. This reframing of rupture as a constructive process as well as being a destructive force paves the way for a fresh understanding of refuge. The book proposes a form of spatial justice that transcends physicality, the narrative dives into the depths of human memories, trauma and displacement, underscoring their role in spatial practices. With an emphasis on place-wounding and place-making, this vision of spatial justice champions a palimpsestic approach, urging a proactive integration of these concepts into spatial and urban studies. The resulting spaces of refuge transcend the meaning of shelter and encapsulate other forms of action: those of resistance and reclamation. In addition to the introduction provided in the paragraphs above, the spatial structure of the book is divided into five further sections.

Chapter 1, 'The positionality of protracted rupture', positions the book conceptually and delves deep into the methodological approach and the ethics associated with it. The chapter critically defines architectures and spatial practices within the concept of rupture, siting them between vernacular informality and humanitarian forms of inhabitation. It further identifies 'difference', which is integral to the meanings of 'justice' within these spatial practices (Young 2011). Utilizing 'frames of war' (Butler 2009) as a lens, the chapter conceptualizes and underscores the dialectical nature of rupture: on one hand, it signifies trauma induced by war and violence, on the other, it embodies the spatial practices formed in response to such traumatic conditions. This dichotomy positions rupture both as an unfamiliar disruption and as the familiar coping mechanism, echoing the dynamics between spatial violence and its subsequent spatial adaptations. The chapter places emphasis on the multifaceted notion of refuge. While conventionally tied to displacement, at its core, refuge captures both a static place-based practice and acts of drifting and mobility in seeking refuge. The chapter casts a focused spotlight on the struggle of Iraqis over their geographies. It provides an immersive deep dive into Iraq's history with violence. By framing the broader narratives of foreign invasion, sectarian violence and the rise of ISIS against the more localized frames of refuge and displacement, the chapter sketches a multidimensional picture of the spatial practices emerging from Iraq's layered past.

Of pivotal importance, the chapter introduces a novel use of deep mapping methodology. This approach goes beyond mere data collection, underscoring the integral roles of memory, storytelling, reflexive activism and autoethnographic methods. Deep maps emerge as dynamic tools that delve deeply into trauma layers, memory and latent spatial possibilities. They transcend mere representations, unearthing untapped terrains and democratizing the realm of knowledge production. Deep mapping encapsulates traumatic narratives, memories and lived experiences, amplifying often silenced voices within communities. In conclusion, the chapter seamlessly integrates discussions on the different scales and perspectives emerging within urban and domestic practices. It posits that the spatial practices explored are characterized by fluid transitions between domestic, urban and border spheres, resonating with the inherent resilience and adaptability of Iraqis. It further sets the scene for the following chapters and unpacks people's struggle to protect themselves and the frames through which their struggle, trauma and creativity are negotiated, remembered and imagined.

Chapter 2, 'Siting trauma spatially: Negotiated and centralized spatial responses from the Global North and South', explores how we locate spatial trauma (focusing particularly on geo/spatial-trauma [Pain 2021]) and violence by initiating a dialogue between different types of structures – whether shelter, dwelling or refuge. The chapter examines, from the perspectives of both the Global North and the Global South, how pre-war preparations, civil and military defence, and warfare strategies altered home, domestic, urban and camp sites. It uses examples of shelters and spaces of refuge created ahead of the Second World War and Cold War in Britain, Europe, America and Japan to express how such spaces affected people's lives, instilling both fear and comfort. In contrast, the chapter brings into focus the Global South's more informal and immediate refuge-making spaces, spotlighting the disparity in spatial responses between the North and South. Amplifying these discussions are voices from experts in architecture and spatial practice, shedding light specifically on the Middle Eastern context. The chapter argues that despite their geographical diversity, war-induced traumas universally manifest as spatially influenced, locally shaped and politically varied experiences, offering avenues for expanded models of alternative spatiality.

The chapter presents a fluid map, illustrating the boundless, fragile and prolonged plasticity binding the book's core themes. This fluidity resonates with the intricate territorial and ethnic tapestries of the region in question, focusing on Iraq. Emphasizing the significance of scales and perspectives, the chapter underscores the need to critically assess the geographies of spatial practices, tracing their evolution and positioning in a global context. The chapter culminates by emphasizing the criticality of the origins of these scales and perspectives, as they contribute to constructing an expanded model of a just spatiality, while comparing perspectives from both the Global North and South.

Across Chapters 1 and 2, knowledge is further located and positioned through analysis of interviews with key thinkers and practitioners from the fields of architecture and spatial practice. These individuals engage in knowledge creation in the Global South in relation to notions of dwelling, refuge and heritage through historicity and postcoloniality, to cultivate a new sense of spatiality in response to trauma.

Chapter 3, 'Creative negotiations in spaces of refuge and memory: Material objects, home and domesticity, the urban and borders', unthreads the conceptual complexity, creativity and multiplicity of spatial practices for refuge-making put forward in the first two chapters. These responses to trauma and negotiated intimate memory are explored through four scales: material objects, home and domesticity, the urban, and forced displacement in borders and peripheries (camps and informal settlements) relevant to the impact of the event. Featured heavily in this chapter are processes of deep mapping and memory-work with cognitive maps, supported by the lived and felt experiences of Iraqis (inside and outside Iraq) as described in interviews. The chapter delves into the diverse meanings of refuge, as well as other spaces and structures of negotiated belonging, seen here as sites of resistance. It goes on to map, both ontologically and topologically, concepts such as the making of intimacy, home, domesticity, the urban and borders. It further examines the interplay between material objects, home and urban geographies, and the enduring search for refuge amidst the chaos of war and violence in Iraq. With the backdrop of violence, these objects and spaces undergo a transformative journey, marked by distinct discursive and performative practices highlighted through the creative practice of mapping. Terms such as ruptured domesticity, urban warfare and forced displacement encapsulating the disruptions to life experienced between 2003 and 2023, are unpacked through textual and creative practice.

The practice of map-making becomes pivotal, with maps envisioned as intricate frames, capturing and portraying traumatic memories across time and space. Drawing from Paolo Boccagni's (2022) perspectives on 'homing practices', and the palimpsestic map-making method, memories are layered to offer multi-dimensional narratives. A series of fifteen maps charted by Iraqis (textually and visually) emerges, standing as a testament to the hardships faced and as a celebration of the resilience and adaptability exhibited in the pursuit of refuge. Concluding the chapter are reflections and projections on the future of spatial practice marked by trauma.

Chapter 4, 'Architectural structures and disrupted memory of refuge in relation to time', examines, through case studies, how time and memory have an impact on places of resistance and spaces of refuge. It also analyses how the longer duration of some conflicts can alter the architectural structures associated with them – from shelters to blast walls, to the reappropriation of derelict buildings for refuge during political protest, to informal settlements and other structures and events. The narrative is organized thematically around three core concepts: sudden rupture, ruptures of mobility and movement, and temporal rupture. These themes are critically aligned with the conceptual framing of rupture put forward in Chapter 1. The chapter sheds light on the way in which time, memory and protractedness during times of rupture, trauma and violence can strip spaces of refuge of their integral and quintessential characteristics. In other words, in some cases these can shift from being spaces of protection (refuge, safety, agency, etc.) to volatile and threatening zones. The case studies provide a profound understanding of how architectural spaces can embody different uses and functions, dynamically responding to both sudden and protracted events over time, especially amid war and violence. Key to these narratives are both violent and peaceful social actions, which result in diverse, emergent spatial practices. By dissecting the different scales of violence, the chapter underscores their inherently political and social nature, showcasing the multifaceted relationship between temporality and the protractedness of trauma, and how they manifest in various spatial structures.

Equally crucial are theories of memory, touching on both individual and collective memories and the intricate processes of remembering and forgetting. These theories intertwine with the historicity and creative imaginaries of place-making, emphasizing the creation of spatial knowledge that bridges the past and future. Furthermore, the chapter explores in depth the social, political, environmental and spatial frames of trauma and violence in a cross-sectional way, exposing a spatiality of multiple scales. It also emphasizes the ethics of care in the making and remaking of refuge. This is done through concepts that are collectively and ethically constructed, for example, return (i.e. to violated homes and cities), otherness, memory-work and imagination. The chapter sets out to build a theoretical discourse concerning knowledge building and sharing that is performative across spatio-temporal frames.

The book's conclusion, 'A manifesto for structures of refuge in spatial justice', puts forward a manifesto of spatial justice rooted in the trauma of the Middle East which recognizes spatial approaches that, under the influence of protracted rupture, must negotiate with multiple actors, powers and geographies. This takes the form of a palimpsest approach, both textually and spatially, and provides lessons for alternative practices that constantly challenge societal, political and environmental injustices. Such practices emerge from examining a multiplicity of spatial structures of refuge within architectures and geographies in times of war and trauma.

This book advances the field of spatial justice (Soja 2010) within the discipline of architecture in the context of Iraq. It does so through empirical fieldwork and critical reflexive and performative practice, working in particular towards producing a just framework for architecture in the context of postcolonial spatial practices of the Middle East. It further contributes to human geography and sociology, especially concerning the volatility of the concepts of home, domesticity, urbanity and their associated geotrauma. It also develops post-war and conflict urban studies in its focus on memory-work and the three scales of spatiality in relation to time. It thus puts forward a new practice of spatial justice as a socially rooted approach to building structures of refuge for the future, particularly for post-war and conflict development projects. More specifically, it harnesses the collective memory, as well as the lived and felt experiences of people who are making and remaking their lived and imagined environments. The emergent practices of spatial justice are derived from a research practice based on the ethics of reflexivity while emphasizing a plurality of views from the ground up as it uncovers structures of refuge.

1 THE POSITIONALITY OF PROTRACTED RUPTURE

At this initial stage of the book, it is worth noting that positionality is key to the development of its arguments, its conceptual framing and its contextual point of view. This chapter develops the concept of positionality within the context of Iraq and thus starts with a declarative stance on the types of architectures and spatial practices that are relevant to this book. It then goes on to situate the study within reflexive feminist, postcolonial and post-structuralist thought. It places a multidisciplinary lens over the methodological approach of deep mapping (Roberts 2016), which is further applied across all the multimodal fieldwork methods and ethics used throughout the book. Then, with the help of other researchers and practitioners in the field, this chapter frames the book's key conceptual performative and topological notions, drawing connections between them through a palimpsest approach. These notions include protracted rupture, trauma, refuge, struggle over geography, memory, justice, creativity and imagination. Furthermore, the chapter frames protracted rupture in spatial terms within and between vernacular informality and humanitarian living. The chapter concludes with a history of the struggle of Iraqis to find refuge, as well as with a review of some relevant research that deals with similar struggles, also explored from a spatial perspective.

Spatial practice in *Rupturing Architecture*

Throughout the book, I use the term architecture (with a lower-case *a*, and sometimes in the plural – architectures) to emphasize the different approaches to the making of architecture and spatial practice that emerge from the ground up, both locally and socially, in response to trauma and violence. A research-based spatial practice, this book hinges on the multiplicity of spatiality (domestic, urban or border) and the socially engaged action associated with such spatiality. It examines how spaces of becoming provide spatial possibilities that are constantly open-ended, negotiated and reimagined, and how the methods for creating these practices pivot on agency and collective activism (Dodd 2019). This requires spatial practice to be attuned to social formation and reformation in any given context (Liggett and Perry 1995). As a field, then, spatial practice sits broadly at the convergence of art, architecture, design, urban planning, anthropology and sociology. It draws on interdisciplinary and transdisciplinary knowledge of these practices that is performative and calls for spatial justice. In *The Production of Space*, Henri Lefebvre (1991) puts forward a nuanced theoretical thesis of social space. Lefebvre (1991: 413) draws distinctions between space (as a philosophical term) and spatial practice whereby the 'former can only be formulated on a theoretical plane, whereas the latter is empirically observable' and furthermore, 'described and analysed' across multiple spatialities: architecture, planning, urbanism and so on. Edward W. Soja (2010) emphasizes the interdependence between the sociality and spatiality of space where neither stands in isolation from the other. He posits (Soja 2010: 19) that 'Space is not an empty void. It is always filled with politics, ideology, and other forces shaping our lives and challenging us to engage in struggles over geography'.

The fields mentioned here are concerned with this kind of Lefebvrian spatial practice, which attends to the actuality and locality of the spatiality and organization of everyday life and 'urban reality' (Lefebvre 1991: 414). While this book certainly frames spatial practices within the conceptual strata of a socially produced space, it also aims to actively situate such spaces within the context of Iraq – its locality, its spatial reality and its struggles, past and present – rather than remaining in a purely theoretical space. This concept sits more comfortably with Doreen Massey's (2005: 130–1) concept of place as a 'spatio-temporal' event that is open and 'woven together out of ongoing stories', and 'as a particular constellation within the wider topographies of space, and as in process, as unfinished business'. The openness of spatialization and temporality within space and time (see Henri Bergson on *Matter and Memory* [1988]), lead to what Rob Shields (2013: 94) terms 'spatial struggles'. These occur in the process of trying to understand the production of 'counter-spaces', those of resistance and refusal to submit to the dominant spatial orders and codes of societies (Shields 2013: 94). Soja (2010) delves into the intricate relationship between spatiality and social justice. He emphasizes the significance of space and its geography in understanding societal disparities and the fight for equity where justice 'has a *consequential geography*, a spatial expression that is more than just a background reflection of a set of physical attributes to be descriptively mapped' (Soja 2010: 1). By engaging Iraqis' troubled history with traumatized geographies, we uncover struggles with historicity and memory in the making of spatial practices of refuge, that ultimately reveal glimpses of justice.

As a field and as a process for understanding the production of space, spatial practice is built upon Lefebvre's (1991) triad of space as something that is 'perceived', 'conceived' and 'lived'. More specifically, the triad assumes spatial dialectic relations between the 'social practices' that are perceived, the 'representations' of spaces related to what is conceived (such as architectures and cities) and 'representational spaces' – in other words, the associated notions, images and symbols that communicate conceptual meanings in *lived* space (such as with structures of refuge) (Lefebvre 1991). It is not possible to speak of one aspect in isolation – one cannot be untangled from another. Soja (1996: 60) extends the dialectic nature of Lefebvre's concept of space into a critical strategy of 'thirding-as-othering', proposing a 'Thirdspace' that negates binarism (such as 'either/or') and introduces an 'in-between' positionality (such as 'both/and also …'). This post-structuralist 'thirding' serves to disrupt and deconstruct permanent constructions, and produces an accumulative approximation, or what Soja (1996: 61) describes as 'a cumulative trialectics that is radically open to additional othernesses, to a continuing expansion of spatial knowledge'. I give a concrete example of Soja's concept of 'Thirdspace' in the spaces in Baghdad that emerged out of the systemic deployment of blast walls throughout the city. In this example, it becomes possible to reflect on how Iraqis navigated this challenge creatively as they forged complex networked spatial practices of mobility and refuge (Murrani 2016). Here, the word 'spatial' seeks to expand rather than to replace the word 'architecture'. It does so in a similar way to its intended use in *Spatial Agency* by Nishat Awan, Tatjana Schneider and Jeremy Till (2011: 82), where actions and interventions take place alongside negotiations and deliberations involving the politics, representations and appropriations of structures and agency that 'bring about the empowerment of those involved'. In describing 'other ways of doing architecture', Awan et al. (2011: 82) refer to the processes of spatial production as being simultaneously proactive and practical, noting: 'Spatial agency shows how negotiation, tenacity, imagination, participative spatial encounters, and one's own understanding as a morally responsible actor, might together lead to a different and more ethical understanding of spatial practice.'

These acts of negotiation, imagination, participation, agency and ethics are what frame the processes of spatial production and spatial practice as political in nature. 'Political', here, does not refer to the structures and governance of politics, but instead encompasses a broader understanding of the negotiations and interactions that are fundamental to public life and civil society (Dodd 2019). Feminist spatial practice, for instance, posits that practice should seek to provide 'ontological reframing, re-viewing (or re-doing) differently, and cultivating forms of creativity that emerge from an experimental, performative and ethical orientation to the world' (Schalk et al. 2017: 15). These are the methodological challenges negotiated and imagined across the chapters of this book.

Also fundamental to this book is the notion of pursuing refuge as an act of resistance – it conceptualizes refuge as resistance against the loss of agency or life. This notion is inherently political, and the spatial practice emerging from this process could therefore be categorized as a kind of political othering or 'practicing otherwise' (Petrescu 2007). It is difficult to define a moment where the 'spatial turn' first came to the fore within the field of architecture and spatial practice, particularly in relation to the Middle East and North Africa. Explorations of spatiality in relation to the historicity of the Middle East in the context of architecture are particularly present in the work of Gehan Selim (2017: 68) as she calls for the legitimization of traditional people-led spatial practices of authentic quarters in Cairo, and connects this legitimization to the preservation process of social fabrics within the city.

Although the term became widely used with the rise of globalization, which created conceptual changes within the humanities and social sciences as they began placing further emphasis on the spatial dimensions of place, space and the built environment, this supposedly global 'spatial turn' did not take place in Iraq and the nearby regions for another twenty years. Political oppression, war, conflict and economic sanctions meant that Iraq's priorities lay more with social dimensions than they did with spatial dimensions. The social and spatial appeared to be separate entities until the beginning of a series of protests across the region, defined as the Arab Spring (Brownlee, Masoud and Reynolds 2013) in the early 2010s. This originated in Tunisia, Egypt, Libya, Syria and Yemen, then rippled out a few years later into Iraq (amongst others) at the height of major wars and violence.

In the context of this book, I seek to situate myself within the positionality of relevant conceptual framings and thought, and to take inspiration from earlier work that ties together the entanglement of spaces of refuge and resistance with the memories and imaginative geographies from marginalized and mostly muted sites and communities. In his analysis of his two seminal works, *Orientalism* (1979) and *Culture and Imperialism* (1993), Edward Said (2000) speaks of 'imaginative geographies', which are representations and projections of the 'Orient' as perceived by externals (or 'colonialists', for Said) that exist somewhere between memory and place, as opposed to the actual context of these geographies. As this book is written in English and primarily aimed at an English-speaking audience, my goal is to untangle and at times challenge such imaginative geographies, not in an attempt to separate the real from the unreal, but rather to unveil the difference between what is externally perceived and what is lived and practised internally within the sites and events of this book. In terms of an insider researcher looking in, Ammar Azzouz (2020) illustrates this point explicitly when he contrasts the voices of Syrians imagining and reimagining the reconstruction of their own cities with those of major international investors and key players in large-scale international development projects. When he writes, 'Reconstruction can be seen as a new form of re-destruction and a process that damages the memory of the city instead of preserving it' (Azzouz 2020: 723), Azzouz stresses the dangers of neglecting the voices of communities. This is something that Hiba Bou Akar (2018) predicted concerning Beirut, in which violence was fomented by the political and religious-led planning that created geographies of otherness and segregation. Therefore, a positionality and ethics of insider research that pivots on reflexive processes that emerge from within (Greene 2014) is pertinent for this book. This concept is contextually framed in Chapters 1 and 2, and later materialized through the spatial practices emerging from the voices and stories of participants and communities suffering from the protracted trauma of war, conflict and displacement.

Deep mapping and the ethics within

Importantly, declaring the positionality of this work as 'inside research' does not negate the wealth of outside research conducted by researchers who have no prior knowledge or shared characteristics (cultural or otherwise) with the participants and communities they study. In fact, the binary division between inside/outside research itself is a flawed concept (Breen 2007), especially with regard to the positionality of an 'indigenous-outsider' researcher (Greene 2014). This occurs where the researcher has prior knowledge and shared cultural values and characteristics with the community they are researching – which could either be seen as a reductionist approach or, conversely, labelled by the community as outside research. This is further complicated by the difficult positioning of a researcher who happens to be on the outside at the time of conducting the research (which is the case in this book), when the fluidity of this positionality is viewed both internally and externally (by participants and communities within, and readers and critics on the inside and outside).

I must remind the reader that, although this book is written in English, it looks beyond the Euro-American-centric framework concerning structures of refuge and the circumstances that created them. Instead, the book achieves a more appropriate framework through a blended postcolonial, post-structuralist and feminist approach (both from the Global North and South), combined with the lived and felt experiences of people and places struggling with the injustices of colonial pasts. This book enacts a just spatial practice that is centred on, as well as negotiated and constructed critically from, the raw material of remembering, tied as it is to place. bell hooks (2009: 5) asserts the processual characteristic of memory and place-making, stating: 'We are born and have our being in a place of memory. We chart our lives by everything we remember from the mundane moment to the majestic. We know ourselves through the art and act of remembering. Memories offer us a world where there is no death, where we are sustained by rituals of regard and recollection.'

Several factors have led to my decision to conduct this research remotely. These include the uncertainty of the Covid-19 pandemic and the ensuing disruption to travel and fieldwork, the unstable political situation in Iraq, and the fact that the research focuses on events and situations that happened in the past, some of which I witnessed (although their protracted nature remains raw). My remote research methods tapped into several recently developed multimodal approaches to data collection and visual production for reflexive activism and qualitative fieldwork (Smith 2012). The data collection that relies on memory and storytelling involved processing fieldnotes (Emerson, Fretz and Shaw 2011) and conducting textual analysis of critical literature as well as online interviews, accompanied by online probes (drawings, maps and photographs of home, as well as other buildings and spatial practices of refuge). From these interviews, translations, transcriptions and fieldnotes, I was able to elicit and critically and reflexively engage in qualitative textual and thematic analysis. Autoethnographic activism (aimed at amplifying indigenous unheard narratives; Smith 2012: 226) features heavily in some of the case studies and storytelling surrounding the lived and felt experience of war. As stated earlier, memory-work and critical analysis of personal reflections dominate the autoethnographic methods of research. Although the majority of the Iraqi interviewees are professionals in the fields of architecture, planning, anthropology and creative practices, most of these individuals were not acting in a professional capacity during the 2003 invasion of Iraq, the 2006–8 sectarian violence or ISIS's atrocities and the Yazidi genocide in 2014. In light of their professional roles now, they have been able to reflect on their spatial responses then, as well as recognize their subsequent acts of resistance in remobilizing the emergence of spatial practices of refuge for the future.

As well as being a methodological approach, deep mapping is a practice. It is a *performative* practice that explores, traces and constructs knowledge from diverse sources – historic, spatial, social, through memories and so on – all of which are considered equal, and all of which serve to amplify marginalized voices (Springett 2015: 624). The concepts of deep mapping and deep maps were developed by scholars in the spatial humanities to reflect the complexity and overlapping that occurs between ontological and epistemological approaches to spatial narrative (Bodenhamer, Corrigan and Harris 2015). Deep maps are held to be simultaneously a process and a product, as well as a platform of reflexivity that engages with the way agency, memory, identity and imagination constitute spatial narratives:

> Deep maps are not confined to the tangible or material, but include the discursive and ideological dimensions of place, the dreams, hopes, and fears of residents – they are, in short, positioned between matter and meaning. They are also topological and relational, revealing the ties that places have with each other and tracing their embeddedness in networks that span scales and range from the local to the global.
>
> (Bodenhamer et al. 2015: 3)

This type of deep mapping implies a kind of agency, as it moves beyond the representation of the world or the imposition of power structures, and into the uncovering of potential and the unfolding of hidden or unimagined grounds (Corner 1999: 213). The resulting maps constitute a process of creative practice that is always in the making, always negotiating possibilities, memories and, in the case of this book, trauma.

From the perspectives of architectural and spatial practice, deep mapping and deep maps are, respectively, the process and product of a cross-section of conditions. These include spatial, political, temporal, ecological and psychological conditions that represent, identify and enact within a place, coupled with the spatial imaginaries, memory and agency of people with lived and felt experiences of that place. In the context of this book, deep mapping digs into the layers of trauma and violence that mark a place, producing maps that transcend an area's usual descriptions and representations. The practice of deep mapping thus cuts through the material and conceptual representations of storytelling and memory-work, while simultaneously signifying and amplifying the muted voices within the communities who negotiate the places, sites and events that unfold across time. In doing so, deep mapping democratizes the production of knowledge and confirms the fluidity of the researcher's position in relation to the researched, making it a relationship of creative practice. In her work, which taps into Iraqis' muted cultural imagination, Ruba Ali Al-Hassani (2021) asserts the power of storytelling in connecting story to justice and peacebuilding practices. She writes:

> Persuading survivors of war and conflict to engage in storytelling and active listening is to persuade them to revisit trauma. It must be done with caution, consider their readiness, and provide safe space for story engagement. When storytelling is done in safe spaces where listeners are actively engaged and equal sharers of power, it can heal everyone involved.
>
> (Al-Hassani 2021: 514)

Throughout this research, I have taken into consideration the traumas the interviewees have endured and asked them to share only what they feel comfortable with. These narratives are accompanied by deep maps, also known as 'cognitive maps' and 'counter-maps'. These are a set of embodied representations of temporality and refuge spaces in states of precariousness that Iraqis charted cognitively through their memories of war, conflict and displacement. Together, they build a collective picture that brings us closer to understanding the spatial emotions and traumas shared between 2003 and 2023.

Shields (2013) warns of the dangers of confining the notions of 'conceptual mapping' and cognitive maps to the material and geographical landscape, which can result in intuitive evidence being overlooked as conceptual maps contain more than the material world. He describes 'conceptual mapping' by postulating,

'They are also surely matrixes which function as "mappings" of the social cosmos' whereby 'people are located not only "in space" but "in society"' too (Shields 2013: 94). Often, these 'counter-maps' stand in opposition to the usual state-imposed geographical representations that are driven by a 'politics of bordering and ordering' (Campos-Delgado 2018: 490), hence they are considered 'counter-' or 'anti-' as a rejoinder to this mindset. The maps in this book each tell a spatial story of how the trauma of war and violence have been spatially negotiated, remembered, imagined and created in homes, cities and borders, in the pursuit of refuge. The emergent maps are fleeting and constantly made and remade as people remember details, therefore, they do not constitute accurate accounts and representations of the reality of the past. However, collectively they can and should be viewed as spatial possibilities and practices of refuge-making.

Spatial stories are the articulations and enunciations that emerge from lived spaces that become zones for practice, as events are remembered and retold (de Certeau 1988: 130). In this book, the stories and memories shared constitute the spatial practice of refuge imagined, lived and represented in the form of maps. The events and narratives contained within these spatial stories do not conform to chronological order, but rather offer performative ways of dealing with trauma as a palimpsest of history, events, memory and agency. To deal with traumatic events chronologically would be to go against the natural function of memory as it retrieves, recalls and actively retells moments in our lives that transcend time. The spatial stories constructed and the case studies discussed in the book will therefore follow several complex and profound key themes that influenced people's lives, rather than insisting upon a historical timeline. Following Daniele Rugo's (2023) contribution of art practice as a new method of understanding conflict, these spatial stories that take the form of maps serve to disrupt particular meanings associated with violence and, rather than representing moments of trauma, construct different frames of knowledge surrounding the events experienced by the interviewees.

Said (2000: 185) reminds us of the significance of collective memory when he asserts that it 'is not an inert and passive thing, but a field of activity in which past events are selected, reconstructed, maintained, modified, and endowed with political meaning'. The maps produced in this book are saturated with political meaning, arising as they do from the accounts of indigenous, individual Iraqis, whose collective narratives and memories of spaces of refuge were created and negotiated throughout years of war, conflict and displacement. Together, they contribute to the indigenization of both the process and the content of mapping as a spatial practice of world-making (Rose-Redwood et al. 2020). The maps are co-constructed within the unpredictable dynamics of creative knowledge creation, as it is shared between researcher and interviewee. Interviews are always unpredictable, especially in research on conflict and war, and as such they place a significant ethical weight on the researcher's shoulders in the form of the inevitable changes interviewees will experience throughout the process (Kostovicova and Knott 2022). For example, the process may trigger in the interviewee painful personal memories, grief over lost loved ones and/or communities, or make them feel vulnerable to stigmatization or incrimination if they were to share sensitive information. The inevitability of such unpredictability and change requires both the researcher and the interviewee to continuously question and reflect upon the data being shared. As such, the interviewees must become reflexive participants in co-creating the ethical framework of the research. In the case of this book, such reflexivity is practiced through the positionality, identities and shared knowledge (Chilmeran and Hedström 2021) arising from the data collected and manifested via storytelling, which is thematically aligned with the maps produced. From the process of sharing knowledge production with the fifteen Iraqis, a set of themes have emerged reflexively positioning the analysis of the interviews and synthesis of the maps and the associated visual elements of the research.

By deploying a creative, multimodal methodology of visual, textual and reflexive critical analysis through memory-work, this book aims to define the parameters for a just spatial practice that could, in the future, aid post-war and conflict responses by engaging traumatized people in the construction of their environments. More specifically, it reveals and examines people's spatial practices of refuge through the conceptual framework of *rupture*. Rupture, in this book, is identified through two dialectical expressions: first, it represents the spatial, psychological and social trauma and destruction brought about by war and violence, and inflicted on people and their built environment; second, it represents the place-making and spatial practice of creating refuge in response to those same conditions of trauma. This dialectic nature of rupture presents it as both cause and response, unfamiliar and familiar. It is the trauma caused by spatial violence (unfamiliar) *and* the creative spatial responses to that same violence (familiar).

Conceptual underpinnings

The word 'rupture' is usually associated with a medical emergency relating to the sudden material breaking or bursting of something that should be acting as a single entity, often caused by violent strain or tension (Waite 2012). Yet rupture has roots deep within philosophy and the epistemology of evasive structures and systems that are disrupted (Machiavelli's situationist disruption), broken (Hobbes' destructionist break) or interrupted (Hume's empiricist interruption) (Kingsmith 2017). Following Spinoza's 'dual aspect' theorization of rupture, Martin Holbraad, Bruce Kapferer and Julia F. Sauma (2019: 1) speak of 'critical rupture' being inherently negative, while at the same time able to function 'as a positive or dynamic impulse towards escape, redirection, reconstitution and sometimes renewal', giving it a destructive and generative potential. They affirm that the process of rupture tends to negate dominant narratives of modernity, including notions of resistance, and 'can act instead to reveal instances in which interference in dominant narratives is more strategic than resistance' (Holbraad, Kapferer and Sauma 2019: 18). This dual aspect of rupture goes beyond oppositional dialectics and instead engages with the plurality of difference, as well as all forms of disruption to power.

As they age, cities, their architecture and the built environment in general suffer from several ruptures, mostly from natural causes. At the macro level, these ruptures are visible in the deterioration of infrastructure, and congestion or high demand over housing owing to increases in population. At the micro level, we see cracks appearing in exterior walls and paint, leaks emerging between the joints of different materials and other signs of wear and tear. However, nothing ruptures cities and their architectures more completely than repetitive, massive impact damage through war or violence. Buildings are damaged beyond repair, often permanently altering the complex nature of their existence within their urban context. In the context of Iraq, like many other countries troubled by violence over a long period of time, this rupture is not an individual, isolated event, as in the work of Charishma Ratnam and Danielle Drozdzewski (2020), where rupture signifies a point in time that forces a movement. Neither does the rupture experienced in Iraq represent any one-time material change to a familiar and harmonious environment. Instead, it is a protracted rupturing, which could be associated with the concepts of 'slow violence' (Nixon 2011) and 'geotrauma' (Pain 2021), as well as 'domicide' (Porteous and Smith 2001) and 'urbicide' (Abujidi 2019). It is a kind of 'chronic trauma' (Pain 2021) that is spatially situated, yet drifts when traumatized people migrate or are displaced, making it a collective, social phenomenon, as well as temporarily permanent, as in Nixon's (2011) 'slow violence'. Although Nixon's work is mainly situated within the environmental humanities rather than geography and architecture, the material embodiments of violence discussed in his work can clearly be applied to the spatial rupture discussed here. This is particularly the case when viewed from the post-structuralist and postcolonial feminist perspective of 'chronic urban trauma', as presented in the work of Rachel Pain (2019).

As her work relates to housing dispossession and displacement, Pain's (2021) context of trauma is predominantly urban, hence the insertion of the term 'urban' within 'chronic trauma'. This book considers the urban and the domestic together alongside their theories and application as *spatial*. This is not to suggest that these two scales (urban and domestic) are undifferentiated, but rather to assert that the spatial practices discussed in this book have the tendency to slide, transition and change between the domestic, the urban and the border. In this context, the same applies to the notions of 'domicide' and 'urbicide'. Domicide refers to the deliberate destruction of a home against the resident's will, with the accompanying consequences of 'eviction, exile, expropriation, displacement, dislocation and relocation' (Porteous and Smith 2001: 12) at the domestic scale.

Urbicide, on the other hand, relates to the act of killing cities and the deliberate annihilation of urbanity that extends beyond the geography of the city and into social life. It is a term originally coined in the 1960s, but which later gained traction during the Bosnian War and the siege of Sarajevo (Coward 2009), as well as the obliteration and erasure of settlements in the West Bank in Palestine (Abujidi 2019: 23). In this study, the ability to move between, over and above the domestic and the urban allows for narratives and case studies to be connected from the inside out (from the domestic looking at the urban scale) and the outside in (from the urban peering into the domestic scale). The protractedness of rupture in Iraq adds further complexity to the conditions explored here, and requires us to understand and critically define the fact that all of the situations, events, buildings and spaces discussed exist within a context of continuous change, rendering everything volatile, incomplete and dynamic. This is precisely how I wish the reader to see the architecture and spatial practices discussed in this book – from the homes altered during war and violence to the appropriation of buildings, all for the purpose of seeking refuge. Here, we see rupture both in spatial trauma, violence and destruction, and also in the creative spatial and social changes that occur in response to that violence, including the negotiations of trauma and the spatial possibilities it affords.

Pain (2019: 389) observes that there are important syncretic and characteristic overlaps between her concept of 'chronic urban trauma' and Nixon's 'slow violence', in that they both emerge 'from continuous misuse of structural power and have incremental and cumulative effects in certain settings'. Pain further critiques Adrian Lahoud's (2010: 19) concept of 'post-traumatic urbanism', which describes trauma as the sudden and unpredictable impact that shatters people's situatedness in life, by highlighting the difference in temporality between Lahoud's 'sudden' trauma and that of 'chronic' or 'slow' trauma/violence in hers and Nixon's work. She adds, 'The trauma created by slow violence not only oscillates over time, but becomes magnified where the source of violence continues and proliferates; trauma becomes, in turn, a powerful force sustaining the effects of violence' (Pain 2019: 393). Presented this way, trauma is a dynamic phenomenon that can be rooted just as much in place as it is in the psychological mind and the material body. Psychological philosopher Catherine Malabou (2012: 6) connects trauma to wounds that pierce through protective barriers, not in the material sense, but psychologically; for example, in the passage of time after war and conflict, where memory and violence can be reactivated in what she terms 'affective conflict'. In *What Should We Do with Our Brain?* Malabou (2008: 12) champions the philosophy behind brain 'plasticity' and what it means for the brain to be able to shape one's identity or be reshaped and changed by past traumatic events. She expands on this concept in her later book, *The New Wounded: From Neurosis to Brain Damage* (2012), where she situates plasticity at both the extremes and the conjunctures of receiving form (sculpting with clay), giving form (plastic surgeon at work) or destroying form (through war, accident, etc.). As such, plasticity manifests itself through its flexibility in constructive and destructive shaping (Malabou 2012: 17). Malabou's plasticity certainly resonates with Pain's description of the process of wounding, where she states; 'Wounding is spatially and temporally dynamic, working both metonymically (via social ecologies of place and loss of routines) and psychologically (via residents' intimate relationships with the city)' (Pain 2019: 390). These conceptual framings certainly resonate with Black and postcolonial analyses of trauma as socially and collectively experienced processes (Fanon 2001) of resistance (hooks 2004) in which temporal and spatial dimensions are in constant negotiation with one another.

Rupturing Architecture considers the multiple layers of trauma as perpetually tangling and unravelling in time and space, echoing Pain's concept of 'geotrauma' (2021). The coupling of time and space with trauma and violence, along with the socially collective nature of the experience, is fundamental to the ways in which traumatized people resist, negotiate and respond to trauma and violence. On the one hand, this coupling renders trauma timeless and placeless, situating it primarily within the body (Adams-Hutcheson 2017: 105), and, on the other hand, it provides the potential for change and the emergence of new spatial practices. Like 'geotrauma', protracted rupture serves as a framework through which we can examine and afford spatial possibilities to the refuge-making practices that emerge directly from trauma and violence, fuelling resistance and plasticity. Pain (2021: 974–4) explains this coiling of place with the experience of trauma in community rebuilding, stating:

> Geotrauma describes, then, the relational clasping of place with the experience and impacts of trauma. As a noun, clasp indicates the mutuality of the grip of place and trauma as an interlocking mechanism, while as a verb, clasping implies that this grip is ongoing and continually remade. So the spatial contexts and relations around traumatized people, communities or nations may variously hold trauma in place, contribute to retraumatization, or help to establish freedom and the rebuilding of life after traumatic events. In turn, trauma and traumatized people alter those contexts and relations in ways that tend not to be very visible.

Within the humanities in particular, postcolonial trauma studies have critiqued the tendency towards Euro-American-centric approaches to analysing trauma in a non-Western context, for example in recent work on Post-Traumatic Stress Disorder (PTSD), a condition identified in US war veterans that is not necessarily fully applicable in a non-Western context (Craps et al. 2015: 907). This critique brings attention to the specific spatial context of Iraq, which has been situated throughout its history and more recent past in an oscillating position between imperial, colonial and postcolonial understandings of trauma. Most of the events discussed in this book have either directly or indirectly resulted from trauma inflicted by the West. As with Afghanistan, Iraq is just one such example of the phenomenon, and while it is difficult to homogenize postcolonial trauma studies, it is further impossible to untangle them completely from Western understandings of these conditions. PTSD features heavily in both trauma and memory studies in psychiatry and in the humanities. The fields of geography, urbanism and architecture have also engaged with the disorder and its implications for people, spaces and cities (Pain 2021), yet few scholars have explored Post-Traumatic Growth (PTG) spatially as another manifestation of the plasticity of trauma. PTG is well studied in clinical and applied psychology, and although Pain (2021) alludes to growth as she speaks of freedom and rebuilding life after trauma, it features very little, if at all, in the fields of geography and architecture.

Psychological studies have highlighted the positive changes that may result from the struggle to negotiate trauma, viewed as personal growth rather than a return to normality (Tedeschi and Calhoun 2004). This occurs in a complex coupling between trauma and memory, triggered by remembering or re-experiencing trauma. It is not, however, to be confused with resilience – the ability to cope with trauma and return to a pre-traumatic state. Instead, PTG refers to a personal transformation, where the individual gains positive psychological benefits that transcend the ability to resist and not be damaged by trauma (Tedeschi and Calhoun 2004: 4). PTG requires specific 'actions', which involve the ability to negotiate trauma (especially in the pursuit of refuge), to develop personal growth and to lower stress (Henson, Truchot and Canevello 2021: 7). But growth is not a linear process, and not all growth can be considered positive. This is highlighted in a few PTG studies, where growth has sometimes led to aggression and additional violence (Henson et al. 2021: 7). PTG is further determined by the severity of the trauma and stress upon the individual, as well as the temporality and duration of suffering and its reoccurrence (Pat-Horenczyk and Brom 2007: 384). As such, growth can only be categorized as yet another syncretic characteristic of the plasticity of trauma and memory, and it should therefore be approached with caution. PTG is therefore discussed carefully in this book through the lens of creativity and imagination in spatial production, as well as through memory-work.

The coupling of trauma and memory is fundamental to this book, as the act of analysing them pivots on our ability to deconstruct and reconstruct lived and felt experiences of war, conflict and displacement in past and present events. It is therefore paramount that I highlight the hypothesis that has dominated all my past work and is present in this book. The hypothesis posits that there is a complex and incomplete dependency between people's creative and spatial responses to trauma and violence, and that this is connected to the ways in which they are psychologically affected by and able to process that trauma through memory. This is not to suggest that the trauma of war gives people better coping mechanisms or makes them more resilient than others, nor does it suggest that war makes people more creative (although there is research that shows a correlation between stress and creativity; Byron, Khazanchi and Nazarian 2010). Nevertheless, the impact of psychological trauma on the brain and memory in relation to creativity has always fascinated me and shaped my way of thinking, which planted the seeds for this book.

In order to engage fully with memory, we must approach it as a triadic meta-concept: memory of lived and felt experiences, memory of events and memory of place. In so doing, I follow the work of geographers, anthropologists, sociologists and psychologists who deliberately overlap these three types of memory in the form of a palimpsest. There is an emphasis in this book on Middle Eastern and North African (MENA) scholarly perspectives on memory-making, where it is considered to be a political act, in which storytelling is a fundamental tool of resistance and a way to construct meaning and collective memory (Roccu and Salem 2019: 221). For example, Selim (2022: 477) explores an important 'nexus between politics, memory and urbanism' in the context of the built environment and cities in the MENA region.

In particular, this research finds that memory of lived experiences (Frechette et al. 2020) is connected to the plasticity of the brain, presented through PTSD and PTG, and embodied and inhabited though creativity and imagination. Memory of events, on the other hand, is situated in the temporal nature of the rupture caused by trauma and violence of war, conflict and displacement (Makdisi and Silverstein 2006). Lastly, memory of place manifests itself in material and spatial damage (domicide and urbicide), as well as the changes and negotiations (collective resistance and spatial imaginaries) within places of refuge that emerge in response to such spatial violence. This book seeks to uncover the spatial practices that are made and remade by memory-work and 'spatial imaginaries' (Davoudi et al. 2018) or 'imaginary geographies' (Said 1993). These concepts are considered here to be collective models of spatial architecture, design and planning that appear to be fundamental to the creation of a just society.

Owain Jones (2011: 876–7) asserts that, in geographical studies, this entanglement and complexity of memory transcends the basic processual actions of encoding, storing, recording and retrieving experiences whether these acts of remembering happen sequentially or in parallel, voluntarily or involuntarily (un/consciously), and ultimately embody space and time performatively. Furthermore, he situates the collective imaginative and creative aspects of memory in the performativity of practice, embodied as it is both spatially and temporally, where 'Memory is a key means by which the present is practiced' (Jones 2011: 879). Deeply connected to the idiosyncratic plasticity of the performativity of memory is its fragility, especially concerning the lived and felt experiences of vulnerable and traditionally excluded communities as they remember and engage in storytelling about the wartime events that have affected them (Drozdzewski, De Nardi and Waterton 2016: 449). Psychologist Paula Reavey (2017: 107) highlights this interdependency between the context (which she refers to as the 'scene') and the 'narrative' (or storytelling) as 'geographies of memories' and 'memoryscapes' – in other words, 'the material objects occupying space that interweave with multiple narratives about the past'.

Steven Brown and Paula Reavey (2015) further explain that this interdependency between scene and narrative makes memory an activity that is constantly emerging from its roots in space, and therefore it is in need of an 'expanded model of memory' that positions remembering as an extended act within a scene. Neuropsychologist Catherine Loveday (2018: 64) further explains what this expanded model of memory means, and how it is constructed and deconstructed:

> Each time we remember a moment from our life we construct it anew. We do this by using the building blocks of episodic memory – recollective feelings of being somewhere; and semantic memory – concrete knowledge about our world … and about our personal history … Memories are almost never 100 percent accurate, and all memories are malleable and changeable.

This expanded model of memory certainly aligns with that of chronic trauma, as described by Pain (2019: 392): 'Every type of trauma displays an unpredictable non-linear trajectory, characterized by temporal dysphoria; time is warped, it moves both fast and slow, trauma can lay dormant for long periods, and the effects of earlier violence are reiterated most sharply at certain points when memory is revisited.' Although aligning memory-work and trauma is a complex task, I must assert here that, for the purpose of this study, the acts of deconstructing these narratives and accounts and reconstructing the spatial practices that emerge are more important than ensuring that the memories of these traumatic events are accurate.

Amid the friction and slippage between memory and trauma lies a space for creativity and imagination that emerges directly from the effect that trauma has on our ability to recall episodic memory in a linear way (Thomson and Jaque 2019: 216). On three previous occasions, I have explored such a hypothesis that couples memory and trauma with spatial creativity. The first occurred in an urban context, and involved interpreting Baghdadis' creative responses to the constant changing of location of Baghdad's blast walls (Murrani 2016). The second involved mapping the mobility of refugees across borders in Europe and the innovative ways they navigated their treacherous search for places of safety (Murrani 2019). The third constituted a participatory action research project that involved working with displacees (refugees and asylum seekers) in England to visually map what home and homeland meant to them (Murrani, Lloyd and Popovici 2023). On an epistemological level, creativity is a complex and multifaceted construct associated with processes, products and behavioural traits, the representations of which are bound by, shaped by and dependent on the constraints placed upon individual creators (Haught 2015). The *Oxford English Dictionary* defines the adjective 'creative' as 'involving the use of imagination in order to create something' (Waite 2012). Further to this, creativity is often associated not only with imagination but also with inventiveness, innovation, originality and resourcefulness, all of which expand creativity into a meta-model beyond the created product itself.

Importantly for this book, this meta-model engages creatively with 'everyday creativity' (Richards 2010), meaning that it seeks out negotiations of creativity that lie within the research approach, the context being researched and people's responses to trauma and violence. The act of imagining, as a mental process, can be both performative and pragmatic as it combines practical problem-solving with nonlinear narratives that emerge from episodic memory (Feng et al. 2017). For the processes of imagining and creativity to be realized in everyday life, the spatial dimension of justice needs to be illuminated. Just as trauma and memory are integral to spatiality, geography is essential to the concept of justice. Injustice manifests within and through geography (Soja 2010) and spatial practice, making it inherently connected to the intertwining of trauma and memory. In *Theorising Justice*, Stephen Przybylinski (2023: 191–2) articulates justice in spatial terms, identifying overlapping connections between concepts of space that are simultaneously 'absolute', 'relative' and 'relational', alongside the flexibility of scale and its relevance in 'examining how space is produced'. He also highlights the importance of considering a 'politics of scale' in its construction and the significance of this analytical approach, asserting that 'scale serves both as a measure for bounding analyses and as a concept to explain certain socio-spatial processes' (Przybylinski 2023: 192).

Echoing feminist philosopher Iris Marion Young (2011), justice displaces the notion of equitable distribution of wealth, land, and territory by embracing frames of difference instead. Anna Stanley (2009: 1000–1004) further elucidates how frames of difference serving as an analytical tool for oppression 'might shift the lens of environmental justice scholarship away from distributional explanations of injustice towards critical engagement with the politics of meaning that structure environmental practice':

> The work of differentiation, producing relational meaning, and relationally positioning subjects and objects in networks of distinction is a thoroughly spatial set of processes. Difference making takes place not only in space through the relational positioning of objects in space and in relation to already coded spaces, but draws on spatial tropes, categories, and imaginaries to construct and create difference.

Similarly, the spatial practices remembered, imagined and created in this book are socially constructed and contribute to producing difference within the politics of scale and power dynamics, based on Iraqis' lived experiences of trauma and memory. These various scales and social relations do not always yield geographies of just spatiality. Soja (2010: 5) cites examples such as the South African apartheid and the Palestinian occupation, amongst other instances of marginalization and environmental injustice, describing them as 'spatiality of (in)justice', and further argues that these situations 'affect society and social life just as much as social processes shape the spatiality or specific geography of (in)justice', particularly in how spaces limit the possibilities for rights and freedoms to be practiced. Recognizing that space and social relations are both produced by and produce just and (in)just frames of difference enables the integration of the analytical framework of spatial justice with that of trauma and memory, emphasizing the complexity, uncertainty and dynamics of the frames through which spatiality unfolds.

The spatial practice examined in this book operates within the blurred space of imagination that exists between the lived and felt experience of trauma, on the one hand, and what is being imagined and expressed through episodic memories of events and situations, on the other. This in-betweenness is manifested both through the object and place of refuge and the act and movement of seeking refuge itself.

The idea of 'refuge' is widely associated with refugee-hood (denoting the noun 'refugee') (Cole 2021) or the act of seeking refuge (indicating movement through use of the verb 'to seek') (Pasquetti and Sanyal 2020). Yet refuge in its etymological sense is 'a place or state of safety from danger or trouble' (Waite 2012). If we accept the plurality of its spaces and states of being and becoming, we can allow the word to represent and transcend both the idea of a fixed place of refuge (such as women's refuge for domestic abuse), and the spatial and social acts of resistance that bring people out of one traumatic place into another, safer place. Therefore, refuge as a concept has simultaneous access to nounhood and to verb-making. Elena Fiddian-Qasmiyeh (2020) highlights the importance of spatiality in refuge-making practices in a way that moves beyond the historic and geographical lens of 'narratives of crisis' and instead urges us to trace 'historical and geographical resonances' alongside 'relationalities, continuities and discontinuities' that are particularly relevant to displacement (Fiddian-Qasmiyeh and Berg 2018: v). Fiddian-Qasmiyeh (2020: 4) further adds that the spatial mode of analysis concerning refuge 'involves developing nuanced understandings of the ways that spaces such as cities, towns, camps, reception centres, markets and schools are (re)constructed, shared and controlled by different actors throughout processes of displacement – and of the significance of scale, which requires that equal attention be given to actors and processes across micro-, meso- and macro-levels'. In this way, this book locates the creation of everyday structures and acts of refuge-making within creative practice and, in return, examines their spatial possibilities through the creative methods of storytelling, mapping, drawing, photographing, collaging and so on, to engage with the relational disjuncture along the way. Everyday creativity and spatial practice share an important characteristic in that they both use imagination in the remaking of spaces and world-making beyond what is already made, shared and experienced. As such, they therefore engender new performative, reflexive and topological spatial practices.

Siting rupture across and between vernacular informality and humanitarian living

Rupturing Architecture examines spaces of refuge created by Iraqis in preparation for, and in response to, wartime and spatial violence across two decades. These spaces are usually informal, temporary and engender a surplus of spatial complexity in scale and materiality. Here, we witness the unfolding of more than the 'dual aspect' of 'critical rupture' (Holbraad, Kapferer and Sauma 2019), where the informal assumes 'difference' (Young 2011) into 'everyday creativity' (Richards 2010) and yields various scales of spatiality. These spaces are generally associated with concepts of home and domesticity, and, given the fact that they are situated in Iraq, their informal multiplicity resembles that of the vernacular, the everyday and the familiar to the architecture of the country. 'The term "vernacular architecture"', writes Suzanne Preston Blier (2006: 230), 'over the last half-century has come to represent a farrago of building traditions that lie outside canonical largely Western building exemplars created generally by formally trained architects. From the Latin *vernaculus*, meaning native, indigenous, domestic, or subaltern (*verna* referencing local slaves), vernacular connotes popular as opposed to elite idioms'. In fact, the term continues to receive criticism and debate, countering the monolithic narrative provided by Western scholarly research that associates the term with traditional and primitive buildings, or otherwise 'nonpedigreed architecture' (Rudofsky 1987). The real crux of the concept of 'architecture without architects' (I reference here Rudofsky's famous 1964 exhibition at the Museum of Modern Art in New York and the accompanying book) is in a vernacular that conveys a people's locality, their history, tradition, material culture and ancestral skills.

For a Western audience, the Egyptian architect Hassan Fathy tends to encompass the image of the Orient. In the non-Western context, however, Fathy's vision of a vernacular architecture for the poor in rural Egypt could not have been achieved without his family fortune. He states in his book, *Architecture for the Poor: An Experiment in Rural Egypt*, that one of his dreams was 'to build a village where the fellaheen [farmers] would follow the way of life that I would like them to' (Fathy 2000: 1). While Fathy embraced and celebrated traditional building techniques and methods, particularly the local process of mud-brick making, he viewed the experiment more as an architectural intervention than a locally driven initiative that gave the '*fellaheen*' (meaning 'farmers' in Arabic) people agency. This critical view of Fathy's work has been challenged by Nasser

Rabbat (2003), the Aga Khan Professor and Director of the Aga Khan Program for Islamic Architecture at MIT. Rabbat agreed to an interview for this book in 2022, where our aim was to outline, from a Middle Eastern perspective, the challenges to the production of knowledge in the fields of architecture and social science. Rabbat (2022) asserted that, despite the fact that there are silent or suppressed voices in certain classes, backgrounds, geographic locations, religions or sects, the production of knowledge is not democratically spread over any society. He adds:

> We have to acknowledge that the production of knowledge has historically always been the privilege of the powerful, the rich and the well-educated. Therefore, we cannot take it against Hassan Fathy, who comes from the aristocracy in Egypt and who was born to a wealthy family distant from the ordinary people on multiple levels, that his vision for the *fellaheen*, which he put together in 1940s Egypt, was to make them closer to the lifestyle of the aristocrats. Hassan Fathy was progressive architecturally, yet not class-conscious. He thought up a benevolent, utopian socialist approach, where the elite leads and it is out of the kindness of their hearts that they are going to try to uplift the life of the *fellaheen*. Fathy was not alone in this approach to projects across the Arab world. Colonial authorities and, later on, governments after independence, built housing for the poor where the poor questioned these projects' relevance and viability to their ways of living. You see this from the Carrières Centrales housing project by ATBAT Morocco [1952] all the way to the projects of Doxiadis in Baghdad [1955–8]. Across the Arab world, you see projects like these failing simply because they are not adjusting to the population that is supposed to be the beneficiary of such visions.

Interestingly, the narrative that distinguishes between the architecture of the people and that which is created by architects is increasingly being resisted by Western as much it has always been by non-Western scholars (Oliver 2003). In her seminal work, 'Vernacular Architecture', Preston Blier (2006) frames this highly debated narrative outside the narrow perspective of 'tradition' versus 'modernity' and injects an element of spatio-temporal 'change' into the meaning of the term. This perspective is further problematized as postcolonial planning practices sweep over to modernize cities and urban spaces in the Middle East (Selim 2016). This moved from local to regional to global factors that instilled change, as the term became adopted in psychological and haptic studies as well as in issues of class, ethnicity, political dominance, coloniality and globalization (Asquith and Vellinga 2006). Despite these wide-ranging references to vernacular architecture, spanning as they do from the domestic to the urban and peripheries, scholarship on the subject has been dominated by issues of domesticity and mobility (Preston Blier 2006: 239).

In 'Traditions of the Modern: A Corrupt View', Ananya Roy (2001: 10) discusses the geopolitics of modernity and its multiplicity through the question of tradition and authentication that situates the West in opposition to the 'underdeveloped world', 'Third World' or developing world. In this article, she uses the term 'multiple modernities' to imply a sense of surplus and ambiguity, two conditions that are not immediately associated with 'modernism' or 'modernization' (Roy 2001: 11). She further asserts this position by postulating that 'the idea of multiplicity can be understood not so much as historical diversity but rather as a constantly contested hegemony, a subversion of the singular ideal of the modern' (Roy 2001: 11). Understanding tradition through modernity (and vice versa), considering their complexities, helps us to uproot the concept of the vernacular from the locality of people's history and authentic, indigenous traditions. This, in turn, allows us to connect the concept to the multiplicity of people's mobility and transnational existence. The vernacular, as much to do with the now as it is to do with the past, therefore, embodies the moment while depending on its memory and its different representations, and hence embraces multiplicity, temporality and change. These characteristics are manifested in architecture as well as embodied in everyday creativity and spatial practices across multiple scales, from home to urban, rural and border spaces. The transition between these varied scales of spatiality is one of the distinctive expressions in this book that help us visualize the structure of spatial practices.

Rupturing Architecture acknowledges this multiplicity, in conjunction with domesticity, of the vernacular especially in relation to another term extensively studied by Roy (2005), that of 'informality'. Roy seeks to locate the production of theories and policies on how cities function in the developing world. In so doing, she is not attempting to create a wedge between the Euro-American centric view of the making of cities and that of the developing world, but rather she is emphasizing the need to engage with *informality* and its state of exception from the formal and plannable (on an urban scale) to allow for spatially distributed justice to emerge (Roy 2005: 147). In their edited collection *Urban Informality: Transnational Perspectives from the Middle East, Latin America, and South Asia*, Ananya Roy and Nezar AlSayyad (2004) discuss the importance of transnational perspectives when considering 'informality' in different contexts. By doing so, they move away from comparisons, especially those that place the underdeveloped world in an inferior position to that of the developed world. Instead, they interrogate the urban conditions of informality in one context in order to generate new configurations in another (Roy and AlSayyad 2004: 4). They define 'urban informality' as: 'a process of structuration that constitutes the rules of the game, determining the nature of the transactions between individuals and institutions and within institutions. If formality operates through value, including the mapping of spatial value, then informality operates through the constant negotiability of value and the unmapping of space' (Roy and AlSayyad 2004: 5). Their model for studying informality transcends borders, but is also political, taking into account knowledge divides such as the split between the so-called Global North and Global

South. Their collection presents a post-structuralist model of knowledge sharing that emphasizes transnational conceptualizations of practices (social and spatial) that empower the marginalized as much as they enrich the developed world.

One of the most relevant examples related to the way this book recognizes vernacular domesticity, which embodies a post-structuralist model of knowledge sharing that includes multiplicity and informality, can be seen in the work of Nabeel Hamdi. In *Small Change: About the Art of Practice and the Limits of Planning in Cities*, Hamdi (2004) champions the dialectic practice of participatory development. While acknowledging top-down planning structures, it takes a bottom-up approach to practice that begins with local, collective imagination and creativity and develops globally through incremental small-scale actions. Hamdi (2004: xix) postulates in the introduction to *Small Change* that 'Practice disturbs', and he further describes practice as a triadic 'form of activism' that addresses the complicated messiness of spatial injustice in the world through collective and creative imagination in 'making things happen'. In order to make 'informed choices' and 'create opportunities for change' (Hamdi 2004: xix), we must first understand the context before influencing global change.

More recently, after the 2020 explosion in the Port of Beirut that caused over 200 deaths and displaced over 300,000 people, a group of architects, planners, critical cartographers and educators at the School of Architecture and Design in the American University in Beirut made consolidated efforts to establish the Beirut Urban Lab. This is a collaborative platform of critical enquiry and engaged research in contemporary urbanization that works collectively with urban citizens 'aspiring to just, inclusive, and viable cities' (Beirut Urban Lab n.d.). In this way, their work resembles that of Hamdi, but from a collective standpoint. The projects led by Beirut Urban Lab engage with social and spatial themes, using critical mapping and participatory planning methods to develop a strategy for urban recovery that values informality. Their work centres on the act of creating and imagining multiplicities of change that will develop the necessary practice in order to disrupt and negotiate existing local structures. Like Hamdi's *Small Change* (2004) and Roy and AlSayyad's *Urban Informality* (2004), this book also champions spatial and social equality and justice, identified locally yet applicable transnationally. In *Improvised Cities*, Helen Gyger (2019) provides a history of aided self-help housing in post-war Peru that intersects with concepts of vernacular housing, urban informality and architectural production in relation to agency and the availability of resources. In her work, Gyger (2019: 4) does not address architectural practices alone in the context of providing housing in times of crisis, but instead examines the conflictual interface between 'formal architecture', which she defines as 'an expertise in design and construction' with the 'informal building', understood to be 'substantially cost savings, because residents themselves furnished the labor'. These aided self-help housing projects are typically more dependent on the state and the economic growth of the cities in which they are situated, as they are usually guided by a form of structural formality led by architectural practices. Thus, their conceptual paradigm is rooted in the unbalanced, the marginal, the dependent and the informal, and aided self-built housing in Peru remains at the heart of urban housing developments and the conceptualization of cities in Latin America (Gyger 2019: 24–5).

The journey to understand the multifaceted conceptualizations of vernacular informality has tended to situate it in spatial practices of domesticity and urbanization (home, housing, shelter) as well as mobility (the multiple negotiations between constantly shifting spaces). Operating in cities and on the peripheries and borders, these spatial practices constitute the main subjects of this book and continue to dominate debates on humanitarian living in the fields of architecture, planning, geography and sociology, among others. The field of humanitarian architecture has similarly concerned itself with vernacular tradition, incremental change and development, and can thus be described as a form of practice that is socially, collectively and culturally driven. The appropriateness of the term 'humanitarian' being used in relation to architecture has been questioned, however, all architecture must by definition be humanitarian, if the word refers to the many ways in which architecture can serve a variety of community groups with design solutions to both everyday problems and major crises. At the heart of this debate are concepts of shelter and refuge, and the politicization of architecture itself as it runs through all aspects of life and the built environment (Charlesworth 2014: 4). This book is concerned with the type of humanitarian architecture that relates to 'development', rather than those that are associated with the 'design parachute' or 'fly-in-fly-out' approaches (when agents 'fly in' without understanding the context or consulting those affected, implement preconceived architectural practices and schemes, and then leave) (Charlesworth 2014: 4).

If we take refugee camps as one example, we see that humanitarian design sometimes operates within a system of dependency and helplessness, where the emergency of the crisis appears to justify a sense of transience. But given the lengths of stay and the spatial practices that emerge from within these places, where we see signs of resistance, adaptation and negotiated development occurring on a daily basis, we ought to interrogate the impermanence associated with these spaces (Aksamija, Majzoub and Philippou 2021: 261). With varying degrees of success, humanitarian responses and development initiatives within post-conflict and post-disaster contexts have attempted to engage with this sense of 'localization' regarding tradition and the vernacular. The concept of localization in humanitarian aid, relates to scale in geographical, sociological, political and economic terms. In its essence, localization is 'a relational concept dealing with power relations between the local and the international, the local and the regional, or the local and the national' (Barakat and Milton 2020: 154). As such, the concept can shift and change – the local is not a static entity.

Structures of refuge are diverse – vernacular and traditional, informal and local, implemented through humanitarian aid or emerging creatively through everyday participatory development initiatives. From refuge, we get a material and spatial sense of protection, implying physical shelter from external or unfamiliar conditions. Tom Scott-Smith (2020: 5) couples the term protection with shelter, stating, 'If shelters are structures of protection, there always remains a great deal of flexibility in the dynamics of who is protected, how, and what they are being protected from.' Scott-Smith (2020: 4) further defines shelter within a wider category of spatial structures of sheltering that is considered a process and an activity offering varying degree of protection, veering towards the purposefulness of home, domesticity and other buildings. While I understand the distinction Scott-Smith makes here, as he speaks of specific types of shelters as structures that do not fit within the usual concepts of domesticity or building typologies, I instead consider shelters (as structures of varying degrees of protection) to be in constant spatial and social negotiation with concepts of domesticity and urbanity. Writing on the subject of shelters as structures of refuge and protection for displacees that usually appear on the borders between states, Anooradha Iyer Siddiqi (2017: 521) asserts that these 'borderlands' always manifest themselves in some sort of construction:

> Thus, in spite of their conditions of particularity and situatedness, these architectures make a claim to the universal – not in any flattened embodiments of meaning that lie elsewhere, but rather in the discursive extension of their very materiality as framing and constitutive of the borderland. Moreover, all architectures incorporate and delimit a different border altogether, one less concrete and more conceptual. It spans the distance between the formality of institutions and instruments and the informality of undetermined activity and practices.

Siddiqi alludes to such borderland architecture as forming the starting point for most spatial practice that unfolds while negotiating formal and informal modalities. Camillo Boano (2011: 52) adds to this concept of formality and informality within protection practices as he describes humanitarian post-war/conflict/disaster spaces in the following way: 'the provision of security is simultaneously the production of physical form, the creation of social, cultural and symbolic resources and also, critically, the outcome of a facilitative process in which enablement becomes a central idea. Such an approach fundamentally repositions the role of architects'. This further affirms the notion that the spatial practice of protection and refuge concerns social spaces with 'micro-practices of powers' in everyday life for people seeking protection (Boano 2011: 52).

Struggle over refuge

Iraq's struggle over refuge stretches back centuries, as over the years state power structures and social structures have fallen out of sync with one another. In his book, *The Struggle for Iraq's Future*, Zaid Al-Ali (2014: 103) provides an extensive account of the legacy of oppression and violence since the establishment of the state of Iraq that has driven a wedge between state powers and the Iraqi people. The history of this struggle and division between state power and people is pertinent to this book, as it confirms the protractedness of rupture at political, social and spatial levels. Baghdad in particular has witnessed an eventful history since Caliph Al-Mansur first announced it as the capital of the Abbasid Caliphate in the year 762 CE (Gulick 1967). With its centralized head of state and power, its circular walls and four fortified gates, Baghdad was characterized by its capacity for defence and protection (Petersen 1999). The city enjoyed a period of cultural development (both spatially and socially), which ended when the Caliphate was defeated by the Mongols, led by Hulagu Khan, in 1258. Ever since, the country has been subjected to numerous sieges, battles, wars and conflicts. After the Mongols came the Turks in 1638, in which the Ottomans wrested Baghdad from the Persian Empire, and 1920 brought with it British colonization following an invasion in 1917, which was part of the British Mandate following the First World War. After the official announcement of Iraq's independence in 1932, there followed three coups d'état: the first, in 1958, overthrew the monarchy in favour of the First Iraqi Republic; the second, in 1963, brought with it further military violence caused by divisions inside the political ruling party; on the third occasion, in 1968, the Socialist Arab Ba'ath Party took power in Baghdad. Importantly, the built environment formed a significant part of this politically charged violent history, as lavish palaces and other governmental and strategic buildings are seen as key symbols of power in cities.

This era also saw Saddam Hussein become president of Iraq in 1979, followed immediately by an eight-year war from 1980 to 1988 between Iraq and Iran. In 1990, Iraq invaded Kuwait, triggering the first Gulf War in 1991. Following this war came UN Security Council Resolution 661, which imposed sanctions lasting nearly thirteen years, and caused Iraq (particularly Baghdad) to fall into complete despair. The international economic sanctions set out by UN Security Council Resolution 661 are believed to be the harshest placed on a nation in the late twentieth century (Gordon 2010: 20). Nevertheless, it was not until the 2003 US-led invasion of Iraq that Baghdad and the rest of the country were reduced to a state worse than that following the 1258 Mongolian invasion. The massive bombardment known as 'Shock and Awe' lit and rocked Baghdad and other major targets across Iraq at the dawn of a tremendous war which began on 20 March 2003. It targeted infrastructure, military and industrial bases, palaces and whatever lay in between, and after three weeks, the capital fell to the control of the US-led

Multinational Forces in Iraq (MNF-I). This was marked by the famous toppling of Saddam Hussein's statue in Baghdad's Firdos Square on 9 April (Anderson 2006), and ignited a period of looting and lawlessness, leading to sectarianism and the rise of ISIS in the region. The culmination of this historic account of events delineates the context for this book, providing the reader with a snippet of background to Iraq's violent history. There yet remains, however, a scarcity of information at the granular level – the level of the everyday for people and their cities, their stories of struggle for protection and survival. This book attempts in part to fill this gap from a spatial perspective, as it focuses on spaces of refuge.

Embedded in Iraq's history of violence, this book provides a wealth of examples of injustice, but also demonstrates the richness of ordinary people's responses to the trauma inflicted upon them – all through an architectural and spatial lens. While we have addressed some of Iraq's recent eventful history of violence, a wider view of its context and history would include the establishment of its early civilization, its natural resources of crude oil and other minerals, its two famous rivers (Tigris and Euphrates) and its strategic location. The country sits amid an important network of conflicting geopolitical powers: it is west of a strong Middle Eastern religious influence (Iran), south of a different type of political power (Turkey), north of yet another (Saudi Arabia and the Gulf region) and in close proximity to Israel and Russia. Its distinct, traditional architecture is eroding from neglect, even while its ancient remnants of early civilization are listed amongst the most endangered UNESCO heritage sites. In *Seeking Spatial Justice*, Soja (2010: 13) suggests 'seeing the search for social justice as a struggle over geography', a notion he borrows from Edward Said. To expand upon Soja (2010) and Said's (1993) complex notion of 'struggle over geography', I am suggesting a struggle *with* and *within* geography that is constantly negotiated and ruptured (made and remade), to begin to unpack critical spatial practices from the perspective of Iraqis themselves. Anthony Shadid (2006: 15) echoes this struggle in his seminal work, *Night Draws Near: Iraq's People in the Shadow of America's War*, where he sheds light on ordinary Iraqis' narratives as they prepare emotionally for the US-led invasion of Iraq and its aftermath, describing Baghdad as 'a city of lives interrupted, its history a story of loss, waiting and resilience'. In his work, Shadid (2006) situates an entire country in a place of waiting, waiting too long to receive significant change or improvement for its people or future.

As well as having their lives interrupted, every single Iraqi found themselves in great need of shelter and refuge from war and violence, affecting their mobility within neighbourhoods, cities, across the country and beyond. People were on the move in what appeared to be a constant process of seeking refuge at relatives' houses or in shelters, escaping expected targets and travelling to neighbouring cities. The lack of documentation and statistics regarding houses damaged and destroyed during the bombing offensive exacerbated what was already a housing crisis at the time, with Baghdad alone identifying over 50,000 homeless people by the end of 2003 (IRIN News 2005), and Iraq as a whole being short of 1.5 million homes (a number that had risen to 2.7 million by the end of 2019; Al-Mamouri 2020). This constant search for shelter and refuge made Iraqis agile in their mobility and movements, a skilful characteristic that was put to the test several times, especially during the sectarian violence of 2006 and 2008, where cities became ethnically segregated. It would take another stand-alone project and accompanying monograph to map the mobility of Iraqis in search of shelter and refuge over the years of war, conflict and displacement, showing nonlinear routes drifting out of and returning to wounded cities. Yet the core focus of this book seeks to understand the context that shaped the structures of refuge and the struggle over (and with) geography in these 'wounded cities' (Till 2012). Karen E. Till (2012: 12) presents the possibilities that can arise from reimagining violated cities through memory-work and place-based ethics of care, where she postulates: 'When individuals return to places that have witnessed pain and violence, but are now being cared for and may offer care, they can be again surrounded by living memory and emotional attachments, providing a safe space for personal self-reflection, discovery, and change'. Veena Das (2007: 7) similarly follows Till's ethics of care with the idea of 'a descent into the ordinary' and the everyday, to trigger healing and recovery from trauma. *Rupturing Architecture* engages with such everyday narratives and case studies that embrace the notion of *return*, a return to rebuild and to re-establish life, in a material and cognitive sense, through memory-work.

In *Frames of War*, Judith Butler (2009) considers the different frames through which war is selectively and continuously constructed, presented and positioned. She defines 'frames of war' as 'the ways of selectively carving up experience as essential to the conduct of war. Such frames do not merely reflect on the material conditions of war, but are essential to the perpetually crafted *animus* of that material reality' (Butler 2009: 26). She further adds examples of such frames, such as 'the frame of the photography' and 'the framing of the decision to go to war', the 'framing of immigration issues as a "war at home"', and among others, the contingency and precarity of the lives and social structures facing political turmoil, war and violence (Butler 2009: 26). If we apply Butler's concept of 'frames of war' to the context of Iraq, focusing specifically on the segments of history affected by war and violence over the first two decades of the twenty-first century, we see that these frames shifted and changed from that of a foreign invasion and an occupation to sectarian violence amongst Iraqis, followed by a war waged against the rise of ISIS and a genocide at the hands of ISIS members. These socially, religiously and politically motivated frames overlap and jar heavily with the alternative frames of spatial practices of refuge, of segregation and of displacement that were also occurring simultaneously. Each chapter in this book attempts to situate the case studies and their associated narratives of lived and felt experience through their relevant, precarious frames. Examples of such overlapping frames have been critically constructed before in the work of Zainab Bahrani (2008), Robert Bevan (2016) and Rosie Bsheer (2017), in which the precariousness of architecture and buildings is viewed against the rhetoric of their permanence, especially in relation to violated memory and heritage. These frames portray architecture as the material physicality of the politics of war and violence, something Eyal Weizman (2017: 6–7) refers to as 'elastic geography' in relation to the shifting and changing frontiers of the Separation Wall between Palestinian and Israeli territories.

Weizman's *Hollow Land* (2017) grapples with the plasticity of the notion of 'frontier architecture' – architectural and landscape features that are used to maintain border changes – erected in this case by Israel to violently dominate Palestinian land. Ho*llow Land* catalogues the ways in which military fortifications, settlements, checkpoints, walls and even airspace have been utilized to maintain Palestine as a constantly surveilled war zone. Weizman explicitly focuses on how conflict mutates cities as well as the material culture of a population living under the constant threat of violence and war, and centres his research around the architecture imposed on Palestinians in their everyday lives. Like Weizman, Lebbeus Woods (1993) produced a manifesto or pamphlet entitled *War and Architecture*, concerning post-conflict spatial creativity in Sarajevo in the midst of war between Bosnia and Herzegovina, from 1992 to 1996. In this work, Woods considers the two dominant responses to rebuilding a city after war damage – restoring the pre-war city or beginning afresh – and dismisses these strategies in favour of maintaining the 'scars' of the city as a wounded organism. In doing so, Woods joined an organized group of local architects who had already begun their observations and documentation of the shelling of the city and its destruction during the violent four-year siege. Sarajevo's architects were thus directly participating in what Armina Pilav (2020) terms 'architects in war' engaged with the 'city at war'.

Several similar studies to those of the Sarajevo architects have also emerged from the Middle East by local architects and planners from Lebanon (Al-Harithy 2010), Syria (Al-Sabouni 2016) and Palestine (Abujidi 2019). Their scholarly work engages deeply in discussions that concern the impact of conflict and war on the built environment and on collective memory and the future lessons architects and planners can learn from spatial violence. This book emerges from a progression of work within the disciplines of architecture, planning and/or geography on the impact of war and violence in Iraq beginning with architectural heritage under violence and major architectural movements in Iraq's history (Alslik 2008), and moving into questions of sectarian (Damluji 2010) and territorial politics in cities (Rashid and Alobaydi 2015), as well as architecture and national identity (Merie 2021). Interest in these areas was equally matched by other Iraqi creative practitioners, who joined those in the diaspora in working on trauma that 'not only destroys but creates' in a volume that reclaims resistance through imagining, creating and opposing the oppressive structures of power (Al-Ali and Al-Najjar 2013: xxvi).

Rupturing Architecture dwells on the very essence of imaginative and creative expressions of resistance to violence and trauma, while acknowledging Iraq's historic significance and its heritage, as well as the transnational collective identity of Iraqis. This chapter puts forward the foundational concepts and methodological framework of the book, focusing on the critical role of positionality in understanding architecture and spatial practices in Iraq amidst war and violence. It employs deep mapping and a multidisciplinary lens, influenced by reflexive feminist, postcolonial and post-structuralist thought, to explore key notions, in particular, notions of trauma, memory, refuge and justice within the context of Iraqi struggles. Through examining the historical and contemporary impacts of conflict on Iraq's architectural heritage and identity, as well as the creative expressions of resistance and the pursuit of justice, the chapter lays the groundwork for a deeper investigation into the socially and locally driven architectures that emerge in response to trauma.

2 SITING TRAUMA SPATIALLY: NEGOTIATED AND CENTRALIZED SPATIAL RESPONSES FROM THE GLOBAL NORTH AND SOUTH

At the start of war, people's senses are overwhelmed by an onslaught of haunting sights, sounds, fears, responsibilities, hopes and feelings of despair. Depending on the traumas previously endured by these witnesses to war, these shocks serve either to create new trauma or reveal old trauma as they reverberate and resonate within their bodies. The traumas discussed in this book are political, social and spatial. Bombing campaigns, sirens and shelling during times of war, urban conflict, ethnic cleansing, genocide, protests and revolutions all form powerful triggers of psychological and social trauma, marking the spatial realities of domicide, urbicide and displacement. This chapter scours deeply the spatiality and locality of trauma by examining the ways in which it has been historically embodied within spatial structures of shelter and refuge. It first explores how the West responded to the spatial trauma of war on the 'Home Front' (particularly in Britain and the United States), how governments in the Global North instructed their citizens to protect themselves from air raids during the Second World War and, later, how these same governments conveyed the new threat of nuclear explosions and radioactive debris during the Cold War. The chapter situates these negotiated and centralized responses alongside the informal and of-the-moment structures of refuge that emerged in the Global South.

Discussions around this disparity in spatial responses to trauma from the Global North and South are supported by interviews with experts and thinkers in the field of architecture and spatial practice, offering particular insight into the context of the Middle East. The chapter concludes that, wherever in the world they may occur, the traumas of war, conflict and displacement are similar in that they are spatially induced, locally negotiated and politically diverse, and simultaneously afford possibilities for expanded models of alternative spatiality. It is crucial, however, to critically examine the somewhat arbitrary geographical divide that categorizes regions into the Global South and Global North, or the West and the East, amongst other dichotomizing terms. The origins of such classifications are deeply embedded in racism and coloniality, which ascribed hierarchical value to certain groups over others (Khan et al. 2022). Despite their contentious roots, these distinctions still offer utility. They facilitate comparison, reflexivity and positionality, which are essential in confronting and resisting the myriad injustices present in the world. This analytical framework is particularly pertinent in addressing the trauma discussed in this chapter, allowing for a more nuanced understanding and response to spatial manifestations of trauma. Through this lens, the exploration of spatial justice and the development of alternative spatial models become enriched, prioritizing diversity, equity and inclusion.

Locating trauma

If trauma were a single event consisting of cause and effect, then the act of locating it would allow for the process of recovery and healing to take place. The trauma discussed in this book, however, cannot be considered a singular experience associated with a specific place or time. Instead, it is trauma that is located temporally and spatially both everywhere and 'elsewhere' (Coddington and Micieli-Voutsinas 2017), and considered 'otherwise' – what Cathy Caruth (1995) describes as being connected to other places and occurring in other times. 'The trauma is a repeated suffering of the event, but it is also a continual leaving of its site', writes Caruth (1995: 10), yet even a return to the original site of trauma alters the experience of that place, just as remembering the site triggers different (even retraumatizing) experiences of trauma. In this chapter, our understanding of trauma follows the framing set out by Kate Coddington and Jacque Micieli-Voutsinas (2017: 3), who postulate that, 'Framing trauma through its location elsewhere allows for the conception of its movement across places, spaces and times, and recognizes how it is relationally experienced across scales, bodies and emotions'. As we traverse the spatiality and temporality of traumatic experience through acts of remembering and re-siting, we find that locating that trauma 'elsewhere' reveals the precarity of its positioning both in and out of place, as well as its embodiment and disembodiment within that place. This confirms the origin of trauma as a multiplicity of time and space with unmappable topological qualities that do not conform to Euclidean geometry and Cartesian coordinates (Blum and Secor 2014).

In *Mapping Trauma: Topography to Topology*, Virginia L. Blum and Anna J. Secor (2014: 105) develop the topological structure of trauma from the philosophy and psychoanalysis of Sigmund Freud and Jacques Lacan, arguing structure to be 'at once cause and effect of physical repetition phenomena'. These repetition phenomena, which occur in response to trauma triggered out of place and nonlinear time through the acts of remembering, dreaming or revisiting the physical space, are considered the framework through which we can explain the structure of trauma as topological (associated with the interconnectedness of relational and malleable characteristics of space) rather than topographical (space that is localized, mappable and measurable). Trauma can remain in the subconscious for years and seep out in a different context, yet its structure is always associated with a spatiality – a space of multiplicity. Blum and Secor (2014: 115) explain, 'we have shown that trauma – trauma conscious or unconscious, whether domestic or on the battlefield – by its very nature defies temporal linearity and the Cartesian grid. Instead, trauma works as a topological constellation, a set of unconscious coordinates that upends the passage of time and the verities of space'. This structure complements trauma's somatic qualities, which Gail Adams-Hutcheson (2017: 111) speaks about in *Spatialising Skin*, where she views trauma through the metaphor of skin, a substance in which somatic qualities transcend the 'interior-exterior, nature-culture, mind and body' and instead slide into the different scales of embodied possibilities inherently linked within these concepts, 'allowing focus on borders, envelopes, boundaries, fluidity, porosity and similar spatial vocabularies'. To contextualize this topological quality of trauma in the context of Iraq's recent history is to explore the manifestations of trauma on the Iraqi people, whether they stayed, were forcibly displaced or chose to emigrate. Those who stayed had to deal with concepts of survival, domicide and urbicide; those who were forcibly displaced encountered notions of loss and questions of return; and those who emigrated to live in the diaspora experienced a longing for home. Each of these types of trauma overlap temporally and in conjunction with their multiple spatiality.

In its causes, effects and manifestations, spatial violence in war-torn cities parallels the multiplicity of repetition phenomena relating to trauma. The reality of spatial violence is that it is diverse and ambiguous in its nonlinear impact on people, cities and the other forms of violence it perpetuates. In peace and conflict research, it is vital to recognize the patterns of ambiguity surrounding the structural forms of violence and their interconnections, as they require diverse and specific policy responses in order to counter it (Elfversson, Gusic and Höglund 2019: 85). Andrew Herscher and Anooradha Iyer Siddiqi (2014: 269) go further to locate spatial violence within the roots of the history of architecture and the built environment, characterizing architecture as an agent of violence, not simply the subject of it. This activates the meaning of violence within architecture as a primary source of knowledge and world-making. The spatial violence expressed in *Rupturing Architecture* engages in diverse ways with this notion of knowledge-making within spatial practice, sometimes in a manner that seems contradictory. It does so, on the one hand, through the informal and formal making of spaces of refuge, and, on the other hand, through the destruction of these same spaces, as well as the challenge of historiographical spatial violence in relation to the protracted rupture and trauma within domestic, urban and border spaces. In *All Over the Map*, Michael Sorkin (2011) argues that spatial violence is a political manifestation of urbanism. The example he uses is the destruction of the West Bank refugee settlements by Israeli forces, which he posits to be an 'act of urbanism' that is wedged in between other forms of spatial violence and manifested in the constructions of illegal Jewish settlements and Palestinian retaliation to the occupation (Sorkin 2011: 58).

In attempting to articulate the relationship between trauma and architecture, Teresa Stoppani (2016) raises several questions. These are intrinsic to the genealogy of architecture as a process and a practice of making that can both traumatize and be traumatized. Stoppani's discussion, however, falls short of fully incorporating the structure of trauma and violence into the porousness of architecture beyond the means of representation, design and practice of making and cultural production. Bernard Tschumi (1999) speaks of a different type of violence – not that of material destruction, but in a metaphorical sense, expressing the intense interrelation between people and the spaces they occupy. Instead of relating violence to particular styles and movements within the discourse of architecture, Tschumi connects architecture's violence (violence done both to architecture and by architecture) to events and the actions within those events. He further emphasizes the coupling of architecture and violence by adding:

> 1 There is no architecture without action, no architecture without events, no architecture without program.
>
> 2 By extension, there is no architecture without violence.
>
> (Tschumi 1999: 121)

As a discourse, practice and cultural production, architecture has a long history of being treated as the subject of power (e.g. in the grandiose palaces in Iraq) and/or trauma (e.g. in the destruction of key buildings with cultural value as sites of the ingrained trauma of war and violence). Yet in times of flux such as war and violence, these sites and buildings do not remain the same, nor should their pre-war status be reinstated after the trauma has ended. War and violence alter cities as much as they change people, therefore any consideration of post-trauma building should take into account the irreversible changes that have also made their mark on people. Woods' (2015) drawings of Sarajevo have been criticized for fetishizing violence in architecture (explored in an article by Aarati Kanekar [2010: 789]), as they seemed to glorify the trauma inflicted on the city's buildings. He later responds by explaining that what he was suggesting was not a blueprint for a scarred city that could be replicated in other traumatized cities, but rather three conceptual principles, each of which must be led locally. These were presented as a way of categorizing the types of buildings destroyed to be either restored (in the case of cultural buildings), demolished or reconstructed; further, 'the salvageable building stock must be used to build the "new" city' (Woods 2015: 201). Woods' manifesto for the slow reconstruction of post-war cities was not meant to be used by the people but rather as a way to reinstate the authorship of restored, demolished and newly designed buildings, spaces and cities to local architects. Pain (2019) describes trauma as being hard-wired in places, making them sites of 'chronic trauma' that have the capacity to re-traumatize and therefore potentially shift and change, embracing possibilities for healing and rebuilding (Pain 2019). *Rupturing Architecture* examines the principles of Woods' slow manifesto, not from the perspective of the architect, but rather from the point of view of the people and their spatial practices, within which Pain's chronic trauma is soft and hard-wired, located, created and negotiated constantly over time.

Two archetypes of spatial trauma are discussed throughout this book: one is triggered by socio-political and external structures, and the other is triggered by people's spatial responses to socio-political forces. The first type of trauma is represented and portrayed through the physical impact of war (bombing, shelling and destruction at scale), conflict and sectarian violence (looting, kidnapping and ethnic cleansing), and the resultant displacement of people (uprooting and moving within/between cities, to camps or out of the country) (Wimmer 2003). This type of trauma is similar to that described by Kenneth Hewitt (1983) as 'place annihilation' – namely, domicide and urbicide. The second type of trauma happens simultaneously, in a palimpsestic manner, across and between all the triggers listed above: it is represented in the performative and layered changes people must make to their built environment when seeking refuge. This is performative because the emerging spatial practices are nimble in their responses to change, transforming old familiar places to new ones. These practices both resist destruction and are yet destructive themselves, as they break the structures (material and social) of the built environment at a smaller scale (from a room in a house to a strategic entrance into a neighbourhood, etc.). The layered, embodied performativity of this second type of trauma absorbs people into a constantly negotiated state of creative and innovative world- and place-making, a practice that is antithetical to Hewitt's (1983) 'place annihilation'. An attempt to locate trauma would defy the purpose here, because its performativity is crucially connected to the fact that new and alternative spatial practices are constantly being created.

Dwelling, shelter and refuge

Dwelling, shelter and refuge are concepts that are entangled socially, spatially and anthropologically with notions of home, habitation, being and becoming in the world. In this section, I attempt the challenge of retheorizing these concepts anew, paying particular attention to meaning, representation and expression from a critical, postcolonial perspective, rather than a Euro-American one. This section therefore cuts a cross-section through the more widely referenced literature on dwelling and home by writers from the West, placing them in dialogue with writers from the East (in this context, West and East are loosely connected to the Global North and South respectively – this is explored further in the following section). It is not always possible to map this dialogue, particularly within the context of the Middle East and North Africa, but nevertheless it is fair to say that, whenever this cannot be done, this is due to the fact that they (like most of the Global South) have had to invest a considerable amount of time and energy in developing a unifying, postcolonial national identity (Kumaraswamy 2006). It is arguable that this is highly influenced by a shared language (mainly Arabic, although there are other languages and dialects and different ethnicities across the region), as well as a shared struggle in the form of colonial resistance, symbolized over the years in Palestinian resistance to oppression and occupation.

From the Western perspective, the seminal essay 'Building, Dwelling, Thinking' by Martin Heidegger (1992) dominated the architecture scene in the latter half of the twentieth century in its coupling of the concepts of dwelling and building. In this work, Heidegger (1992: 362) relates dwelling to the fundamental characteristics of being in the world, as with shelter, home and the everyday (Lane 2007). While Heidegger conceptually connects dwelling to being, Paul Oliver (1975) explores similar connections through an anthropological lens as he considers sheltering to be another spatial practice of the everyday, indigenous and vernacular form of dwelling and being. Among others, both Heidegger and Oliver chose to clarify their position, resisting the assimilation of the notions of dwelling and shelter into pure architectural forms, and indicating instead that both concepts should incorporate acts associated with everyday being in the world. Building on Heidegger's notion of dwelling, Tim Ingold (2000) defines his 'dwelling perspective' as not only being in the world, but also occupying the world that is formed around interactions with the built environment – to which I would add becoming and evolving in the world (see further relevance to Nelson Goodman's 'worldmaking' [Goodman 1978] as a form of everyday spatial practice [Murrani 2017]). Such a formulation reverses Western thought and focuses on the process of dwelling instead of the form of inhabitation. Ingold (2000: 186) sees this to be the defining statement of his 'dwelling perspective' stating: 'the forms people build, whether in the imagination or on the ground, arise within the current of their involved activity, in the specific relational contexts of their practical engagement with their surroundings.

Building, then, cannot be understood as a simple process of transcription, of a pre-existing design of the final product onto a raw material substrate'. Later, he affirms his opposition to the idea that form constitutes the ultimate object of design, postulating, 'To the contrary, a dwelling perspective ascribes the generation of form to those very processes whose creativity is denied by that perspective which sees in every form the concrete realisation of an intellectual solution to a design problem' (Ingold 2000: 186).

For the majority of the Arabic-speaking world, the second half of the twentieth century experienced the concepts of dwelling and shelter as being directly associated with concepts of home, tradition and vernacular with respect to postcolonial nation- and state-building and identity (Jackson 2016). Many architects, such as Ihsan Fethi (Warren and Fethi 1982), Rifat Chadirji (1986) and Nabeel Hamdi (1995), among others across the region, indulged in a type of architecture centred around traditional and vernacular practices. Mohamed Gamal Abdelmonem (2017: 35) affirms that such spatial practices are constantly tested against different social and spatial modalities both within and outside the home, moving beyond form, image and architectural features, towards the creation of new practices that occupy spaces and are negotiated around everyday life in communities and cities. Such understandings of home and dwelling function as acts of resistance, and resonate with the emerging architectural work across the region that is politically engaged in, and responsive to, the cultural production of the emerging urban conditions that transcend notions of identity, authenticity and tradition (Andraos and Akawi 2015). The volume, *Open Gaza: Architectures of Hope,* edited by Michael Sorkin and Deen Sharp (2021) features the work of a number of emerging visionary researchers who have created spatial interventions that imagine a better place for the Gazans and Palestinians experiencing limitations, violence and warfare in the face of their traditional ways of dwelling in and inhabiting the city (Sorkin and Sharp 2021). These acts of resistance echo bell hooks' (1990) expression of 'homeplace' as 'a site of resistance'.

Although hooks' 'homeplace' piece (1990) speaks of a different form of resistance – one that is driven by racial inequality – the domestic entanglement of dwelling, home and women's spaces evident in her work resembles those of the private and public gendered spaces in the Middle East. In hooks' work, concepts of dwelling, shelter and refuge quickly overlap each other in a palimpsestic way in the gendered spaces of domesticity. The spatial practices of homeplace discussed in this book resonate with hooks' (1990: 43) depiction of 'the construction of a safe place' that allows for nurturing and for affirming resistance against oppression (in hooks' case, against racism and white supremacy). 'This task of making a homeplace, of making home a community of resistance,' adds hooks (1990: 43), 'has been shared by black women globally, especially black women in white supremacist societies'. Although narratives of homeplace depicted as sites of refuge, nurturing and affirmation exist, so do counternarratives that explore trauma and violence within homeplace (Brickell 2012). But before we delve deeper into the different typologies of homeplace, I would like to address the parallel narrative of gendered spaces of refuge, dwelling and home from a Middle Eastern perspective.

As practices, dwelling and homemaking share links with scholarship on architecture, where descriptions of homeplaces take on a literal translation of the spatial practices that occur within the home. At times, these descriptions acknowledge the gendered roles associated with certain spaces, or other dynamic and constantly evolving routines where spaces and functions collide, change and transition. For example, in the Arabic-speaking world, these transitions can be dictated by several factors: climate (sleeping on rooftops in summer and inside in winter); roles and occupations (crafting, preparing food, teaching, etc.); or family dynamics and rites of passage (marriage, divorce, immigration, death, etc.). Dwelling as a practice is constantly negotiated in response to such internal family dynamics, and of course external factors can impact upon these, such as the political state of the country. Early scholarship on home and dwelling in the field of architecture by Warren and Fethi (1982) acknowledges the origins of the relationships between gender and home formation, and how these play significant roles in the making of Iraqi society. In her book, *Women and Gender in Iraq: Between Nation-Building and Fragmentation*, Zahra Ali (2018) adds that religion, political power, kinship, social class and divisions between urban and rural ways of living all contribute to the construction and fragmentation of the nation. Viewing these through the lenses of feminism and gender, Ali (2018: 48) further adds that 'being a woman is also being positioned within these groups and that ethnicity, sect, religion, class, location, kinship relations, and political and symbolic powers are all gendered in multiple and complex ways'. It is important to acknowledge, therefore, that in Middle Eastern society, gendered spaces and roles cannot be further removed from the linear view of the 'Orient' presented by the West, explored in detail in Said's (1979) work.

Nevertheless, these spatial practices of dwelling, home and domesticity are not free from oppression, gendered power imbalance, abuse, eviction and, pertinent to this book, the slow violence caused by protracted social, spatial and material ruptures. In her article 'The Idea of a Home: A Kind of Space', Mary Douglas (1991: 289) affirms that a home is not the sum of its functions, but rather the starting point for localizing some form of space (material or immaterial) that is 'under control'. Although she briefly mentions hierarchy and authority within the home (as opposed to centralized and authoritarian control), Douglas seems to return to the representation of home as a space connected to community without elaborating further on the part of control. Alison Blunt and Robyn Dowling (2006: 22) delve further into the idea of control, speaking of the home as a politicized site of oppression and resistance, and of feeling and emotion, as well as being a material place and a spatial imaginary. They further assert that home is made through 'home-making practices', where it 'is a process of creating and understanding forms of dwelling and belonging' (Blunt and Dowling 2006: 23). Katherine Brickell's (2012) work, *Geopolitics of Home*, brings further clarity around the issue of home as an intensely political site, calling on geographers to 'make space' in geopolitics for concepts and meanings of home. Brickell makes a compelling argument that imposes the geopolitics of warfare onto the spatiality of the domestic home and the people who dwell in it. She presents three overlapping themes that dissolve into one another, connecting lived and imagined notions of home to geopolitics: warfare at home (e.g. domicide, the bulldozing of Palestinian homes); home(land) and nation (e.g. transnational belonging and diaspora); and the domestic worlds of geopolitical actors (e.g. safe houses or public domesticity protests such as the Occupy movement) (Brickell 2012).

Brickell builds her arguments on the work of Massey (1994: 167), among others. Relevant to this study is Massey's rejection of the problematic and nostalgic association of home with 'stability, oneness and security' and its boundedness to notions of belonging and identity. Instead, Massey (1994: 167) ties notions of home to social relations that are 'in space', 'across space' and 'always have a spatial form and spatial content'. She then elaborates further on the complex relationships between 'particular social relations' as they interact with 'particular locations' that 'in turn produce new social effects' (Massey 1994: 167). Given this complexity, Massey confirms the contestation of 'identity of place' at home to be an identity in flux, responding to juxtapositions with place and social interrelations, and therefore 'unfixed'. She adds:

> They are unfixed in part precisely because the social relations out of which they are constructed are themselves by their very nature dynamic and changing. They are also unfixed because of the continual production of further social effects through the very juxtaposition of those social relations. Moreover, that lack of fixity has always been so. The past was no more static than is the present. Places cannot 'really' be characterized by the recourse to some essential, internalized moment.
>
> (Massey 1994: 169)

This continual production is ruptured and spatialized constantly by events and actions through time and space, a process described by Brickell (2012: 585) as '"Making spacing" for home in geopolitics' while 'paying attention to the mutual imbrication of geopolitics and home rather than re-instating binary divisions between them'. The concept of home as a place of shelter providing a unified sense of domesticity as homeliness is therefore thrown into question by the spatializing of modern warfare within the home.

In his seminal work, *The Location of Culture*, Homi Bhabha (1994) warns of the danger of fetishizing or romanticizing past identities and indigenous cultural heritage prior to their subordination and colonization by other cultures. Instead, he calls for 'presencing' and a sense of 'estrangement' – a 'relocation of home and the world – the unhomeliness – that is the condition of extra-territorial and cross-cultural initiations' (Bhabha 1994: 13). These notions of 'estrangement' and 'presencing' resonate with Vilém Flusser's (2003: 25) concept of 'unsettledness', which describes the essence of displacement and the loss of home (and homeland) and all that is familiar (*Heimat* in German) as a struggle amongst the rest of the world and all that is unfamiliar (Murrani 2020). Bhabha (1994: 13) traces this struggle between home and the world in his concept of 'homeliness', where 'recesses of the domestic space become sites for history's most intricate invasions. In that displacement, the borders between home and world become confused; and, uncannily, the private and the public become part of each other, forcing upon us a vision that is as divided as it is disorientating'. Such an 'estrangement' to home and 'presencing' in the world renders home as a site of resistance, where multiple spatial practices, however disorientating these might be, emerge. Moving beyond considering home as a site, a notion, a place, Paolo Boccagni (2022: 14) adds the *-ing* suffix to the word home, 'acknowledging some "mobility" in the very meaning of home' that encompasses 'home *as a place*', 'home *in the making*' and 'home *as becoming*'. As a category of analysis and practice, then, 'homing captures the experience of home as an open-ended endeavour that may never result in full and stable achievement, particularly for those with more fragmented life and housing trajectories' (Boccagni 2022: 14). This oscillating tension between 'homecoming' and 'becoming home' is what Boccagni (2022: 14) describes as the ultimate embodiment of 'homing' as an 'ontological struggle towards inclusion, recognition, and achievement of the ability to make oneself at home'.

In their article, 'Inhabitation as More-than-Dwelling', Camillo Boano and Giovanna Astolfo (2020: 569) argue that the meaning of dwelling should be recentred in the 'rubric of "inhabitation"', which would represent 'a contribution to the much needed re-centering of dwelling to include intersecting forms of caring, repairing and imagining the future, as a relational practice occurring in marginal and fragile environments and constituted by multiple incremental and transformative acts with the ultimate purpose to hold and resist marginalisation'. The spatial practices that unfold in the following chapters in this book are framed by Boano and Astolfo's concept of entanglement of different types of inhabitations and dwelling in forms of care, repair and imaginings, Brickell's concept of the geopolitics of home and hooks' concept of sites of resistance. These are considered across three sliding scales, from domestic to urban to the border/periphery, where the multiplicity of 'more-than-dwelling' (to borrow Boano and Astolfo's phrase) yields spatial practices that are not only constantly negotiated but also permanently changing from sites of resistance to sites of shelter and refuge, as well as sites of trauma and violence. The idea of shelter, then, carries this multiplicity, moving beyond the basic needs for inhabitation into the world, as frequently seen in humanitarian forms of shelter.

As we have seen, the dynamism of the concept of refuge means that it suggests the motion of fleeing as much as it does the making of a shelter, lending it a performativity across time and space. In *Narrating Refuge*, Colette Daiute (2017: 5) presents a compelling argument that situates the concept of refuge between purpose and responsibility, noting that it is affected by political, social, spatial, economic, and environmental dimensions in a 'complex zone of participation'. Daiute considers refuge to be 'a process of interactions' that 'invokes a scene with multiple persons in diverse roles, with diverse purposes and resources, engaged in activities, across dimensions of space-time. When mapping a zone of refuge, we identify a system of structural relations – causes, consequences, and participants' (Daiute 2017: 5). Moreover, narratives around refuge require us to shift away from the simple rhetoric of meeting basic needs, being adaptable, being cost effective and, in the case of humanitarian shelter, being easy to erect and transport. Instead, we must begin to engage deeply with the quintessential negotiated materiality of refuge, its spatiality, its performativity (as fundamentally social and political), its limitations and its challenges concerning purpose, resistance and responsibility. The spatial practices of homemaking and homing are thus political, and the processes of dwelling, shelter and refuge constitute negotiations and performativity that transcend more-than-inhabitation.

Divisions and overlaps on a fluid map: From north to south, east to west and back

Iraq continues to be shaped by colonial, national and international political borders, cultural and religious meddling, as well as its own struggles. When trying to situate it within contemporary geographical terms, we fall into the folds of a fluid map that is part of the Middle East's larger narrative. Although the term 'Middle East' has been contested (the middle of what, and east of where?) (Culcasi 2010), other terms such as the Arab World or Arab-speaking world exclude a large Kurdish portion of northern Iraq and Syria, not to mention other ethnic and religious minorities such as Assyrians, Yazidis and Sabian Mandaeans. Another categorization considers the Middle East and Northern Africa (MENA) as one entity; while not specifying further distinctions, this categorization also includes the states of Israel, Cyprus and Turkey. In addition to this, the definitions of Middle East and Near East are sometimes used interchangeably, and may include or exclude Iran. Naturally, all of the countries within these definitions hold different (and sometimes opposing) social struggles and beliefs.

Owing to the state's level of wealth and development, Iraq is also included within another potentially Western categorization: the Global South (as opposed to the Global North). The Global South is situated within the rhetoric of 'rich versus poor' and is therefore related to other labels such as the developing or 'Third' World, yet Global South further implies a certain resistance to hegemonic forces and powers (Nilsen 2016). The division itself is drawn from a Euro-American-centric, Western imperial and colonial perspective. Boaventura De Sousa Santos (2016: 238) writes about the difficulties of avoiding and escaping this Western framework while paradoxically writing in a colonial language, and urges us instead to engage with it rather than 'imagining ways of escaping it'. As Santos (2016: 238) asserts, enabling such contradictions makes space for 'epistemological hybridity' – in other words, 'different ways of knowing' that 'call for different forms of social agency', coupled with a different epistemological language of 'grammars and objectives of social transformation'. In this way, we can understand the folds of the map and the contradictions they express.

In 1958, Iraq formed part of the Arab Federation alliance between Iraq and Jordan. Between 1989 and 1990, Iraq was also briefly part of the Arab Cooperation Council with Egypt, Jordan and Yemen, which was dismantled after Iraq invaded Kuwait. Iraq has also been included in literature on the Arab Gulf countries, united by a valuable natural resource shared within the region – oil – which continues to shake the socio-economic and geopolitical development of the region to this day. In *City of Black Gold: Oil, Ethnicity and the Making of Modern Kirkuk*, Arabella Bet-Shlimon (2019) charts the making of a city in northern Iraq from its colonial roots to urbanization through natural wealth, taking into account its rippling scale of influence and the formation within of ethnic divisions.

Clearly, if we go back in history, we find that it is difficult to define the region. This is certainly in part attributable to the way the countries in the Middle East (as well as Africa and other parts of the Global South) were divided on the map by imperialists and colonists without the involvement of indigenous people (Barr 2011). On 19 May 1916, the secretive Sykes–Picot Agreement was founded between the British and the French, dividing the Arab-speaking world into smaller territories – the modern day Middle East – in order to gain control over the Ottoman Empire (Fromkin 2001). Another perhaps equally complex factor in the fluidity of the region as a geo-entity is the ethnic and religious diversity spanning the MENA region, which may have contributed to the bordering and ordering of territories.

In his essay, 'The Arab Condition', Said (2004: 273) asserts that 'despite their many divisions and disputes, the Arabs are in fact a people, not a collection of random countries passively available for outside intervention and rule'. Said (2004: 274) describes the Arab condition itself as a kind of nationalism that encompasses predominantly Arab and Muslim diversity and pluralism, which if realized would constitute a nation stretching between North Africa and the western boundaries of Iran. In describing the region as a nation whose geography is dictated by ethnic and religious nationalism, however, Said overlooks the deep-seated internal hostilities within the region that are driven by the marginalization of other ethnic and religious minorities outside the Arab/Muslim identity. In her book, *Displacement and Dispossession in the Modern Middle East*, Dawn Chatty (2010) highlights a number of forced migrations that have occurred in response to the repercussions of pan-Arab movements. One particularly strong example is the Kurdish case: divided across four different countries, Syria, Turkey, Iraq and Iran, Kurdistan is shaped by the involuntary movements of people over a divided land (Chatty 2010: 8). This struggle is further complicated by the fact that parts of that same land, especially in the north of Iraq, belong to other indigenous ethnic groups such the Yazidis and Assyrians.

It is, therefore, truly difficult to underpin the region with labels that fully unify its people. For that reason alone, it is wise to accept that whenever a label is necessary, we must first acknowledge the region's multiplicity in a fluid map that is conditioned by colonial historicity, ethnic diversity and multiple forms of struggle. Rather than using Said's unified Arab condition, then, work on spatial forms of practice should refer to a fluid map of the region that embraces difference and diversity in its multiplicity at several levels – social, ethnic and religious. In this book, I have attempted to do exactly this in the way I portray the projects and case studies, for example, in organizing them by their local rootedness to people and through a geography that is dynamic and diverse, even within one country such as Iraq.

Just as fluid as the map of the region are the scales and perspectives from which this research has developed. Scale matters, of course, when distinguishing whether something has socio-geo-spatial impact at the local or global level. So too is perspective vital in enabling the reader to critically assess how spatial practices and their geographies are shaped and positioned in a relational context, from north to south, east to west and back again. Nevertheless, we must question where these scales and perspectives originated and how each relates to the context of the spatial practices discussed here. Hence, the emphasis here is on the setting up of a critical dialogue, between scales and perspectives, that is situated in and across, emerging from and within the Global North and Global South.

Spatial responses: Views from the North

When working on the performativity of trauma and the fluidity of the map in which it happens, we can identify two types of spatial practices working in tandem: those that are offensive, violent and destructive; and those that are defensive, protective and creative. This section crosses and meanders between these types of spatial practice, as explored from the perspectives of the Global North. It begins with a historical account of how the West prepared for both the Second World War and the Cold War, and the types of spaces of refuge they created on the Home

Front (e.g. fallout shelters and bunkers). It then goes on to expand on a more sinister narrative concerning sites of defensive and innovative military practice and training (such as producing replicas of cities) and the material presence of forms of defence (such as blast walls). In revealing the diverse spatialities in these defensive, protective and creative practices, this section sets the scene for expanding the model of spatiality that will guide Chapter 3.

In 1939, Britain went to war with Germany, and the Home Office began to rally their efforts for protecting civilians by publishing a booklet entitled *The Protection of Your Home Against Air-Raids* (The Home Office 2012). The booklet, which is still in print, was addressed to all households in Britain and offered instructions for and precautions over how to secure refuge-rooms. In that same year, the Home Office began liaising with the steel industry to produce an air raid shelter for the protection of citizens from blasts and debris, known as the Anderson shelter. These were mainly acquired by small houses with no access to a basement (Wade 2011: 18). Describing the Anderson shelter, Stephen Wade (2011: 19) explains that it was 'a simple concept: two curved sides of corrugated steel were placed in a deep pit, and then earth to a depth of at least 15 inches was placed on top. They were meant to house six people. Six of the panels were bolted together and there was a drainage sump. The height was 6 feet and they were 4 feet 6 inches wide'. The Anderson shelter was designed for houses with a small garden, but those without access to outdoor space needed an alternative, indoor shelter – thus the Morrison shelter was born. Designed in 1941, the Morrison shelter consisted of a long tabletop bolted onto a steel frame with metal mesh sides, and was much smaller than the Anderson shelter at only '2 feet 6 inches high, and 6 feet 6 inches long' (Wade 2011: 25). Both shelters were produced free of charge for low-income households, and both were delivered on site along with an accompanying leaflet with instructions for assembly.

Protecting civilians on the Home Front was thus a priority for the British government, who, in addition to these single-family-use shelters, also provided communal shelters in parks, hotel basements and the London Underground system. In his book, *Air-Raid Shelters of World War II: Family Stories of Survival in the Blitz*, Wade (2011) provides an anthology of air raid shelters that serves to highlight survival stories from the Blitz during the Second World War. From these stories, readers gain insight into shelters as places that encompassed all things, where passing time was a challenge: besides sitting, waiting and flinching at loud explosions, the occupiers of these shelters played musical instruments; read *A Christmas Carol*; played cards, backgammon and chess; and tried to amuse their children (Wade 2011: 42). Unsurprisingly, Wade's descriptions of these activities closely resemble what Iraqis did to pass the time as they hid from the rockets and shelling that took place during the Gulf War, the 2003 US-led invasion of Iraq and the proceeding violence that engulfed the country. But while Iraqis sat, waited and flinched at loud explosions that shook the ground beneath their feet and shattered their windows, they had to invent their own spaces for refuge. This is in stark contrast to the way the British government supplied people with both private and public shelters, however complex and at times disorganized that process may have been. Not only is there a striking difference between British governmental help and that offered by Iraqi, Syrian, Yemeni or Afghani governments, but this has been further exacerbated by the weight and size of the trauma endured by the people.

Similarly, during the Second World War and throughout the Cold War period, Western governments encouraged architects and planners to design strategic spaces across their cities for refuge from air raids and the threat of nuclear blasts. The inspiration that utopian imaginaries gave architects and planners was seen by the architectural profession as being of equal significance to the drive to protect civilians. Adam Page (2016: 119), describes this moment in urban history for architects and planners, stating, 'It is the interaction of unpredictability, fantasy and anxiety that shaped the imagined futures sketched out by architects and planners in this period'. That being said, while the Air Raid Precautions Department (ARP) set up by the UK's Home Office in 1935 made significant efforts to design architecture for emergency and civilian defence, few designs made it to the real world. Page (2016: 127) asserts that, besides the civilian evacuation from cities scheme, there was a return to previously used measures of protection: 'When war was declared, the return to shallow trenches dug in parks, windows boarded up and sandbags stacked in doorways and on street corners revealed how, despite all the debates, very little defensive architecture had made it off paper'. Nevertheless, the strategies implemented to counter a threat that never materialized during the Cold War years, such as bringing trenches to the Home Front, building air raid shelters (e.g. the Stanton shelter) and placing what became known as 'gas chambers' (Moshenska 2015: 125) in schools, had a significant impact, particularly on children's understanding of warfare and the memory of these specific spaces of refuge. These spaces of refuge took on different attributes and forms of representations. Air raid shelters had specific structures: the Stanton shelter consisted of semi-sunken curved concrete segments, resembling a cross-section of a gothic arch; 'The Gas Van' spaces were more temporary structures like tents or mobile vans, although they were sometimes a more permanent room. To those who experienced them, these structures left a painful and sinister memory that cannot easily be forgotten (Moshenska 2015: 132).

The European civil defence, which brought the trenches into the Home Front, continued to haunt its people for years after the end of the Second World War. Sweden, for example, only stopped manufacturing air raid shelters in 2002, however these were mainly used as domestic storage units (Bennesved 2020). In his anthology on the historiography of what he termed a 'sheltered society', Peter Bennesved (2020) constructs a new chronology for civil defence in Europe, focusing on the differences and similarities (both material and psychological) between Sweden and the rest of Europe (the UK, the Netherlands, Germany) regarding their responses to new technologies in warfare. He focuses on the ideas and construction of air raid shelters and spaces of refuge from nuclear attacks that sit alongside the complex processes of certain societal trends (Bennesved 2020: 387). Meanwhile, during the years after the Second World War and into the Cold War period, the United States encouraged a do-it-yourself security plan for building fallout shelters, which both perpetuated certain gender stereotypes and revealed insecurities about the Cold War period (Lichtman 2006). During the 1950s, civil defence architects took inspiration from humanitarian and environmental responses to natural disasters as they dealt with the myths of imminent nuclear war. This tended to take one of two approaches: 'urban dispersal or atomic bomb shelters', though the two often overlapped in scale and location, depending on whether the environment was suburban or urban (Monteyne 2011: 2). According to David Monteyne (2011: 20) the similarities between the responses to a nuclear atomic bomb and to that of a natural disaster 'participated in the production of a particular reality in which nuclear war could be seen as a natural outcome of contemporary geopolitics'.

The year 2020 marked the seventy-fifth anniversary of the dropping of the atomic bombs by the American B-29 bomber Enola Gay on the Japanese cities of Hiroshima and Nagasaki. This event precipitated the end of the Second World War. In the 1940s, community-built air raid shelters looked more or less the same in terms of simplicity of structure and construction, whether in the East or the West. The most common community shelters in Japan were called '*bokugo*' (small dugout bomb shelter), and these were pit-like trenches covered with bamboo and a thin layer of earth, dug beside houses. In addition to these were a few concert shelters, as well as domestic cupboards, which acted as makeshift shelters for families who had no access to public shelters (Atomic Heritage Foundation 2017). The natural landscape also plays a major role when it comes to refuge, and this can clearly be seen in the impacts these bombs had on the cityscapes of Hiroshima and Nagasaki. The hills, mountains and uneven topography of Nagasaki protected some of its inhabitants from the initial blow of the atomic bomb; the flat landscape of Hiroshima, however, meant that the damage travelled much further from the point of explosion. Because of this fact, warfare structures of refuge and protection are usually built in anticipation of a blow that is unpredictable in terms of impact and aftermath. Japan's '*bokugo*' structures had no chance of surviving the atomic bombs, and the images of the survivors of these bombs (called '*hibakusha*') instilled fear in the West. They began building fallout shelters in anticipation of a war that never materialized, but that created an atmosphere of panic nonetheless.

There is, however, no denying that aerial bombardment alone managed to annihilate cities across Europe and the Pacific, especially Japan and China. This fact inspired Kenneth Hewitt (1983: 275) to call for geographers like himself to form their own 'black book' (like biologists' 'red books' and ecologists' 'green books') containing 'the places of violence and places destroyed or nearly destroyed by human agencies'. Strategically, place annihilation from aerial bombardment usually stems from a city's reachability rather than its importance, leaving 'little possibility of avoiding the destruction of great historic and cultural products of urbanism' (Hewitt 1983: 275). The Second World War left cities across Europe (particularly in Germany, Britain and Italy) and the Pacific (specifically Japan) in ruins, yet as wars continue to rage across the world, it appears that we have not learned any lessons. We could not possibly fit all the place annihilation in Afghanistan, Iraq, Syria, Libya, Yemen and more recently Ukraine into one 'black book' – rather, we require books and maps containing spatial stories of people's struggle with the traumatic lived and felt experiences of those spaces.

While civil defence in the West was concerned with fallout and air raid shelters, food storage, preparing homes and evacuating children, its military counterpart was practising the latest warfare technologies on sites designed to resemble the 'micro-geographies' of urban combat (Graham 2007: 121). In 1941, Churchill's war cabinet altered the fate of several idyllic valleys and villages across the southwest and southeast of England, using them for military training ahead of D-Day. In 1943, Tyneham Village on the south-west coast of England was acquired by the Ministry of Defence (MoD), displacing 225 people, and used for firing ranges and training troops. While clearly not an unprecedented requisition, the village's uniqueness lies in the fact that it was never handed back to its people. To this day, its fourteenth- and fifteenth-century homes have been left derelict, and the village rendered a ghost town. In the 1970s, public and political pressure mounted on the government to release the site from military hands, and in 1976, the public was permitted greater access through the site to the beach and other areas, but certain by-laws concerning development have since prevented the village from being fully restored (Wright 2021). This state-designed action to evacuate citizens without offering them immediate replacement homes has struck people in the UK for decades. Tyneham is no longer alone in this forceful identity shift, as in the early 2000s the Metropolitan Police Specialist Training Centre acquired Gravesend in Kent (on the south-east coast of the UK). Since derelict houses in Gravesend had been left abandoned owing to a lack of government funding for development, the small town was vulnerable to becoming a 'fake town' for riot police training. Gravesend has become another abandoned town, leaving inhabitants of neighbouring villages finding that their homes are not worth as much as expected and hard to sell.

Also in the 2000s, the so-called war on terror brought with it new battlegrounds to explore, away from the Home Front in the West. In *War and the City*, Stephen Graham (2007) highlights the difference between the political violence on replicas in the twentieth-century city compared to that of the twenty-first century. According to Graham (2007: 123), the former became grounds for 'urban annihilation through total war', while the latter were designed for training troops for urban 'military occupation and counter-insurgency warfare'. Graham speaks of the scale and detail of these replica sites as they popped up across the West, particularly in the UK, the United States and Israel, and to a lesser extent in Singapore. He describes a 'hidden archipelago of mini-cities' (Graham 2007: 122), containing distinctive architectural features such as minarets and mosques, some containing even finer details such as washing lines, looped recordings of calls to prayer, donkeys and Arabic graffiti. Graham describes at length some of the largest US 'urban-warfare' complexes, such as the Joint Readiness Training Centre at Fort Polk in Louisiana, constructed between 2003 and 2005. This centre featured eighteen Iraqi villages built over 100,000 acres, and involved details such as kebab stools, mass-graves filled with rotting bones from a local butcher, 1,200 actors dressed in Arab clothing and playing the neutral civilian or the insurgent/'hostile', screenwriters to write their 'character sheets' and a stream of 44,000 Iraq-bound soldiers (Graham 2007: 125).

In addition to these simulated realities, sites and constructs seamlessly interweave into digital gaming and simulation technologies, able to produce hyperreal visualizations used for surveillance and attack that map directly onto the built environment. Graham (2007: 129) notes that these urban warfare complexes create an 'army of gamers' who respond to the power of immersive simulation, equating 'these environments with "terrorism" and to stress that they need "pacification" or "cleansing" by military means'. Such replica cities are examples of spatial practices of violent warfare, and they typically include concrete blast walls of different sizes that divide and split thoroughfares, controlling movement and choice within certain communities and delineating spaces for humanitarian corridors. These spaces will be explicitly explored in the context of Iraq in Chapter 4. The focus of this section has instead been on the Global North's spatial preparations and responses to potential threats of trauma and violence. It reflects on the ways in which power and politics play significant roles in civic responses to war or the threat of war.

Expanded model of spatiality: Views from the South (with a focus on the Middle East)

Little can be said about the help offered by the Saddam regime to its people in the lead up to any of Iraq's numerous wars from 1980 to the 2003 US-led invasion. Ghada Alslik (2022), Professor at the School of Architecture at Baghdad University, explains that the regime offered no material or financial means for Iraqis to protect themselves or their homes, stating:

> They were more concerned with protecting certain governmental buildings and universities, but they also dug trenches for people to stay there for

> neighbourhood guarding. People in Iraq took care of themselves. They dug wells in their gardens. People collected dry food, they filled buckets and pots with clean water. People also organized themselves to buy generators to support electricity for several houses. They now have lots of rechargeable equipment, but we still need electricity.

The situation in Iraq of course requires more drastic measures than making electricity available, yet according to Alslik, there has never been a strategy or plan to improve the dire conditions across the country – especially concerning the shortage of housing exacerbated by years of internal displacement. For Alslik, the struggles within the profession are a direct reflection of the struggles of the people of Iraq. Through interviews with professionals in the field, this section finds collective themes and uses them to build an expanded model of spatiality that captures the multiplicity of practices around change and resistance in Iraq. These interviews include discussions with architectural theorists and historians (Nasser Rabbat and Anooradha Iyer Siddiqi), practising architects (Ammar Azzouz, Sandi Hilal and Alessandro Petti from Decolonizing Architecture Art Research [DAAR]), and educators and researchers (Ghada Alslik and Camillio Boano), whose work focuses on the Global South. It is important to note here that these categorizations should not define each individual interviewee, as their work crosses multiple disciplinary and methodological boundaries. Certainly, they are all researchers and educators. The above categorizations only represent the lens through which their portfolios of work moulded the themes in this section and the chapter that follows. In total, the six interviews conducted create a vantage point from which knowledge can be generated to produce a postcolonial world of just and inclusive spatiality. These interviews pivot around four main themes that stretch and overlap with one another: refuge; temporality; choice and memory; and a future vision for a just spatiality in times of war and violence.

In particular, the concept of postcoloniality has dominated the six conversations. Rabbat (2018) emphasizes its importance, specifically the impact of Said's orientalism, on the creation of new frames of knowledge within the discipline of architecture (particularly in architectural history). He elaborates on this in our interview:

> Postcolonialism could have been a liberating moment, not just from the hegemony of the Western frames of knowledge, but also from the traditional and local [referring to the Arab world] ways of knowledge. It should have opened doors for alternative ways of constructing epistemes. Instead, postcolonialism has hindered the ability to produce knowledge in the Arab world in the fields we are talking about [architecture, sociology, urban history and other social science disciplines, etc.]. Yet postcoloniality is a necessary

> step that we [non-Western intellectuals] needed in order to come out of the colonial frame of mind and to cleanse our body of knowledge from its inherited colonial prejudices and knowledge structures.
>
> (Rabbat 2022)

Sandi Hilal, visiting Professor at Lund University, and Alessandro Petti, Professor of Architecture and Social Justice at the Royal Institute of Art in Stockholm, are the founders and directors of the international artistic and architectural practice, DAAR. Hilal and Petti further unpack this entanglement between colonialism and modernity, as the issue lies at the heart of their work. DAAR's *Refugee Heritage* project (2015–21) challenged UNESCO's 'claim of objectivity that is present in the concept of heritage' by submitting to them a dossier that dismantled colonial universalist thinking and argued for giving agency to marginalized communities (Hilal and Petti 2021). Petti remarks that the project 'seeks to reorient heritage towards non-hegemonic forms of life and collective memory' (Hilal and Petti 2021: 34) within the context of the Dheisheh refugee camp in Palestine, and forty-four other Palestinian villages. Located in the West Bank, south of Bethlehem, the camp was established in 1949, and is home to over 8,000 Palestinians. In an interview featuring both DAAR directors, Hilal lays out the relationship between colonialism and modernity:

> The promise of colonization was … 'We are coming to civilize', and modern architecture in particular has been a very important tool to convince people of Western superiority. Modernity and colonialism are two sides of the same coin. Colonialism offers people the myth of becoming modern and civilized. Therefore, anything that is not modern is backwards. An example I can bring is the design we made for a neighbourhood in Gaza. The local authority there was absolutely convinced that Gaza needs multi-storey towers, seven floors each, meanwhile Gaza does not have continuous availability of electricity, and therefore elevators do not work properly. Yet they were convinced this was the way to go because this is the way of thinking that modernity and colonialism actually brought to Palestine. Instead, we decided to look at what Gaza already has, and observe how people are creating their spaces, but because of how modernity affects decisions, decision makers were blinded to the values of the organically led agency that Gazans have, and how their agency has transformed their life experiences and their architecture.
>
> Our work for the nomination of Dheisheh refugee camp as a World Heritage site is based exactly on people's agency to transform their own lives and to say that decolonization and demodernization are two sides of the same coin. We also needed to re-question our aesthetic values, as well as put forward a dictionary of new terms for practice, because our existing values were built throughout

> the colonial machine (i.e. our educational systems) and, therefore, it becomes crucially important to re-evaluate these values for a more just architecture.
> (Hilal and Petti 2022)

In another interview, Camillo Boano, Professor of Urban Design and Critical Theory at the Bartlett Development Planning Unit, UCL, untangles this very problem – the educational system as it relates to the profession of architecture. Boano (2022) states:

> The architectural project has always been a solution-based and not an analytical form of practice. Its basic structures are entirely solution-based, to some extent lacking theory and critical reflection. This complete separation between a theory of criticality that is not attached to a solution hinders the ability to critically provoke the present condition towards future development. Shifting this narrative of solution into a spatial narrative that has history and criticality towards multiplicities of practices is difficult, yet it is one of the possible ways forward, to reclaim and reconcile the full meaning of spatial practice, which includes architecture.

It is possible to explore, from multiple angles, this fundamental issue of reframing multiplicity in spatial practice as a core concept and methodological tool in architectural education. In a 2022 interview, Anooradha Iyer Siddiqi, Professor of Architecture at Barnard Art History and GSAPP, Columbia University, speaks about creating knowledge through the spatial narration of history. She notes that this is especially important when exposing objects and architectures that change function, meaning and representation over time. Siddiqi (2022) further frames this narration through the lens of multiplicity in temporality, referring to Mrinalini Rajagopalan's (2017) *Building Histories: The Archival and Affective Lives of Five Monuments in Modern Delhi* as an example where the built environment, architecture, spaces and objects agglomerate and evolve depending on how they are prioritized and historicized by different regimes of power over time. When they are co-created through the lens of temporality, incompleteness and multiplicity, structures of architecture and spatial practice introduce an array of often novel alternative spatial possibilities into the field, especially in times of crisis. Boano (2022) asserts how war challenges the rigidity of the architectural profession:

> Looking at the idea of completeness within architecture or spatial practice that is definite, precise and in total control of the rules and processes, as the proxy definition of what architecture is, at least in a practical sense, a less critical or less open lens. Completeness assumes a different gesture when we speak about conflict or war. The context of war challenges the ontology of completeness.

> Therefore, anything that is shaped within this ontology is doomed to failure because it is proposing something that is useless for the individuals and their lives in such conditions, but is also because it is unable to meet the very fundamental act of design. War, to me, is the perfect example of design intentions. Yet at war, these intentions require inversion, where the focus shifts from forms to processes, from internal to external relation versus the structure.

Meanwhile, Petti relates this problem to modernity, stating:

> The figure of the professional architect that emerged in the Global North, is very recent, around a hundred years old. Yet we have been building cities for centuries. We need to put into question the very idea that sets people's agency against architects' professionalism without paying attention to past and present forms of architectural practices when cities are built organically without the professionalization of the construction processes. We need to reclaim our collective ability to build our environments without separating the process between people's and architects' agencies. I think it is peculiar to give agency to a specific profession. Modernity has created these divisions and not only in architecture. It is helpful to unlearn what has been imposed on us and then to look at spaces similar to the refugee camps, where the agency of transforming the space is taken back by the inhabitants. But importantly, without falling into the trap of romanticizing the so-called 'informal architecture', another category invited in order to discredit everything that is not built by professionals. We must not forget the deprivation and violence from which refugee camps have emerged. But exactly because they were borne from a kind of collapse of modern society, something else is emerging from them that, on its own, is important to understand in order for us to relearn how agency to build your own space and environment is regained.
>
> (Hilal and Petti 2022)

Hilal adds that, while focusing on an alternative type of pedagogy in the form of a collective dictionary:

> There are moments where we see people, especially refugees, using their architecture as a way of continuing their survival and their struggle, and all that is needed from architects is to step out and try to understand what is going on, maybe by offering a way of thinking together. This formed the basis of our practice, acknowledging that, in refugee camps, there are so many things we do not understand when relying on knowledge acquired from architectural pedagogy at university, where mostly architecture seems to stand alone. But in practice, we had to understand what is going on exactly in that production, in relation to the people themselves. Concepts of ownership, or

lack of it, are completely different, and private and public are non-existent in the context of camps; people might build their homes, but they do not own them, and somehow people start to manage their own collective spaces and lives. Therefore, in order to understand architecture in the camps and what goes on inside them, and how architecture is part of a bigger picture here, we need to create a new dictionary with new concepts and vocabularies, and this has been the mission of DAAR from the beginning, in particular the collective dictionary produced by 'Campus in Camps' participants, an experimental pedagogical program established in Dheisheh from 2012 to 2016.

(Hilai and Petti 2022; see Campus in Camps 2012)

Petti agrees with Rabbat that a necessary step towards understanding the value of agency beyond the rhetoric of Western conceptions involves acknowledging the need to engage with colonialism, for example in the division between tangible and intangible, when speaking of heritage. Petti explains:

> It has to be said that the very division between tangible and intangible is a Western conception. Material objects do not exist without their immaterial aspects, and vice versa. At the beginning of the Refugee Heritage project, representatives of UNESCO were trying to understand what was in our dossier that ticked the boxes of folklore and of values that existed before 1948. Instead, we have been interested in understanding the material and immaterial culture of exile produced from 1948, the year of the beginning of the Nakba, till today.
>
> We were very conscious of the colonial influence in the UNESCO framework. Nevertheless, for us, sticking to UNESCO categories and values was a very pragmatic, political decision, in order to ground our conversations. We needed to challenge these modernist assumptions and the very categories that were put forward by the colonial framework, while simultaneously trying to open up a different, richer and maybe more diverse understanding of heritage. Also, we focused on who has the right to define what constitutes heritage and how people are involved beyond rhetorical participation.
>
> We see our work as part of a longer struggle that has been mobilized in Palestine for decades, in which heritage is seen as a way to resist and re-exist independently from Israeli colonization and continuous demolitions.
>
> (Hilal and Petti 2022)

Hilal adds:

> We recognize UNESCO as a colonial machine, but we must not forget that there are many people that are challenging the structure from inside. Among them, Jad Tabet, a former Lebanese representative in UNESCO, who was an influential supporter of refugee heritage. He was the one who proposed to not only nominate

> the one camp, but make a serial nomination together with forty-four villages of origin, which refugees were expelled from. Indeed, we have to recognize such efforts from inside UNESCO that have been working to decolonize its structures. It is, therefore, crucially important to recognize alliances between local individuals and large organizations such as UNESCO, where these individuals are working hard to break down colonial structures and decolonize systems.
>
> (Hilal and Petti 2022)

Boano (2022), on the other hand, responds to the question around informality and other terms that dictate a certain way of framing knowledge as follows:

> There are two answers to this question, one which is a Marxist view of the world, defined as a set of relations. For example, I am not interested in the notion of informality unless it is able to reveal specific relation to inhabitation. The other version constructs a value around sets of negotiations taking place between different actors claiming certain things such as identity, for example. These two frames of knowledge become problematic when they are set in a static regime of rules. Beyond the linguistics, we need to think differently about the existence of the informal by asking questions about the formal practices that are legitimized by a system of capital. I become resistant to using the word 'informality' because it is a proxy of marginalization, a proxy of specific regime of aesthetic. Yet it remains positive currency as a potential important element to construct subjectivity around marginality, liminality, imagination of the future.

Terms such as 'informal' versus 'formal' are difficult to separate or define. Siddiqi (2022) rejects these terms, arguing that they are imprecise, especially when talking about complex contexts where all structures of normative political economy (i.e. from which the terms formal/informal originate) are upended. Speaking of her ongoing project *Insurgent Domesticities* (Siddiqi and Tadiar 2021), Siddiqi (2022) adds that, in a highly tense and traumatic context such as war, the meaning of such terms could not be defined, nor should they be seen as a linear process of relations, particularly in the context of domesticity. Siddiqi further considers domesticity to be an empirically conceptual and methodological tool, especially in the context of protracted violence and war, positioned as it is between the collaboration and coercion that acquire diverse roles and representations in different scales of spatial practice. On a similar subject, Boano (2022) approaches dwelling and inhabitation slightly differently, as it relates to his previous work with Astolfo concerning inhabitation as a continuous struggle (Boano and Astolfo 2020). Boano (2022) notes:

> Inhabitation is a continuous struggle [within the context of displacement in camps], while dwelling is a given condition. Although it is widely acknowledged that dwelling as a verb implies process, it is still a given de facto in the

Heideggerian sense that dwelling is being. Inhabitation is a struggle for life that continuously transcends different territories that somehow take reflections of dwelling without creating domesticity at the level of the architecture or the infrastructure, but by making it more political in the ecology of their territories' own relation. Unlike dwelling, inhabitation brings with it the idea of the future as a fundamental component in the process of inhabitation, a future that calls for an imagining of real possibilities to have a structure to life and to be able to determine that too. Therefore, displacement is not only the possibility, it is the impossibility of dwelling where resistance to the impossibility or even imagining that possible future, which is the future of stability. Here we go back in full circle to dwelling and the application of inhabitation as a kind of moment in place where there are challenges on the levels of ideas and scale, not only transcending the humanitarian field alone, but reaching other disciplinary boundaries including architecture and urbanism too.

Ammar Azzouz (2022), architect and architectural critic and analyst at Arup, London, and an Honorary Research Associate at the University of Oxford, reminds us that this very struggle for inhabitation is both a personal and a collective trauma, intertwined with memory:

> At a time of war, there is a memory boom, and because the past is being destroyed, there is an urge to reconstruct it. This is not only because of the international organizations or funders concerned with memory projects, but it is rather because, at a time of war, people are eager to return to a different time, a time where the old pieces of their history were still together. But when the past is erased and this memory is being threatened, people feel a sense of rupture, and with that sense of rupture, they want to bring back different slices of history and the past to the surface. To remember that once upon a time there was a city, once upon a time there was a place, there was a community that maybe is no longer there, and maybe that place is no longer existing. In times of violence and war, definitely, memory becomes so critical and very important as a response to the erasure of existence. But memory becomes more critical than before the war, because before the war people took it for granted that things will always stay the same and everything is safe and fine, but when the grounds are shaking, when the foundations of that society are being destroyed, memory becomes very important.
>
> People in times of conflict and war want to return to a home that might be imagined or built to remember that, once, there was a time when there was peace. That nostalgia could be channelled through an archive or by collecting maps, images or music and food in an act of remembering. Architecture is critical here, because it is about how the city looked … and how the community lived in its spaces and places; what were the places they lived in, and what did the streets look like? All these moments become very important.

In times of war, notions of displacement, exile and return are at the heart not only of political discussions but also of architectural dilemmas, especially in relation to destruction, preservation and reconstruction. In their collective dossier, *The Destruction of Cultural Heritage*, Karimi and Rabbat (2016) speak about this very complex relationship between the obliteration of the architectural monuments and heritage of the Middle East, and the impact this has on cultures, philosophies and historiographies. Rabbat (2022) adds to these factors the pressure placed on the profession during times of war. As an example, he refers to the calls for reconstruction in Syria, stating:

> Reconstruction is an existential question for architects. If this question was posed to architects as professionals operating under dictatorships that empty cities of their civility, then they would have no other choice as service providers than to respond in the affirmative to demands of reconstruction. But architects as human beings and citizens have to reject the notion of reconstruction on the ruins of others' lives.
>
> (Rabbat 2022)

Azzouz (2022), who has written extensively about architects' struggle with notions of reconstruction verses repair and preservation, adds:

> Notions of regeneration and reconstruction are global problems, even after World War Two in Coventry in the UK, and similarly after the Civil War in Beirut. In both of these cities at different time scales, the reconstruction destroyed more in the city centre than the war itself. The construction here is seen as a new way of destruction. There are attempts – for example, in Beirut, there is a building called Bait Beirut [House of Beirut], which preserved the memory of the war itself and tried to make a place for reflection – but I think on the scale of the city, it is a very tiny example to say we wanted to remember instead of escape from that history. Similarly, in Berlin after the fall of the Wall, the idea at the time was to forget there was a wall dividing Berlin. It was described as the 'wall of shame'. After ten years, almost all of the wall started vanishing from the city, and suddenly after one decade many started to say, 'well, the wall is part of the story' and 'the wall is telling us who we are and who we were and who we want to be', but it does not mean that if we bury that memory that we have buried it from our mind. Now there are efforts to preserve every single piece and even try … to recall where the wall was … to tell the story. The war is a tragic part of history, but it is part of the story. It is not the solution to bury the past beneath the ground without dealing with questions of accountability, justice, freedom and rights. It does not mean that if we rebuild the city in the new way, that it will become the end of the struggle or the conflict.

I like the work of the artist Louise Bourgeois, where she would collect her old clothes and sew them again and again and again. This was a concept about notions of care and repair. For many architects, it might be tempting to say, 'let us start from scratch and destroy everything; the city was old enough and we need new infrastructure and to build a new face, we need to start a new life', which constructs a new imaginary world, and in that process layers of memory and meaning are destroyed. This happens even when people have good intentions. Even good intentions can lead to harm and can lead to damage. In the region [the Middle East], there is a lack of confidence when we look from the Global South to other cities that are global or international .... But what architects could do is to push back, make space for alternative futures and try to reserve and repair and look at the notion of care and rework, rehabilitate, retrofit and recelebrate who we are and our heritage, without feeling that other cities built towers so we have to do the same. We have our own heritage and our own memory, and we should be proud of them, and we should preserve that story and tell it again. Therefore, there is a huge responsibility to make a space of awareness that the old does not mean we are looking back and not forward ... but the past is telling us who we are and where we are moving forward towards, and how we can build on it rather than destroy and start all over again from scratch.

In the context of war and conflict, then, architects struggle with what to do with destroyed cities, as well as notions of choice: the choice to preserve, to reconstruct, to leave or return. These issues are particularly pertinent to people who are internally displaced or living in camps. Hilal asserts:

> When we were living in Palestine, practising and working there, even within a very strange context filled with oppression and destruction, we found that our work was about construction. This is how we responded to the Israeli occupation – by being active in terms of having agency to build and think, to have our own agenda and to begin to construct buildings such as a university, a square, the school our own daughters went to. Yet, when we arrived in Europe, it was almost the opposite. We felt the need to begin to deconstruct and unlearn modernity and to start to relearn what it means for us to be a collectivity, to be neighbours, to be an extended family, bringing back these values for a society that decided to abandon it, and that convinced all the rest of the world that this was the right thing to do. The moment that you need to deconstruct something, you are actually opening a space for other things to be constructed, the same with learning and unlearning. It is extremely important, especially for a practice of architecture, that we learn not to be worried about moving between construction and deconstruction as a way of understanding colonial heritage.
>
> (Hilal and Petti 2022)

To this, Petti adds:

> One of the main risks in working within camps is normalizing them, and thereby undermining the right of return. In the course of the project [Refugee Heritage], we realized the importance of nominating Dheisheh refugee camp, together with the forty-four villages from which refugees were expelled .... Making the nomination of the camp entangle with the villages of origin was a way for us to keep the right of return at the centre of the project. We called this 'returns', rather than 'return', in order to open up ... different practices of returns instead of one individual narration. Edward Said understood that any notion of return needs to include exile. Therefore, for us, it was important to mobilize a stereoscopic vision for architecture, which meant forcing architecture to operate in the camp and in the villages of origin at the same time. This opened up a completely different scenario, in which people were no longer forced to choose to be here or there, but instead could finally have an existence that can be both here and there at the same time, emphasizing a mobile life. In this way, we understood that, at the centre of the right to return is freedom of movement – that is the basis not only for refugees but for all humanity. A freedom to find and make life by making connections that are not tied or confined within nation-state borders.
>
> (Hilal and Petti 2022)

Fundamentally, any deliberations about the future of a destroyed city are tied to the lives and futures of those who have been forced to flee their homes and countries in search of refuge and protection. In the process of seeking refuge, however, lies an important element of choice – or lack of it. This may manifest as a choice to return, a choice to migrate further, or a choice to stay and rebuild. Where I write 'protection' above, I consider it in its rudimentary sense, meaning refuge, shelter and safety. Like Siddiqi, Boano (2022) argues against the use of the term 'protection' in any legal sense, when used in relation to domesticity:

> Protection is a very intimate dimension that deals with the fundamental possibility of choices. You lack protection when you only have a limited amount of choice, where there is only one place to stay away from the line of fire or the escape route where you can move to. Protection must be reconsidered as a room of manoeuvre to having more space rather than a space that protects. Protection is the possibility to escape. It is not a fixed thing to a place. The movement allows protection, not the fixity. Architecturally speaking, this shift in the thinking provokes a contestation to the fundamental interpretation of protection as something that is internal-looking and spatially fixed. That is what notions of incompleteness or incremental spatial practice are attributed to.

The expanded model of spatiality conveyed across the following chapters keeps these issues at its heart: the temporality and multiplicity of notions of refuge and inhabitation, choice and mobility, collective memory, and the fates of destroyed cities. The architects interviewed describe their personal views and experiences of war and violence alongside their visions for a future of a just spatiality, where the emphasis is on investment in the next generation, in collective storytelling and in small changes that ripple over time. In 'Baghdad: Images and Memories', Alslik (2008) declares that, if she survives the war and violence engulfing Iraq at the time, she will have witnessed a new image of the city of Baghdad, mixing familiar and unfamiliar forms of trauma. Reflecting back in her interview, she states:

> The first image I cannot call an image, as you lived it with me and … somehow it was chaotic. There was a lot of violence and a lot of security precautions, which made the city [Baghdad] a warfront. This first image lasted about eight years, till 2011, during which the image of the city was one of warfront, of deterioration of services and destruction that made the city look much like a big, backwards village. The second image started in 2012, where there was some stability, with less security precautions and no American troops on the ground. People started to rebuild, yet unfortunately, these buildings did not follow building regulations, nor they were designed with a vision, and as a result the city looked random, without focus or a clear vision for an urban scene. More recently, in the last three years, young architects have started building a better image for the city, especially in the housing sector. But we do not see this happening on a large scale or in big projects.
>
> My image of the city is a sad image, yet it is a city that is rising from a long history of violence and destruction and can only get better. But for me, professionally, it is only managing to open its eyes now and has a long way to go.
>
> Investors are not investing in the production cycle of life, where you need a variety of buildings and industries as well as cultural and educational organizations to make a society. Instead, investors in Iraq, who hold power and control within municipalities, are building for consumption only, building malls. Baghdad has thirty to forty malls, and similar numbers of restaurants and cafés are popping up across the country on a regular basis.
>
> There is hope in the new generation, yet there is currently no practical or theoretical guidance for them, and that is a dangerous state to be in.
>
> (Alslik 2022)

Azzouz asserts the significance of multiplicity and incompleteness in storytelling, as well as the importance of memory – collective and individual – when exploring new dimensions into the impact of war and violence in current and future contexts. In so doing, he affirms the necessary absence of there being one particular beginning or ending to the story about Syria (or elsewhere) suffering oppression, violence and war:

> I lived in a time in 2011 where the tanks started entering the city and snipers were positioned in different parts of the city on tower blocks. The streets were blocked and there were checkpoints, making ... movement across the city very difficult. Even walking to the university would be a challenge. Every time I left my home, I would know that it might be my end. Slowly, the city was changing, but not in a way that I would directly link the built environment to the violence. Now that I am distant and I have read about military urbanism and about the weaponization of architecture and the built environment, I would notice that yes, the snipers were allocated carefully at certain points so that they could view and target certain neighbourhoods. Now I would look at the streets as barriers, as borders inside the city that separate different sects from each other. I remember now the checkpoints, how they were tools to control people's movement and limit the interaction between different communities from different backgrounds. I would not necessarily have noticed how all the links emerged slowly at the time, I would not have noticed the posters and graffiti that were part of the ideological brainwashing of the entire community. But now, with some distance, with eyes as an outsider, I can read things more differently. Of course, with a lot of reading, connections emerge strongly.
>
> It is not one person's mission to tell the story of Iraq or Syria, it is a collective work of cultural effort, but we need to push more and more to tell different stories and to enable a space for different voices, because we grew up in a place where there is only one big story, brought to us by a political landscape that does not allow different voices to emerge. Now, maybe with exiled voices, we have started to understand each other differently, because there is more freedom and space for listening to different voices that we would not have listened to if we still were in our own countries.
>
> (Azzouz 2022)

Using spatial interventions, we can emphasize this kind of multiplicity in storytelling and people's agency and work to disrupt the usual mainstream ways that architects tend to respond to crises. Providing routes for opening up the possibilities of these multiplicities might also help us to develop critical long-term solutions to global challenges, through, for example, collective action and adaptable reuse. Petti and Hilal put forward a visual image of what a just spatiality might look like. Petti begins:

> During winter in Sweden, where we live at the moment, lakes freeze, becoming compact, solid surfaces of ice. In spring, during sunny days, you can hear the deep and scary sound of ice cracking, yet you do not see where these cracks

> actually are. But you definitely perceive the sound, that apparently this very solid piece of ice is fracturing, and you should not walk on it when you hear the sound, as it can collapse in seconds. I imagine that, intentionally or sometimes unintentionally, similar practices to ours can create cracks into the present that suddenly change the conditions in which we live and create space for something else to happen.
>
> (Hilal and Petti 2022)

Hilal adds:

> Maybe at the core of our practice is a very messy situation that is hard to describe, but when we are working in collectivity on projects in complex contexts, it is like we are holding a candle, or a small light that can help somehow. What is hard is keeping that candle lit the entire time, allowing people to never go back to darkness. Perhaps working collectively and over long periods of time, we can light several candles over the course of multiple projects, but as soon as these projects finish, this collectivity is turned off, and it becomes hard for the people we work with. I would also imagine that what we want to do requires a lot of effort and, indeed, pretending that we can bring everybody on board can potentially be a violent act, and instead we should pay a lot of attention to what people need to be ready, to be on board or to move on. It is hard to speak about the impact of our practice without remembering what effect the complex influences, the cracks in the ice and the candles that went out, leaving someone in the dark, have had in the context of the projects. These cracks and candles are places for possibilities as well as tensions, and should really be examined and cared for because they impact people. That is how our architectural practice is responding to crises.
>
> (Hilal and Petti 2022)

A just spatiality would position architects as creative facilitators, who make spaces for collective, local possibilities, for change (in all its multiplicity) and difference to emerge. These just spaces are messy, unpredictable, and always in the making. Our expanded model of a just spatiality simultaneously allows for negotiations and resistance between people, places and events to occur throughout the processes of making, wounding and transgressing. In this chapter, researchers and practitioners collectively affirm the need for fresh perspectives to enable the nuances and abundance of the spatial practices of trauma to be conceptualized, analysed and materialized. The task of the following chapter is to acknowledge the different scales and vantage points from which this spatiality can be drawn out.

3 CREATIVE NEGOTIATIONS IN SPACES OF REFUGE AND MEMORY: MATERIAL OBJECTS, HOME AND DOMESTICITY, THE URBAN AND BORDERS

Building on the conceptual framework and methodological positioning introduced in Chapter 1, as well as the exploration of the nuances of difference and multiple spatial practices of trauma presented in Chapter 2, this chapter delves deeper into examining these spatialities across various scales. To unpack the word 'refuge' more deeply, it denotes both a process and a product: a process of mobility, interaction and negotiation, and a product of intimacy, materiality and space unfolding in time. Daiute (2017: 11) adds that:

> narrating may enact refuge, when opportunities to narrate are supported in the context, allowed to be flexible (that is not just one narrative), and orient to future possibilities rather than only the past. Because such narrating interacts with contexts, especially as different genres pull those contexts into the text, family and community may or may not support narrating as refuge.

The process of map-making that accompanies the narratives in this chapter forms part of the practice of researching refuge, and is used here as a methodology for a critical enquiry into spaces of refuge. These maps bring into focus the heretofore muted Iraqi voices as they have struggled against violence and sought refuge over many years. As they challenge dominant power structures both inside and outside Iraq, telling different, more personal, indigenous stories of war and violence experienced on the ground, they should therefore be considered counter-maps (Rundstrom 2009).

This chapter is centred around storytelling, narration and mapping as forms of refuge, and this therefore makes it possible for us to understand refuge to be a form of creative action, whether in the form of resistance, making, justice or otherwise. Specifically, it allows us to reflect on history, on our positionality within certain contexts, and on movement and mobility towards the future. As such, refuge here means something akin to 'social imaginary', as described by Henrik Vigh (2006: 483), an action not to be equated with 'fiction or fantasy' or an 'image or a representation' but rather 'the world perceived as real, to perceptions of the real and to people's praxis within'. In order to unpack this web of possible processes and products, this chapter puts forward a series of themes that emerge from deep mapping and thematic analysis of fifteen interviews with Iraqis from all over Iraq. These interviews were conducted as part of a project entitled 'Ruptured Domesticity: A Visual Narrative of Domestic Responses to War in Iraq' (Murrani 2023), which was funded by the British Institute for the Study of Iraq (BISI). The interviews were thematically analysed and mapped visually, and were published in a visual online archive on the eve of the twentieth anniversary of the US-led Invasion of Iraq in March 2023. A public exhibition of the maps, along with a talk, was also held at the Middle East Centre of the London School of Economics (LSE) in April and May 2023.

Across the interviews, it was possible to identify four scales of refuge. The first is on the scale of the interviewees' intimate memories of material objects and non-material notions of refuge within war and violence. The second is the domestic dimension, which contains multiple ruptures to different realms of inhabitation at different scales encountered between 2003 and 2023. The third consists of urban negotiations between vertical and horizontal warfare, violence and urbicide, as they puncture through cities, and push and pull at their margins. The fourth is focused on people's choices and options regarding their mobility and the possibility of escape. This movement evokes a palimpsestic displacement performatively blurring geographical maps that intend to define the urban and the rural, and social maps of places of refuge. In the case of Iraqis, this mobility was mainly internal, yet the interviewees still describe many different forms of internal displacement: taking refuge in derelict and abandoned spaces, buildings and camps; moving between neighbourhoods in the same city; shifting between city and countryside; and being externally displaced. All interviewees agreed to an ethics protocol with regards to sharing their memories of a sense of refuge across Iraq's recent history, unpacked through the past, the now and the future. As addressed in the Introduction to this book, this time frame starts with the lead up to the 2003 invasion of Iraq, passes through the period 2006–8 of sectarian violence and atrocities inflicted by ISIS (also known as Daesh), continues into the 2019 Tishreen Movement and ends with the Covid-19 pandemic, up to 2023. It has of course been important to highlight these momentous events that brought with them monumental change, but it is also worth remembering that not all of

Iraq suffered equally from these events. Nevertheless, these specific events have certainly touched every Iraqi inside Iraq, and, to some extent, outside it too, and changed the face of its map both spatially and socially. The interviewees have picked their spatial moments of focus, which are often dictated by their own regionality within Iraq, to voice their memories and put forward their stories and dreams. To emphasize the speakers' voices and the significance of these moments on their lives, their words appear in long, uninterrupted quotes in the text with minimal editing for clarity. In addition to these, a thematic analysis of the interviews and visual maps charts different scales of intimacies of refuge, ruptures and possibilities towards a negotiated spatiality. These appear in the final section of this chapter. Overall, this chapter charts a spatial unfolding of violence and trauma through the memories of Iraqis from the north to the south of Iraq.

Creativity is deeply ingrained within this framework, particularly when it comes to the actions of negotiating and manoeuvring between varying geographies and refuge spaces. Creativity is also essential to the processes of re-experiencing, narrating and depicting trauma along with its associated actions and negotiations. It becomes crucial, therefore, to appreciate creativity as an integral part of Iraqis' everyday struggle for refuge, while concurrently acknowledging the numerous ways such creativity can be represented during the mapping process. This evolving creative practice lays bare the interviewees' often-concealed traumatic knowledge, while simultaneously fostering new insights into the field of spatial justice. It may even seem messy, but this is only a reflection of the nonlinear, intricate events and traumas that are nestled within shifting geographies, which in turn transform through space-time, memory recall and creative imaginings of the future. The transient nature of the creative practice that underpins this research accentuates the *progression*, rather than *production*, of knowledge-making. The act of mapping thus evolves into a deliberate creative effort to mould spaces of refuge, and doubles as an analytical instrument for understanding its spatial negotiations.

The traumatic disclosures shared by the Iraqis participating in this research have heavily influenced the creative process and the choices made regarding which narrative fragments and stories to incorporate and which to exclude from the maps. This kind of selectivity in representational practices bears political significance, as it underscores the assertion of agency (Marston and De leeuw 2013). In a special issue on creativity and geography, guest editors Sallie A. Marston and Sarah De leeuw present, with caution, a view of the 'situated politics of creative production' for geographers. This requires an understanding of 'the "climate" in which all geographical knowledge is being produced' (Marston and De leeuw 2013: xx). They further state that 'the very acquisition of the skills of creative making, achieved over time and through repetitive practice, in and of themselves are performative of resistance to the temporalities of scholarship' (Marston and De leeuw 2013: xx). A nuanced understanding of the politics of creative practice and creativity within this chapter considers creative making not to be a mere representational tool of war, violence and trauma, but rather, as Rugo (2023: 2) describes it, 'a world-making process'. This 'world-making process' is a creative practice that can define new ways in which 'art's ability to stir emotional responses has been used both to consolidate consensus or cement the status quo and to disrupt and antagonize dominant power structures' (Rugo 2023: 2). The very act of map-making in this project involved tracing traumatic geographies, charting displacement routes, drawing, cutting and layering material and non-material intimacies, as with a palimpsest. The interview narratives went through this same creative mapping process, too, in the search for knowledge on refuge-making practices.

This palimpsestic approach forces the process of knowledge-making to unpack, dig deep and unwind actions, contradictions and distinctions to the trauma narratives that have been shared. Used as a figurative concept by Kimberly A. Powell (2008: 6), the 'palimpsest' is an instrumental tool in analysing 'the ways in which built environments embody social, cultural, and historical narratives of place, highlighting the involuted relations between material, visual, cultural, and social experience'. The term palimpsest is used by different disciplines across the humanities, arts and social sciences, and bears meaning beyond that of its original association within ancient manuscript – such a fact constitutes 'evidence of its metaphoric prowess and possibilities' (Powell 2008: 7). Sarah Dillon (2007: 4) further explores the semantic difference between palimpsest, palimpsestic and what she calls 'palimpsestuous': 'palimpsestic refers to the process of layering that produces a palimpsest, "palimpsestuous" describes the structure that one is presented with as a result of that process, and the subsequent reappearance of the underlying script'. In a palimpsestuous structure, deep mapping uncovers deep layers. Selina Springett (2019: 99) also speaks of a practice of palimpsest creation that is akin to deep mapping, in that that involves more than just the mere tracing of layers of history and reality; instead, she slowly builds layers, 'savoring, juxtaposing, and expanding on each individual story'. This chapter uses this slow practice of palimpsestic map-making to define the parameters of scale, depth and layering of refuge-making under discussion.

Intimacies and scales of refuge

The term 'intimacy' usually aligns itself with concepts of closeness, privacy and the emotionally or sexually close. Here, however, it is used as a tool to emphasize the palimpsestic relationships and intricacies between the familiar and unfamiliar, the private and public, the personal and political, and the local and global within each interview. In feminist discourse, intimacy is used frequently 'as an analytical device to counter the understanding of the intimate as a private, local realm until it is penetrated by external forces' (Wilson 2016: 250). The intimacies discussed in this section transgress the binary concepts of sexuality and gendered spaces, especially those usually associated with Middle Eastern cultures. Ara Wilson (2012: 48) clarifies her intent for using intimacy as a flexible rubric for 'transnational analysis of power', with a 'provisional reference that emphasizes linkages across what are understood to be distinct realms, scales and bodies', which is 'intended to resist ideological reifications of family, sexuality, or community – that is, to avoid recreating forms of knowledge that perpetuate global inequality'. Collectively, the shared narratives of memories, objects and spaces reveal different degrees and scales of intimacies within refuge, and tell stories of trauma, resistance and the resilience of Iraqis.

Ahead of the 2003 US-led invasion of Iraq, different locations within Iraq prepared themselves in different ways. In order to provide in-depth and wide-ranging coverage of how the people in these different areas were impacted over the period of this study, I have intentionally interviewed people who were geographically diverse at the time. With the lack of any pre-organized governmental support on how to prepare for war, Iraqis organized themselves amongst their neighbourhoods and extended networks. While there is some evidence of government-led media support ahead of the 1991 war on Iraq (Cigar 2014), this diminished ahead of the 2003 invasion. As a result, Iraqis in early 2003 were filling up buckets and pots with water, and storing dried and tinned food and non-perishables, including essential cooking ingredients such as rice, lentils and other pulses. Also on the list of essential items was cooking oil, as well as oil for lighting lamps and heating. Some dug wells several metres deep, thinking that the deeper the well the better the quality of water, but most people who tested theirs (including my family) had disappointing results. Lab results returned stating: 'Unfit for human consumption, contains high traces of crude oil.' I remember my father digging holes to the side of our house to bury petrol cans, because he was worried that a bullet might hit the exposed can and trigger an explosion. These items of food and fuel became priority items in every household at the time, and they were the same items people took with them when they were forced to leave for safety when the bombing intensified. Lack of electricity meant that people had to revert back to traditional methods of cooking, using small gas stoves and baking bread in clay ovens (known as *tanoor* in colloquial Iraqi Arabic). Speaking from her flat where she now lives in London, Sanar Hasan (2022), an award-winning journalist originally from Mahmudiyah, south of Baghdad, recalls:

> The first thing my mother did was store bags of flour and dates. Because of the high price of cooking gas at the time, or the lack of it, families decided to return to using the traditional clay oven [*tenoor*] to make bread. Behind our neighbourhood there were orchards and, in that, a clay oven was created and was serving the neighbourhood. Women used to take their dough and go there, sit together and make bread. I used to accompany my mother. I felt it was a strange thing to return to old, traditional ways of cooking. I was a teenager

> at the time. It was an experience I still remember, the smell of freshly baked bread, the children accompanying their mothers, collecting dry wood and sticks, and playing, and mothers talking about everyday life.

Iraqi flat, round bread (known as *khubez* in colloquial Iraqi Arabic) has always been a lifeline for Iraqis. During previous times of tension, unrest and war, bread makers always kept their shops open, and these became spaces of convergence for communities during times of trauma. Because of this, *khubez* became a symbol of refuge, social support and heritage, yet it was always shrouded with its association with struggle and trauma. I asked Abrar Wadi, a civil engineer and feminist activist from Basra, who was born during the brutal UN sanctions, if she has any memory or material object that she associates with the 2003 war. She recalls the trauma associated with war through the image of her mother's bread:

> I have this feeling and a memory from when I was young. We were struggling financially during the war when my mother used to make bread from poor-quality flour, but I used to think it is the best bread ever. I used to walk around the house with a piece of her bread in my mouth all the time. During the early years of secondary school, I ate hardly anything apart from my mother's bread. I gained a lot of weight and my teeth suffered. I was forced to stop eating it because of my health. Now every time I see or smell bread, a painful memory comes to mind, reminding me of the war and the hardship and how I once was addicted to bread.
>
> (Wadi 2022)

Even the tools used before electricity was invented, like the instrument that crushes wheat to make flour, or the clay pot (known as *hib* in colloquial Iraqi Arabic) used to keep water cool, all made a comeback during this time. With only a few exceptions, the interviewees all recall how trauma and the improvised solutions to it made certain gendered activities and spaces more apparent, for example, women became more concerned with providing food, and men with keeping everyone safe and creating makeshift shelters. Improvisations were of course also happening across the gender divides – while women were associated with economizing, rationing and creating different types of food with limited ingredients, they were also integral to the decision-making involved in the creation of spaces of refuge both inside and outside the home. Across all interviews, it is possible to identify social themes such as 'togetherness' and the concept of 'strength in numbers', but what stands out in particular are certain object–body relationships. In other words, how matter became an integral part of the process of refuge.

Karen Barad (2003: 802) reminds us of the performativity of understanding matter not as items of representation but rather as 'matters of practices/doings/

actions', bringing to the fore 'important questions of ontology, materiality and agency'. Barad critiques the social constructivist view of representationalism, which became inseparable from linguistic associations with nature and the image or appearance of anything natural, as it lacks association and embodiment within history. Instead, Barad (2003: 821) writes, 'Matter is always already an ongoing historicity', expanding upon Judith Butler's account of materialization as a process rather than a passive, empty site awaiting activation through the inscription of cultural or representational significance of relationships between the material and its exterior. In describing the performative relationship between materiality and discursive practices, Barad (2003: 829) asserts the interdependency of human to nonhuman relationships in world-making, where the epistemology and ontology of matter are inseparable to world–body space:

> Boundary-making practices, that is, discursive practices, are fully implicated in the dynamics of intra-activity through which phenomena come to matter. In other words, materiality is discursive (i.e., material phenomena are inseparable from the apparatuses of bodily production: matter emerges out of and includes as part of its being the ongoing reconfiguring of boundaries), just as discursive practices are always already material (i.e., they are ongoing material (re)configurings of the world). Discursive practices and material phenomena do not stand in a relationship of externality to one another; rather, the material and the discursive are mutually implicated in the dynamics of intra-activity. […] Neither discursive practices nor material phenomena are ontologically or epistemologically prior. Neither can be explained in terms of the other. Neither has privileged status in determining the other.
>
> (Barad 2003: 822)

Barad's (2007: 141) lens of performative practice allows for a specific reading of objects and spaces that are in 'intra-action' with bodies as they actively seek agency. In the context of this book, agency is not seen as inherent, but rather it emerges from some form of action, dynamism or force, usually in the form of an active search for refuge. In times of war in Iraq, we see that objects and spaces are appropriated out of need, displaying a wide range of discursive, performative practices. The long years of sanctions during the 1990s both enabled and, to some extent, hindered this kind of appropriation. While Baghdadis were digging wells, Iraqi Kurds were preparing themselves for a chemical attack, in the event that Saddam Hussein chose to retaliate against them for allying with the United States. The collective trauma and memory of the Halabja massacre ordered by the Saddam regime in 1988 meant that, in 2003, the Kurds were busy creating chemical masks and sealing their windows and doors with nylon sheets. Dr Rozhen Kamal Mohammed-Amin, herself a Kurd from Sulaimani, is Director of the Digital

Cultural Heritage Research Centre (DCH) and Lecturer at the City Planning Engineering Department, Sulaimani Polytechnic University (SPU). She recalls:

> Because Iraq before 2003 was still under the UN sanctions, there were no chemical masks available in the market, so people had to improvise. We used coal wrapped in ordinary cotton clothes to make masks. These were always with us in the same room where we stayed, as we were anticipating an attack at any point.
>
> (Mohammed-Amin 2022)

Meanwhile, the daily life of Baghdadis was soon interrupted by heavy bombardment. Basma Al-Azzawi (2022), a Baghdadi ceramicist and, currently, a single mother seeking asylum in the UK, told me:

> I was pregnant at the time and only gave birth to my daughter nine days before Baghdad was struck in 2003. My now ex-husband and I were living in our house in Adhamiyah, but when I gave birth and we knew the war is imminent, we left our house and went to live with my parents and brother in Felisteen Street in central Baghdad. My father had a poultry field with a little farmhouse. He was worried about the livestock and the workers, so had to leave us. We were only four adults and my newborn. Felisteen Street was surrounded by several ministry buildings, and we were incredibly worried about my daughter. After the bombing of one of the ministry buildings, we emptied and cleaned a small cupboard that we used to put our shoes in for her small cot to go in, just to shield her from the shattering glass.

After the fall of the regime, in 2003 and 2004, the absence of law and order led to waves of kidnappings and rape. In response to this, people emptied and prepared their rooftop water tanks and clay ovens to be used as safe spaces for hiding women and girls. In these examples, we can see refuge across multiple scales: from the appropriated spaces in and around the home, to the small objects like the tiny book of prayers in one interviewee's wallet that she carries with her at all times, to another's diary containing details of every bomb, explosion and argument within the household. Interviewees recall how certain spaces and objects within their homes took on different attributes, meanings and senses of belonging and identity. Representations of such themes include Yazidi traditional clothing, an Assyrian calligrapher's tools, and one's father's library containing his all-important and defining activism in the form of a Communist Party Pamphlet. These intimate and boundary-making practices provide an alternative view of objects of war (Auslander and Zahra 2018) and violence, a more indigenous practice of historicity. These are unpacked later in the chapter, in relation to violent ruptures within domesticity.

Ruptured domesticity

The country's urban and rural landscapes are still haunted with the residue of criss-crossed tape stuck on windows, and bullet and shrapnel marks on buildings. Days before the 2003 invasion of Iraq, Iraqis were fixing blankets to their window frames to prevent the glass from flying everywhere, and deliberating with neighbours and relatives about the routes that might be taken by invading troops into main cities and neighbourhoods. My family's house was wedged between the main road that leads to Baghdad Airport and the road that leads out of Baghdad and towards the notorious Abu-Ghraib prison. We knew that our area, Amiriyah, would become a battleground – it was only a matter of *when*. Like all Iraqis, we prepared and stored as much as we could, and on the eve of 19 March 2003 we awoke from sleep to the heavy and continuous bombardment on Baghdad. We heard the siren go off (we did not then hear the continuous tone indicating safety until several days had passed), and the four of us (my parents, my younger sister and me) leapt out of our bedrooms and headed for what used to serve as a living room. This improvised shelter was towards the back of the house, with walls against our back footpath, which led to our neighbours' houses. The room had a built-in wardrobe full of bedding and sheets, and a small window that we had boarded up. The sofas had been pushed away, as had the television, which was covered with a sheet, and mattresses lay side by side on the floor, piled with extra duvets and blankets. My father's ear was almost glued to the battery-run radio, but we could only receive a local channel, which played Iraqi nationalist songs, and the Arabic version of 'Radio Monte Carlo', which gave only thinly detailed news. We remained in that room for three days before we began to feel a sense of despair at the unbearable heavy bombardment on the city. What followed was a series of violently ruptured senses of domesticity and refuge that rippled across the country from Baghdad outwards. This is told through the individual stories of people with lived and felt experiences of that trauma.

The memories included here describe multiple ruptures of domesticity, as well as non-domestic refuge-seeking. These are viewed through different modes of 'homing practices' – a term borrowed from Boccagni's (2022: 5) definition of 'home as interaction' rather than 'home as place'. This form of interaction weaves and braids together several alternative homing practices found in the creases of rupture, trauma and violence spanning the years between 2003 and 2023. Iraqis were gripped with the necessity to transform a room inside the house into a safe place. Most of these were spaces thrust to the backs of houses, adjacent to bathrooms, and required the shifting of furniture and blocking up of entrances, amongst other preparations. Although the main focus of this section on domesticity concerns the home, this is not a study of spatiality in relation to gender roles in the architecture of a place, as has been explored in the collection edited by Hilde Heynen and Gülsüm Baydar (2005). Nor is it concerned with the relationship between the interior of a house and its exterior, where the domestic interior serves as a receiving or broadcasting device, as discussed extensively by Beatriz Colomina in *Domesticity at War* (2007). Instead, domesticity is defined here as a set of relations that are material and symbolic (Blunt and Varley 2004), and which reveal different scales of intimacies at local and global levels. As a concept, therefore, domesticity is considered a methodological tool for braiding knowledge (Atalay 2019) and for revealing degrees of intimacies of war and violence. Borrowing from methodologies within Indigenous archaeology (Atalay 2020) and critical geographies of homing as an active form of making (Boccagni 2022), domesticity emerges as a nexus of relations and degrees of intimacies of the rupturing home and a sense of refuge.

What follows are three degrees of rupture, told through the voices of the interviewees. The first concerns the material and memory object/body/space relationships, a scale of rupture that includes the trauma of debris and shrapnel. The second is the act of violation through raids and searches of homes and domesticity in general. The third is the complete obliteration and erasure of homes and identities, at the scale of domicide/geocide.

The first three days of Shock and Awe in 2003 caused different degrees of rupture in Iraqis' sense of refuge and domesticity. Most of these ruptures involved emotional trauma – indeed, the heavy bombardment still remains in the minds of Iraqis – but some were physical trauma, impacted upon specific geographical locations. Dr Zeinab Shuker, Assistant Professor of Sociology at Sam Houston State University, Texas, speaks from Baghdad after fifteen years of exile. She recalls the moment a missile struck near to her family home in Amiriyah in 2003:

> During the weeks of bombing in 2003, the Iraqi Army had a rocket launcher at the end of our street. We felt the sound and impact of that, more so than the bombs and missiles that were falling. Eventually, the rocket launcher was bombed in the middle of the night. That missile destroyed part of our kitchen wall and the windows broke. We were fine, but we had to repair our windows and sort out the kitchen. The neighbours helped too.
>
> (Shuker 2022)

What follows are three accounts from three different perspectives. South of the country in Basra, Abrar Wadi and Dr Nawrast Sabah, Lecturer in Geology of Sciences at the University of Basra, recall a series of ruptures in 2003 that gradually took over ordinary life. First, Wadi (2022) describes the drastic change in domesticity and sense of refuge:

> At that time, I was five years old. We were living in a northern suburb in the city of Basra, close to orchid farms. It was far away from the city centre, so we

did not feel the impact of the attacks on the city. There was no electricity, so we could not follow the news, but our first encounter with war at the time was when my mother and I were walking towards my grandparents' house, which is in the same neighbourhood, and we were faced with military tanks. We could not tell between the American and the British troops. They were handing out canned food, which had no taste whatsoever.

I think at the time, the poor part of the population had no idea what was going on and what the war and invasion brought to the country. There was widespread ignorance among the people towards their country and what was unfolding at the time. This was particularly true at the time of the looting [just after the fall of Baghdad]. I remember the old and the young welcomed the troops – they considered them liberating forces. At the beginning, we felt they had rescued us from a dictatorship. We were now free to visit the holy shrines and practice rituals, which were banned during the Saddam era. We only realized they were not liberators after a long time, through systemic violence across the city and the rest of the country as a whole.

In our neighbourhood, houses were scattered in the land, it was not a heavily built-up area. In 2004, the shelling and bombing of tribal retaliation against the foreign troops reached our area. A lot of families felt their houses were exposed and left for a different neighbourhood. We moved into another house in between a cluster of other houses and had to change the type of roof we had then. It used to be the traditional blockwork [an old ceiling and roof building technique which relies on material surface tension known as *aagada* in colloquial Iraqi Arabic] and we had to change to reinforced concrete. We are a large family; my father has two wives and a large number of children from each wife, therefore we needed two large houses next to each other. We opened a doorway between them during the sectarian violence, so that we could avoid leaving one house to access the other.

Sabah (2022) also notes:

Basra was bombed during the 2003 invasion, especially the centre. Near our house was the governorate centre. This centre was one of the locations that was bombed. I remember this missile vividly, I was standing next to my father and, when the missile hit, I jumped from the blow across the room. Some of our windows shattered and the whole house shook. We were under British control. I remember once I looked at the window and saw a British tank outside our front gate, in the middle of the street. That was the moment that I felt Iraq was occupied and we had no control over the sovereignty of our country. The British troops were targeting Ba'athist cells and houses, meanwhile Saddam's special commandos (Fidaayo Saddam) withdrew into the orchards and agricultural

> lands, these places where two of my cousins were living with their families, so we had to rescue them and they stayed with us in our house. We were about thirteen people in the house. We felt safer in numbers.

Dr Ula Merie, Lecturer in Architecture at the University of Babylon, Faculty of Engineering, Department of Architecture, tells a story of violence that continued to rip through the city of Baghdad from the fall of the regime. This was the infiltration of Al-Qaeda throughout Iraq between 2004 and 2006, and the years of sectarian violence from 2006 to 2008. Her story conveys the fact that ruptures and violence can inflict iterative, nonlinear trauma on people's homes and domesticity. Merie (2022) also notes:

> Before Baghdad fell to the US troops, my father left us because he was a military officer. At the time, the popular army (part of the Ba'ath Party) suggested that we leave the area, given that Dora is south of Baghdad and the district is considered a main route into Baghdad. So we moved to my aunt's house, which was in the Adhamiya area. We left everything behind and only went back in the morning of the 9th of April (the fall of Baghdad) when we heard back from my father. At that time, the looting movement (*Hawasem*) began everywhere, so we were worried about our house.
>
> During the sectarian violence, it was a different story. Our house and its location in the centre of Dora in Baghdad was right in the middle of two neighbourhoods – the south of that neighbourhood was controlled by the Shia militia and the north of the neighbourhood was controlled by the Sunnis. These two parts of the same neighbourhood were throwing bombs and missiles at each other, one of which fell on our house, breaking part of our guest room and the outside fence. My brother and I were inside. There was a huge dust cloud. Our neighbours came to check, but we were okay. We had to leave before the violence got even worse.

Over two decades, debris and shrapnel littered and studded houses and neighbourhoods across Iraq, producing multiple traumas. Although the material presence of shrapnel on walls exists to this day in some neighbourhoods, the physical repairing of other neighbourhoods left a different kind of trauma, both on cities and their people. Ali Al-Baroodi (2022), a photojournalist, translator and academic at the Department of Translation, Mosul University, tells of the lingering trauma of war and violence after Mosul was liberated from ISIS in 2017:

> My house is still riddled with bullet holes, shrapnel and scars. Memories, tangible and intangible, are still all around me. It is necessary to have these memories.

Our bigger home, Mosul, is still carrying the scars of war everywhere. Yet the concept of being home, on its own, is enough to make us feel better.

You would notice a lot of the windows were blocked to protect people from broken glass and shrapnel. Basements in the old city were taken as the primary spaces for protection. An L-shaped basement would be divided into a cooking space and a sleeping space. I found cooking oil and pots and pans left in the wreckage of what was left of these houses when I went with my camera one day. That part of the city was under constant bombing for two months, to get rid of ISIS. For two months, people relocated their entire lives to this microcosm right at the bottom of the house.

On the 26th of November in 2016, the army was marching around our neighbourhood. We thought the battle for Mosul was still far away from us, but all of a sudden, we heard two missiles falling. It was about 50 metres away from my bedroom. The missiles hit ISIS shovels and lorries as they were attempting to create a new road for their vehicles. I found myself on the other side of the room. You will see white spots where shrapnel has hit my room [referring to the second photograph he shared with me]. The next day we decided to change where we spent our time inside the house to a different room. We were sixteen people [family and relatives] then.

The next day, my brother went out to block one of the windows to the front of the house to stop shrapnel from entering in. I begged him to leave it and come back inside but he insisted, until we heard a jet and, within seconds, he was on the ground surrounded by a pool of blood. My nephew and niece thought he was dead and were crying, and his wife too. I got courage from nowhere, went towards him and wrapped his injured arm and took him to a nurse who lived nearby. She said we had to take him to hospital. The jet was still over my head. I was wondering whether it would spare me, like the story of the American pilot of 1991, who was aiming at a bridge in Baghdad and saw a car crossing the bridge and decided to wait until the car reached the other side before hitting the bridge, but this pilot did not spare me. The force of the impact threw me across onto the ground just by the door. I stood up and checked my body to see if I was hit. Thankfully, I was not. I took the car, picked up my brother and took him to hospital. He survived the blast, but he now has a deficiency in being able to fully use his right hand and fingers.

That was the only time when we left the house totally empty. We moved into another house in the neighbourhood while it was raining rockets. That was when ISIS decided to evacuate that entire neighbourhood to use as their military base. It was the only time I bade farewell to the house. I took all the gasoline and food that we had kept in storage to see us through the hard times and moved everything to my cousin's house. When I was about to close the door for the last time, a flash of my entire childhood and adult life and the good times I spent in that house passed in front of my eyes. It was like saying goodbye to a person you love, a person that you have lived with, [he mutters an Iraqi saying: I say farewell to you and wish for God to protect you]. I closed the door and left.

The systematic and protracted violations of homes by those in power (whether the Saddam regime, the invading troops and their coalition, or militias such as Al-Qaeda) ruptured any sense of refuge and domesticity that people used to associate with their everyday lives. Shuker (2022) recalls finding a sense of familiarity in the violence across the years of her childhood and up until she left Iraq as a young adult:

> The home was not safe, that [Communist Party] pamphlet in the house would have got us killed. The school was not safe because I did not trust friends enough to be who I am. My grandmother's house was not safe because my uncle was abducted from his bedroom by the Saddam regime. The street was not safe, everywhere you turned there was a car bomb. This feeling continued even in the USA, especially given the long history of the US involvement in Iraq and what that meant to Americans.
>
> At the peak of the sectarian violence, other neighbourhoods around us were not Shia, so street fighting became more intense. One time we saw Afghans running in our streets. That was one of these surreal moments. I was outside in the garage [usually to the front of the house, like a patio], I opened the door and saw this fighter, clearly not an Iraqi, wearing a dress with a long beard, holding a machine gun, aiming at someone in the street. He saw me, he clearly knew this was a Shia area; instead of shooting me, he just told me to go inside.
>
> Two days later, a bullet got through the library window in our house and into one of my father's books. We used to sleep on the roof because of the high temperatures, but there was a battle going on outside and people were shooting at each other, so my father said we should go downstairs. We went downstairs and found a bullet next to my bed headboard.

During the years of sectarian violence in Baghdad, home raids and searches in strategic locations across the country were taking place constantly, adding to the maps of target homes. Depending on the part of the city and the particular conflict, these raids could have been conducted by the Iraqi military, Sunni or Shia militias, or American troops and their allies. As such, the violation of domesticity occurred at the hands of people on all sides, as long as they had power over civilians. From 2006, when sectarianism was rife in and near Baghdad, Merie, Hasan and Al-Azzawi recall these kinds of occurrences. We begin with Merie (2022):

> Dora was very unsafe. The American soldiers were doing regular checks on houses in the neighbourhood. One time I was alone when around ten US soldiers knocked on the door. I opened the door and immediately they started searching everywhere. They saw my father's photo with his uniform on and they started saying things like, 'You are part of the old regime.' They used to steal bits and pieces from people's houses during these raids. They were asking me questions and others went inside the house to check – they checked and looked inside everything. One of the troops spoke to me softly and discreetly in Arabic, it sounded like a Lebanese accent; he said, 'My sister, go and check your gold, they [the US soldiers] have been stealing from houses.' I went upstairs to check. We had a box with a bit of money put aside and a few pieces of gold. I found a gold bracelet, an heirloom, missing. I went back outside and told them there was something missing and I needed it back. They said, 'No, there should not be anything missing.' They knew that one of them did it. They went out into the garden, and they started checking each other. Later on, they said, 'No, we checked everything.' Meanwhile, a female soldier went upstairs again, came back down asked me if I would like to go up and check again. I went back upstairs and found the bracelet, this time inside the box. It was a terribly unsafe time.

Hasan (2022) also recalls:

> During the days when the American soldiers used to raid houses in the Mahmudiyah area, south of Baghdad, I remember my mother and I used to put our underwear in black plastic bags, just to protect this part of our dignity and lives. They also used to steal whatever gold or money you had during those raids, and no one could complain. My mother used to hide her gold and money inside the freezer. They even once took my pocket money. During these raids, the US troops used to put women and children in one room and take men and boys into another room and tie their hands with plastic cable ties.

Al-Azzawi (2022) notes:

> The Shia militia had a list of names that they were going through, door to door, threatening families – mainly men were affected – then forcing people to leave, and then killing them if they did not obey. So, my parents decided to leave Felisteen Street, central Baghdad, and head outside the country. I had been separated from my husband at the time due to domestic issues, and was still living with my parents, yet could not leave the country with them because my daughter had no passport and, by Iraqi law, I would need to obtain her father's approval for a passport to be issued. I could not get him to agree to it, so I had to find somewhere else to stay.

The complete obliteration of homes came at the hands of groups of Islamic militants, the remnants of Al-Qaeda who called themselves the Islamic State of Iraq and Syria (ISIS), or Daesh. They established themselves in the region in 2004, and were only defeated within Iraq in 2018 after a series of battles across the country. The brutality of the ISIS advances, which culminated in the 2014 fall of Mosul and massacre in Sinjar, has left scars and trauma on Iraqis and their homes, cities and villages that remain to this day. The trauma runs deep, as thousands of Yazidi men and older people were executed and thousands of women and girls were kidnapped, abused and sold as sex slaves, many of whom are still missing. Based in the north-west of Iraq, in the Nineveh province, Yazidis are one of many religious minority groups in Iraq, and they typically live in villages of single-storey mud houses with fenced areas for livestock. In the space of just a few days, their homes and villages were annihilated, which, along with their executions, amounts to domicide and genocide at the hands of ISIS. Two of my interviewees are Yazidi survivors from different parts of Sinjar: Amera Ibrahim, now a biologist, is from the north of Sinjar, and was working as an associate for Sinjar Academy (a charity supporting the education of Yazidis in Iraq); Shahab Sameer is a writer and a member of the General Union for the Literaries and Writers in Iraq, and is originally from the south of Sinjar. Both recall multiple layers of loss – the full experience of trauma of which Caruth (1995) speaks:

> Sinjar is mostly a semi-desert landscape with a mountain that most Yazidis know well, because of their history of seasonal work in farming and keeping animal stock. The route to reach the mountain is treacherous, but every Yazidi knows that this mountain had our backs every time we needed to escape. The edge of the mountain was home to the original villages of Yazidis, before the Iraqi government provided housing away from that area back in the 1970s. Therefore, it remained a familiar place of refuge to many Yazidis. When ISIS attacked from the south of Sinjar, there was no other route for us other than the mountain. All routes outside Sinjar were blocked. Our only option for escape was towards the mountain. Yazidis who knew the mountain well also knew that, once we reached the mountain, other routes and options would be possible either towards the Syrian border to the west or towards the Kurdistan region to the north-east of the mountain. Nevertheless, all of these routes are treacherous, and none of them is fit for cars, only possible for skilled hikers. Remember, we had elderly people, pregnant women and small children. My wife was heavily pregnant at the time with our second child when we made that journey. We walked for three continuous days. We could not take anything with us and the little we took we had to leave behind in order to continue to climb with little weight on us. August is incredibly hot in Iraq, we had no water or

> food, but we had to continue our walk regardless. We were walking with other families and people helped each other.
>
> (Sameer 2022)

> We felt protected and safe in our small village. The Yazidi minority people are simple and peaceful in nature. We were never involved in wars and killings before. When ISIS attacked our village in August 2014, we even had a limited number of weapons because we always avoided conflict. So many of us did not know how to use these weapons to protect ourselves. ISIS took away every sense of safety we had before. When ISIS attacked our village of Sinjar, there was no bombing. Our houses could not protect us as they were operating their offences door to door and street to street. But at the beginning, we stayed in our house. We had a room, which was about 4 by 5 metres. It was small, had one small window, and its door was thicker than the rest of the doors. That was the only safe space inside, but soon after, we had to leave. We left the village, heading to the mountain on foot, even though it was really far away from our village. It took us three hours, but it was the only option for survival. We stayed at the mountain for about seven days. The route to getting there was very difficult, full of heavy and large rocks. We used the caves inside the mountains to shelter, we had little food and water. People perished because of the lack of food and drink.
>
> (A. Ibrahim 2022)

In their work in unpacking the braided complexity of both home and domicide, J. Douglas Porteous and Sanda E. Smith (2001: 63) suggest that domicide signifies the loss of both physical and emotional aspects associated with home and self-identity:

> Domicide, then, may result in: the destruction of a place of attachment and refuge; loss of security and ownership; restrictions of freedom; partial loss of identity; and a radical de-centring from place, family, and community. There may be a loss of historical connection; a weakening of roots; and partial erasure of the source of memory, dreams, nostalgia, and ideals.

Ibrahim's and Sameer's accounts above both touch upon dimensions within this complex definition of domicide (Azzouz 2023). These details form a palimpsest of the different degrees of rupture, both spatial and material, from the violation of home and domesticity to the physical and deliberate erasure of self-identity.

The urban in a spherical space between vertical and horizontal violence

What emerges from these interviews is a clear conjunction between violence and trauma at both the domestic and the urban scales. This section deals with the 'spherical violence' that has engulfed cities across Iraq. This violence can be perceived as spherical because it breaks the Euclidian physical dimensions of geography and geopolitics. Viewed from the perspective of Iraqis on the ground, the US-led invasion of Iraq, particularly its aerial bombing campaign, represents a verticality of violence; contrastingly, occupation, sectarianism and ISIS movements operated horizontally within cities. There is therefore violence being generated both towards and by the urban condition – a fact that highlights a particular case of what Ash Amin (2016: 779) calls 'urban failure', 'based on the assumption that the threat of collective dysfunction confronts all cities insofar as they are complex open systems constantly confronted by turbulence and uncertainty, external and internal'. In the case of cities in Iraq, then, these vertical and horizontal threats and confrontations, both fast and slow, can extend to urbicide (sectarian violence and ISIS), to intimidation by local, national and neighbouring governments and states (soft and hard borders, aggressive responses to peaceful protests such as the 2019 Revolution, etc.), and finally to the responses to all such violence by Iraqis themselves. Iraqi cities have struggled on the verge of failure for decades, especially as their infrastructures and social orders are continually shaken.

Iraqi cities, like many others, conflated the creation of refuge spaces for their expanding population with the urge to contain violence (internal and external). With the expansion of urban centres and peripheries, fortifications and aggressive/defensive architectures and planning tactics have imploded over the years. The strategies for the deployment of blast walls and high fences around governmental and presidential buildings were reflected onto individual houses and enclaves within cities, creating corridors of violence that rippled through segregated neighbourhoods. One such example is the Army Canal highway in Baghdad, which divides multiple neighbourhoods to the east of the Tigris River. In *Planet of Slums*, Mike Davis (2007) pulls out the dialectics of such planning tactics in criminalizing the urban poor to fulfil power grabbing purposes. Davis (2007: 205) refers to Sadr City as 'one of the world's largest slums' in which local young people 'taunt American occupiers with the promise that their main boulevard is "Vietnam Street"'. Sadr is one of the poorest enclaves on the eastern periphery of Baghdad, and has struggled for years with lack of sufficient infrastructure, particularly sanitary water and a working sewage system, amongst other daily needs (Makiya 1998). The enclave was rife with unemployment, which drove young men to organize a militia called the Mehdi Army, filling the power vacuum left after the fall of the regime in 2003. Between 2003 and the start of the sectarian violence in 2006, the Mehdi Army retaliated against the US occupation through any means possible, including the use of suicide car bombs, killing and terrorizing innocent Iraqis along the way. Davis (2007: 206) argues that the criminalization of the poor in Sadr City by the West has set the stage for an orientalist view of urban warfare, with the 'civilized world' in the West versus the 'Eastern Other', with its 'terrorists' nests of Islamic cities':

> This delusionary dialectic of scrutinized versus demonic urban places, in turn, dictates a sinister and unceasing duet: Night after night, hornlike helicopter gunships stalk enigmatic enemies in the narrow streets of the slum districts, pouring hellfire into shanties or fleeing cars. Every morning the slums reply with suicide bombers and eloquent explosions. If the empire can deploy Orwellian technologies of repression, its outcasts have the gods of chaos on their side.

Dr Dhirgham Alobaydi, the Chair of the Department of Architecture Engineering at the College of Engineering, University of Baghdad, resides in one of these neighbourhoods. He has previously published research on the physical spatial networks that dictate certain spatial practices' 'power over' and 'power to' control territories within Baghdad (Rashid and Alobaydi 2015: 192). Alobaydi (2022) explains:

> The Army Canal highway itself is a violent corridor. It cuts through neighbourhoods to control people by limiting their areas and access. The eastern side of the road is a shortcut to isolate and control the Sadrist Shia area. The same thing happened with Amiriyah and Dora – the highways split these two districts to make them manageable to control.

At the start of the 2003 invasion of Iraq, a horizontal means of control and violence collided with vertical warfare, though such vertical warfare was in itself 'flat'. The flatness of the vertical American warfare, as Graham and Hewitt (2013) suggest, is defined by its 'horizontalism'; in other words, in its analysis of urban spaces that disengage with the vertical qualities of urbanization in favour of a top-down, aerial gaze of geopolitical spatiality. This method of 'horizontalism' was tested during the months in which American troops and their coalition forces occupied Iraqi cities, as they became vulnerable to pockets of retaliation, resistance and revenge for their senseless, vertically flat bombardment. They were later tested again during the years of sectarian violence and ISIS atrocities. Alobaydi (2022) continues:

Places that were used by Ba'athists in the past as corridors and fences of control were then used by tribe leaders to provide control and protection to neighbourhoods like main centres, schools and public buildings. During the years of sectarian violence, when the militia (the majority of them young and lacking education) moved from other neighbourhoods in particular to Sadr City, to control other neighbourhoods within the Shia majority. These same spaces became places of trauma and violence.

While the intense vertical violence was concentrated in main cities, other areas and strategic locations around the country were not spared. Professor Jaafar Jotheri (2022), a geo-archaeologist from the University of Qadisiyah, explains what was happening in the city of Qasim, Babylon province, south of Baghdad:

> During the 2003 invasion, bridges were bombed, and some state buildings in Qasim. It was a miliary route from Samawah, Diwaniyah and then Hillah (the southern main route to Baghdad).
>
> After 2003, the coalition forces set up a camp in Diwaniyah (the main city in the Qadisiyah province). We in the Department of Archaeology at the time built a relationship with civil archaeologists, who came with the CF. They tried to rebuild our department and build surveying and excavation excursions. Meanwhile, as this help was going on, there were other foreign interests, such as the coalition forces, who stole a number of original bricks from the Babylon archaeological site. Babylon suffered a great deal of abuse, looting and smuggling over the years.
>
> ISIS did not bomb Qasim, but there were only a few car bombs going off every now and then. Yes, we prepared to fight. There were rumours that ISIS would invade Najaf, Karbala and the south from the western desert. Qasim is close to Najaf, and we thought of the marshes to protect our children and women, but the problem with ISIS was that they knew how to move across urban and rural areas. They did not just use main roads. They were more dangerous than any state threat or military air strike. That is why we decided to fight them if they came to our land.

Over time, the verticality of the urban reached a new depth of trauma and violence, through horizontal infiltrations within cities. Alobaydi, Hasan, Al-Azzawi and Shuker speak about that period of Iraq's history:

> It is hard to recall women walking on their own from one area to another during that time. At any time, a woman could be kidnapped and killed or disappear, so women stayed at home. Before the civil war, the tribes controlled

> the area, and women had the freedom to navigate the area and the city, but during the sectarian violence, the militia controlled the area. Militias are put together based on ethno-religious influences, and when they had control, they removed the tribal groups, stripping away their authority, and they took total control over all neighbourhoods, even the mixed ones. They dressed in black clothes and drove a special kind of car, mainly Toyota and/or Opel. The years of militia control were the hardest years, because of their extreme religious beliefs on both sides – the Sunni and the Shia. Both militias practised their thoughts and beliefs violently: they prevented young men from shaving their beards or wearing necklaces, and further prevented them from dressing in casual shirts and shorts; they forced women to wear the full Hijab and cover their hair, even if they were from other (religious) groups such as Christians and Sabian Mandaeans. Some militias were loved by some locals because they provided public services like water, gas, food and even transportation; however, when they turned to their radical thoughts and violent actions publicly, they were no longer loved.
>
> (Alobaydi 2022)

In these moments of violent intimidation of women, the country regressed several decades in time. This new form of violence, shrouded in religious and ethnic extremism, forced these women into domestic spaces and limited the public use of urban spaces to men only. The physical manifestations of this type of violence were therefore reflected not only in the cities' segregated neighbourhoods but also in the domestic lives of Iraqis, adding significant mental and psychological pressures onto Iraqi society at large.

> Between 2003 and 2004, there was no sectarian violence, but there were attacks by the US troops and the coalition forces across Baghdad, and you did not know when you would be caught in one. Therefore, mobility was difficult in and around the city, and accordingly, we restricted our movement to only the essentials. So we had to make do with what we had for longer periods of time. The US troops had a curfew in place, where after certain hours in a day, anyone outside would be considered a target. They used to use tall buildings or mosques and have US snipers placed in there. Our house was near a mosque and that mosque had lots of attacks by Al-Qaeda (Sunni militants who later became Daesh/ISIS) members, who were against the Mehdi Army (the Shia militia).
>
> (Hasan 2022)

> After the fall of Baghdad in 2003, carnage and chaos filled the streets, especially around us, because of our close proximity to several ministry buildings, which

were looted. My parents' house was on the main road, so we witnessed all the looting in the area (by the group called Hawasim, which refers to all groups who looted and burned buildings across Iraq). We then saw American Hammers and tanks parading the streets. At the time, no one had a mobile, but lots of people were incredibly inquisitive and wanted to get close and speak with the Americans.

During the sectarian violence years, we witnessed another level of brutal violence, religious and ethnic. We are a well-known Sunni family, even though we live in a mixed neighbourhood with Christians and Sabian Mandaeans, as well as Shia neighbours. Our area was taken over by Shia militia, then known as the Mehdi Army, followers of Muqtada Al-Sadr.

Large blast concrete walls littering Baghdad meant that you could be stuck in traffic or stranded for hours on the wrong side of where you wanted to be. I remember for a few years during the peak of the sectarian violence, T-concrete walls were appearing in the streets on a daily basis, and moved around regularly so you could not even assume that what was a route available you could take today would still be open tomorrow. Kidnappings were on the rise, and I did not want to risk it. From 2006, for two or three years, our neighbourhood changed: women were forced and later just expected to be wearing the black *abaya* when they were out. I used to hate wearing the veil or the black *abaya*, especially in the unforgiving summer months in Iraq. Bearing in mind, this was a neighbourhood that had so many secular liberal Baghdadis living there, and it turned into this place that I could not recognize anymore.

(Al-Azzawi 2022)

During the sectarian violence, the city [Baghdad] changed. There were checkpoints everywhere. The problem was, no one knew who was checking at this or that checkpoint. One time at the checkpoint, they [militia men] asked for our ID. We just had to be honest, because you could not really predict what their religious allegiance would be. It was, as it happens, a Shia checkpoint.

Women walking in the street had to cover their head. I refused to put the veil on. One time, we were driving to my grandmother's house in Harthia (about fifteen minutes' drive from our house) and the main road was closed, so we had to take a detour into a mixed neighbourhood. It was so quiet; we did not understand why it was so quiet. Then a guy who was clearly suffering from mental health problems – he was laughing hysterically – asked us what we were doing here. He then said, 'Just turn around and leave.' Immediately after, in this mixed neighbourhood, people started shooting each other and we were caught in the crossfire. My mother was screaming and praying and my father was driving. I was calm – perhaps it was one of those unhealthy reactions to

> such a tense situation. I then said, 'Let us turn around and drive back', as the way in was shorter than trying to find our way out. That incident was almost like a scene from theatre.
>
> (Shuker 2022)

Shuker's account of the trauma of the violently occupied space is further evidence of the complexity of power that transcends and traverses multiple dimensions beyond Euclidean space and geography. Within the fields of architecture and geography, Eyal Weizman's (2017) *Hollow Land* and Stephen Graham's (2018) *Vertical* each provide convincing arguments for the verticality of deep power and violence. Both of these works develop spatially complex and multidimensional illustrations of power and control that have contributed a great deal to scholarship on violence. Referring to these works, Stuart Elden (2013), reminds readers to think of the dimensions volumetrically rather than two-dimensionally; in other words, to visualize power in a three-dimensional spherical space, associated with the geopolitics of territory, border, aerial bombing and urban violence. Elden (2013: 49) asserts:

> Just as the world does not just exist as a surface, nor should our theorisations of it; security goes up and down; space is volumetric .... Most fundamentally, thinking merely straight up and down may blind us to different angles of approach, and the function of the oblique. Only by thinking through all of these aspects can we reflect more profoundly on the politics, metrics and power of volume.

Speaking of the sectarian violence and then the ISIS occupation of Mosul, two natives of Mosul, Ali Al-Baroodi (a photojournalist and an academic) and Raad Sultan (an architect and a PhD researcher at the University of Plymouth), recall the brutality and the similarity in urban warfare tactics between ISIS and the Israel Defence Forces (IDF). Weizman (2017: 193) refers to IDF's tactics as the 'walking through walls' method of 'vertical apartheid'. Al-Baroodi (2022) explains:

> The sectarian violence of 2006 and 2007 affected Mosul, but not in the same way that it did Baghdad, because Mosul is predominantly Sunni Muslim majority. It was not militia against militia, it was terror against civilians. Some Christians and Shia and Kurd minorities were forced to leave their homes and others felt threatened.
>
> Nobody was exempt. The Sunni identity may protect you, but if you do anything against their will, you will be targeted. If you are accused of being a translator for the coalition or the occupier, you are targeted. If you are seen with a certain dress code, you are targeted. My whole department, the Department of Translation at Mosul University, was targeted in 2004.

In 2014, the situation was more violent, ISIS navigated their ways around the city, moving from house to house through the walls, not the streets. They trespassed every single private home in the old town on the riverside. Houses in the old town of Mosul had basements, which became a frequent component of protection from wars and violence.

From Sultan's (2022) point of view:

After the fall of Baghdad, the American troops entered the city, like all cities in Iraq. At first, they seemed to be roaming the city freely, but after 2004, Iraqi patience for true change was running out and pockets of retaliation against the occupation were starting to emerge. During that period, the American troops considered all people walking in the streets as moving targets. We were caught between explosions, like car bombs and so on, and the Americans firing at us. I was caught in the middle several times, where I would be emerging from a side road into the main street and have American troops fire at my car, suspecting it to be a militant's car. These conditions remained the same all throughout 2004 and 2005, where there was little law and order enforced by the state and where we witnessed a rise in looting, killings and kidnappings for ransoms, from which my family suffered dearly.

As an architectural engineer working in the field at the time, I had to stay at home and avoid work, fearing for my life. At the time of the waves of brain drain and ethnic cleansing in the country between 2006 and 2008, doctors and engineers as well as university professors were targeted, kidnapped for ransoms or slaughtered at their front gates. The streets were not safe, and our homes turned unsafe too. You never knew when someone would leave a bomb in the street and run away, and for that bomb to explode and attract American troops firing at our houses, thinking the bomb came from a militant group squatting in a house in the neighbourhood. There was a lot of chaos, chaos in the streets, in the management of bomb attacks and a mess in every aspect of life.

When ISIS attacked Mosul, they used empty houses and moved horizontally into the depths of the city very quickly, but also utilized the basements that are a feature of the houses on the west side of the city. They forcibly evicted people from their houses in strategic locations and these houses quickly became targets, and missiles would aim directly at them. This air warfare was very precise and accurate. Locals started to predict the minute they suspected ISIS in the street; they would evacuate, otherwise they might get caught in the battle. My sister's house was flattened because it was empty and was seized by ISIS. ISIS took all the main roads, so people fleeing had to use mountainous passages and other treacherous roads like Tikrit Road, the Hamrin Mountains and other desert-like paths.

After all of the violence experienced by Iraqis between 2003 and 2019 came the promise of a peaceful revolution – the Tishreen Movement (October Movement). With its heartfelt slogan, 'We want a homeland' (Mustafa 2022), the Tishreen Movement represented a yearning for spatial and social justice for Iraqis like never before. In Baghdad, Iraqis from all walks of society took to Tahrir Square (*tahrir* means 'liberty' in Arabic), which overlooked the Green Zone and the Iraqi Parliament. The Green Zone is also known as the International Zone of Baghdad which was originally the centre of power during the Saddam regime and became the centre of the US-led occupation in Iraq, while the Red Zone refers to all areas outside the Green Zone in Baghdad that were deemed unsafe and unsecured by the military occupation. This revolution began with secular youth calling for a better life: employment opportunities, public sector funding (especially for infrastructure and the rebuilding of cities), and thriving educational and health systems. It was a call for basic demands, for a decent life for the many, not the few, and it transcended sectarian and religious divides. Ali (2021: 540) confirms that as much as the political, societal changes were mobilized through such protest movements 'against sectarian, conservative, hierarchical and social norms'. Taif Alkhudary (2022: 5) adds that the spatial negotiations between protesters, as well as the site of the square, enabled protesters to plan their strategy well, and respond peacefully to the rage of what she calls the 'war machines' (anti-riot police and snipers using live bullets and military-grade gas canisters). One of the symbols of the Tishreen Movement soon became the tall, fourteen-storey derelict building called the 'Turkish Restaurant', which was occupied, appropriated and inhabited by protesters, who used it as a monitoring station to alert protesters in case of an attack. The square became a place both of refuge and violence. Meanwhile, the Tishreen Movement broke out in other sites around Iraq, mainly in the southern cities including Hillah, where a main bridge and the areas around it were blocked by protesters, some of whom lost their lives, while others developed refuge-making practices. Chapter 4 looks in detail at Tahrir Square during the 2019 revolution, providing a lengthy case study on the creative material and spatial making of a revolution. Below, however, are two of the more pertinent accounts from brave female activists, who shared their spaces of becoming during the revolution. Hasan speaks about her experience in Tahrir Square in Baghdad, and Wadi recalls the events led by female activists in Bahriya Square, Basra. Speaking of the people she calls heroes and heroines of the square, Hasan (2022) states:

> They did not just create a city-like environment, but they created a new life. There were several small-scale revolutions between 2003 and 2019, but nothing like the Tishreen revolution. For the first time, the revolution was not political nor religious, but rather it was for the homeland [*watten* means 'homeland' in Arabic].
>
> Before this revolution, ordinary women avoided sexual harassment and would not be seen wandering around the area. The square, all of a sudden,

> became that progressive space of acceptance, not only for all religions but also for all ages and sexes. Women gained freedom in the square. Even the tuk-tuk drivers, who had an instrumental role in transporting injured protesters to places of safety in the square, had a sense of responsibility (even though they were all teenagers) towards respecting women's equal role in the square.
>
> All forms of expression there became a way to revolt: mothers were cooking to feed the protesters who stayed in the square and wash their clothes; people donated food, money, blankets and tents; and artists drew murals on the walls of buildings and the tunnel leading into the Green Zone. There was a collective sense of responsibility and care for one another and for the square itself. Bearing in mind that this downtown area of the city was always a masculine urban space.

Feminist activism in conservative Iraq was, and still is, seen as taboo. Public spaces are masculine spaces, yet the word 'revolution' in Arabic is linguistically female, and women were determined to make its action female too. This type of activism, investing deeper meaning into the action, was used in the many slogans and chants that defined the revolution (Mustafa 2022).

> It started with the university students joining the revolution in Baghdad by revolting in the main square in Basra. During that time, there were very few scattered feminist voices in Basra, but we witnessed a large number of female students who joined the revolution in the centre of Basra, and we felt that was the moment to make the revolution truly female.
>
> We felt an urge to protest as if we were responding to an internal call for freedom and a better life. This gave us strength and allowed us to fight against the oppression – not only that which is imposed culturally, but also the unfairness imposed by the state. The national intelligence and security forces fought us hard, especially at night when the number of protesters would decline naturally. They also forced people to go back to work and study, and used violence and force with rubber bullets and tear gas cannisters that were aimed at protesters. Protesters would escape to the narrow alleyways, and I remember people used to keep their front doors open to provide protesters with refuge. We felt at the time that we had a mission; people trusted in us to make their voices heard and we had to continue protesting.
>
> (Wadi 2022)

The strategic urban warfare that suppressed the 2019 Tishreen Movement across Iraq followed tactics that are often implemented in cities, involving division and dispersal, and instilling fear into the hearts of peaceful protesters by leaving traces of the authoritarian power machine. The divides mentioned here were sometimes intangible. Rumours instilled fear of certain places and potential dismissal from the workplace, and ordinary people soon learned to avoid locations that became associated with violence, effectively creating an informal system of borders.

Over the years, Iraqis have suffered through the implementation of both hard and soft borders in different contexts. In the 1980s, during the Iraq–Iran War, the border between these countries was effectively sealed from the south to the north. In the 1990s, after the First Gulf War, Iraqi airspace became a no-fly zone. This period ran up until the 2003 US-led invasion of Iraq, which imposed a full closure of borders across all directions and dimensions of the country. Meanwhile, between the 1980s and early 2000s, soft borders of power were surfacing throughout the country, mainly demarcating the Kurdish territories to the north and the Shia stronghold to the south. These soft borders were never fully clear, and they remain contested, exclusionary and in some cases violent to this day. They are called soft not because they are peaceful but because their characteristics change over time, shifting, retreating and grabbing not only space but also behaviours, excluding some while including others. In this way, these soft borders resemble the violent corridors that cut through neighbourhoods in Baghdad and elsewhere. One of the main contested territories defined by such soft borders is the northern part of Iraq, indigenous to historic Assyria in the Nineveh Plains, which is now claimed by the Kurds and their centre in Erbil. Because it crushes indigenous communities of Assyrian and Yazidi heritage, among others, the Iraqi government in Baghdad allowed for such a border to flourish. Over the years, that border has warped, stretched and shifted through its land-grabbing tactics. It has pushed and pulled support from certain militarily weak districts such as Sinjar, Shaikhan and Tel Kaif following their liberation from ISIS. Finally, it has placed pressure on ethnic and religious minorities, forcing them to migrate away from their ancestral lands to protect themselves (Aprim 2022). The two following accounts portray the border in different lights: the first is told by Mohammed-Amin, who is from Sulaimani (demographically the second largest Kurdish-Iraqi city); the second is described by Sameer, an internally displaced Yazidi from Sinjar.

> Kurdistan, before 2003, had two sanctions imposed on it, one by Baghdad and another by the UN .... It felt that there was a clear border separating Kurdistan from the rest of the country. Across that border (which felt like a hard border), I heard from family and friends how people were wheeled in large wheelbarrows or the backs of designated trucks (instead of using the cars from the Kurdistan region, which were not allowed to cross the border for security reasons) to the Iraqi government checkpoints. At the height of the tensions between Saddam's regime and the Kurdish region, on that hard border, I heard that blood was taken for sampling for diseases, checking mainly to harass the travelling people from the Kurdistan Region to other parts of Iraq. All tactics of intimidation and

> discrimination were used. These tactics largely stayed in the Kurdish memory until this day, and therefore there is constant anticipation of fear around using and navigating spaces anywhere outside the Kurdish region.
>
> (Mohammed-Amin 2022)

> Sinjar was affected during the sectarian violence just as much as Baghdad was. In 2006 and 2007, Yazidis were cut off from Nineveh province, so all employees who worked in Mosul could not go to work. A thousand Yazidi students at the University of Mosul were transferred to universities in the Kurdish region and none remain in the Arab-controlled province. At the same time, the Kurds started pushing their control over the region by influencing the mobility of Yazidis in and out of Sinjar towards Kurdistan. People were scared for their lives. We felt that we were on the border of a civil war between the Arabs and the Kurds. Until this day, Yazidi students studying at the University of Mosul live in student hostels in Bashiqa [a town outside Mosul, home to the third largest Yazidi community in Iraq].
>
> (Sameer 2022)

Helen Malko (2019: 218) speaks of the cultural genocide at the hands of ISIS and critiques the use of the unbalanced power term 'disputed territories', used by the Kurds. This has an impact on the devastated communities of the north of Iraq, specifically the Assyrian Christians and Yazidi minorities in the Nineveh Plains, who 'remain internally displaced, struggling to gather back their shattered communities and return to their homes' (Malko 2019: 218). Sharing Malko's concerns are members of these two significantly impacted communities: Dr Rawaa Qasha, Assistant Professor and Director of Scholarships and Cultural Relations at the University of Mosul, a Christian from Alqosh; and Shahab Sameer, a Yazidi from Sinjar:

> Situated to the north of Mosul in the Nineveh Plains, Alqosh is home to Chaldean Catholics in Iraq, and also a base for the Communist Party in the region. The town is officially governed by Nineveh, but in reality it is controlled by the Kurds and the Peshmerga [Kurdish military forces].
>
> The state of Alqosh is desperate now in terms of displacement. A large number of people have left the country for good. Fears are rising for the future existence of Christians in the north of Iraq. The more people leave, the weaker the community becomes, where we become prone to vulnerability and to further forced displacements due to ethnic and religious belongings. Turkey, for example, continues to this day in shelling our villages in the north of Iraq, taking territories and local farmers' orchards.
>
> I fear for our identity getting lost in the politics of the region. I was really concerned to what would happen to our monastery [built in 640 CE] if it falls

into ISIS hands. I fear for my childhood memories and the people we knew and the way of life we have been preserving for centuries. My father is a calligrapher and a sculptor. He writes in Assyrian, and so do my brothers, who are also artists and sculptors. Through my father's work, I feel we are preserving our heritage and keeping our identity alive. This is in addition to practising our religion, among our rituals and cultural habits. Not only architecture such as churches, monasteries, traditional old houses and historic arches, but also material objects from an ancient way of life have been preserved and exist throughout the town, all sited across its hilly and mountainous landscape. It is like an open museum and always has been for tourists in particular. My father has several stone sculptures, from the mountain to the centre of the town. We had an old house in the mountain, which had a cave inside it.

(Qasha 2022)

We always had a strong sense of belonging to the land and our community, but the strongest sense of belonging we ever witnessed was after 2003, when Sinjar was in a development boom financially and infrastructurally. This sense was all lost in 2014 after the Peshmerga [Kurdish military forces] abandoned Sinjar and its people. With each day that passes, I feel whatever sense of hope for a renewed belonging we ever had is vanishing before our eyes. With each day, we feel we are second- and even third-class citizens in this country. We feel it when we go to the Kurdish region, and we also feel it when we go to Nineveh province or elsewhere south of that in Iraq.

Sinjar is still vulnerable. Yes, we got rid of ISIS, but it is now under random shelling by Turkey on a regular basis, due to clashes with the Kurdistan Workers' Party [PKK]. Even though in recent years Yazidis in camps have returned to Sinjar in small numbers, now we are witnessing a reverse return, back to the camps, due to the instability there. Politically, there is no clear central governing for Sinjar, just like the rest of the north of Nineveh province.

(Sameer 2022)

If we are to borrow terminology from Graham (Graham 2004: 13) and Elden (2013: 49), we could say here that, from the perspectives of these interviewees, the complex violence described has deep vertical, spherical and volumetric characteristics; however, from the perspective of those inflicting that same violence, it would seem more of a 'flat' and 'horizontal projection of power'. Yet this flat space of power could not remain effective on a horizontal geopolitical terrain, only shooting at moving and static targets located on a grid map from the air. Hence the need to engage with the urbanized terrain at a smaller, closer scale that shakes and disturbs the power of dominance. This is what Graham (2004: 14) calls the verticality that 'breaks down communications' as it 'leads to an increasing problem in distinguishing civilians from combatants'. In the years between 2003 and 2014, vertical violence drove millions of Iraqis from their homes and into internal urban displacement, in camps on the peripheries of cities and borders, or into external migration. Along the way, these people charted new routes of mobility.

Displacement and mobility inside centres, and into borders

At the height of the sectarian violence, ethnic divides alone reverberated, and continue to do so, across the country, impacting the highest numbers of internally displaced people of all time. As of 2022, the UN International Organization for Migration (IOM) for Iraq estimates a figure of over 6 million internally displaced people (IDPs) across Iraq's eighteen governorates (IOM in Iraq 2022). Lack of rebuilding, as well as shortages of housing, infrastructure and public services are just a few of the reasons behind this serious decline across the destroyed cities and devastated villages of the country. But this issue is not local only to Iraq: the modern history of the wider region brims with flows and mobility that have shaped the landscapes and the geopolitical terrains through its routes of displacement. Dawn Chatty (2010) tackles different displacements (internal and external) across the Middle East, and finds that in Iraq alone, there are several displaced minorities. Assyrians, Armenians, Kurds, Palestinians, Jews, Sabian Mandaeans and Yazidis, amongst others, whose displacement and mobility was not only restricted to the peripheries but also crossed the hard and soft borders of cities and nations. Writing about the sectarian segregation of Baghdad, Muna Damluji (2010) affirms that, prior to February 2006, Baghdad represented an ethnically heterogenous place, with only a few exceptions, for example the Sadr City area. Damluji (2010) continues, stating that during the years of sectarian violence the new dimension of spatiality within the city was driven by sectarian politics:

> Shi'a and Sunni militias both engaged in practices of intimidation, kidnapping, murder, and other forms of violence as a means to drive civilians identified with the opposing sect from their homes. These practices were carried out as an explicit strategy .... Displacements were frequently brutal. Residents might sometimes have to abandon their homes within hours, or even minutes, of receiving direct threats .... Following displacement, many families transitioned into informal shared housing arrangements. Commonly, a host family in a relatively safe area would open its home to as many as two or three displaced families. Intended as a temporary solution to the crisis, this often meant that several families had to share the limited shelter, electricity, food and water meant for a single family.
>
> (Damluji 2010: 78)

Compounded by ethnic, sectarian and religious discrimination and cleansing, cities across Iraq struggled to cope with the large numbers of displaced families. A somewhat less explored feature of displacement within research on Iraq, yet one that featured heavily in the interviews, was the concept of the tactics of mobility – a necessity that underpins all refuge-seeking. Violence forced Iraqis to make choices (if they had any), and those with limited options were of course adversely affected – to this day, many are still stuck in protracted displacement. For the few who had choice and options, there were several possibilities for seeking refuge, as well as opportunities for return. Jotheri (2022) describes this condition of seeking mobility as a way of life that many Iraqis had to endure for years, even before the 2003 invasion of Iraq. He recalls:

> Before 2003 we felt safe, but we did feel the existence of the Ba'ath Party in our lives. We have a house in the city and another one in the countryside, but we always had in mind a third option in case of an attack during the old regime. Therefore, we were always thinking of places of escape. People were always prepared to move from the city to the countryside, and if that failed, then people fled to the marshes or the desert.
>
> We were living in Babylon province, in Qasim, which is a small city, and we have a countryside house with land, which belongs to my grandfather. Within this land, we have marshes across the river. Whenever we felt unsafe, we swam across the river to the marshes. People used to take this journey or similar journeys when the state [referring to the old Ba'athist regime] summoned them for questioning or other reasons, and they wanted to escape persecution. We have the advantage of having options and we feel ready to move whenever necessary. In the marshes, we hide in long grass and small shelters can be built from reeds. We wait for food to be delivered to us by other relatives. The marshes saved a lot of young Iraqi men from the firm grip of the state. People escaping the city fearing military attacks head towards the countryside. This happened in 1991 and it happened again in 2003.
>
> After 2003, I witnessed mobilization on a major scale. Lots of people were on the move; we witnessed different accents, different dresses and clothing, the countryside became very busy. Mainly people came from Qasim, and then a significant proportion came from Hila and Baghdad. A large proportion of these families that fled kept a member of their family guarding their houses in these cities, so they were not only internally displaced, but they were also separated from their loved ones. We also know that other people welded their front doors to stop other people squatting inside or stealing their property. At that time, there was a shortage of fuel, so people knew they could not do multiple journeys to rescue their belongings beyond the essentials, so people had to leave their memories behind.
>
> (Jotheri 2022)

The mobilization to which Jotheri alludes offered early lifelines of refuge that many Iraqis sought over the years of war, sectarian violence and ISIS. These were not one-way mobility routes, nor did they occur only once, but over multiple incidents that forced people to move, return and then move again. The frequency, recurrence and chaotic nature of the moves makes the mobilization of Iraqis over time difficult to map. Mobilization here can be categorized as a form of 'drifting', which unsettles and disrupts any 'locatedness', 'comfortable associations' or 'bonds' between body and place (Cairns 2004: 40). Ratnam and Drozdzewski (2020) recognize this disruption as a concept of 'rupture' that finds true expression in the plurality of these moves, routes and diversions, with ruptures found in the detours and the back-and-forth escape routes involved in the search for refuge. Refuge-seeking was further re-enacted in people's mobility from one neighbourhood to another, which happened during the aerial bombardment in 2003, the sectarian violence and during ISIS attacks. Most of these moves, of course, had an adverse impact on the urban make-up of cities, in the form of unplanned densification and the springing up of what is known as 'informal housing' (known as *ashwaiyat* in colloquial Iraqi Arabic) – problems major cities continue to wrestle. This complexity is described in the context of three different cities (Baghdad, Mosul and Basra) in the interviews with Alobaydi, Sultan, Wadi and Sabah:

> We stayed for a while in our neighbourhood in an area called New Baghdad [Baghdad Al-Jidida, Nwab Al-Thubatt, near the Canal Army], and then we went to Diyala Province to protect our kids, women and elders. We went to Shahraban, which is a rural area with many fruitful orchards, farm animals, houses that are distanced from each other, and small rivers providing Diyala's districts with water through traditional methods. We then wanted to return to Baghdad, but the American army prevented us from doing so, so we stayed there for a while (less than one month). Shahraban was safe and quiet because it was controlled by tribal influences, and people knew each other, mostly belonging to three clans, known as Rabeeia, Tameem and Al Jboor. The tribes had a deal between them to stop the fight and protect the neighbourhoods. Tribal influences stabilized certain regions including Shahraban for months after the fall of the Ba'athists and their regime.
>
> We reached Shahraban by avoiding main roads and highways, because we knew these would certainly be the main routes in for the Americans. When we reached the boundaries of the city of Baghdad, we got help from a guide to take us through orchard farm roads [equivalent to country lanes in the UK]. These routes had no checkpoints or stops by either Ba'athists or Americans. It is pure knowledge of local rural agricultural areas that took us to safety. These routes are nevertheless difficult and dangerous, because you have to cross streams and narrow rivers. This same infrastructure of the city and its physical landscape provided refuge and protection for us.

We took several routes on many occasions, avoiding main roads. We used what we call here in Iraq, 'dirty roads' – routes on the boundaries, across streams and other geographical landscapes – rather than paved main roads. These somewhat zigzagging routes connected the main roads to our neighbourhood that is shaped by original planning principles of Islamic architecture. Routes between housing estates were windy and zigzag-shaped [known as *equod* in colloquial Iraqi Arabic, which means knots due to the multiple intersections between the routes] deliberately for defensive purposes and privacy.

Over the past two decades, areas witnessed a wave of densifications. They became divided into smaller units, or built on their gardens and open yards. We now are thinking of moving out of our neighbourhood, because the original owners of the old houses that we grew up knowing have all left to areas in the centre of the city, and now we have a new group of families coming from other provinces, mainly from suburbs and peripheral areas. Now I am also noticing central Baghdad areas are going through densification. This is of course due to the lack of new infrastructure that matches the explosive population increase, we now see 600-square-metre plots in the city centre, which used to be a single detached house with a large garden, divided into six different plots. These six plots would share all amenities, drainage, water supply, electricity and so on. The sidewalks have disappeared because all of these now have been turned into parking lots.

(Alobaydi 2022)

During that dark period of ISIS' chaos and mess, people wished they lived in derelict-looking houses in order not to attract the attention of looters and gangs. Lots of people left their homes and lived elsewhere to protect themselves. There was a lot of movement and displacement internally, inside the city, but also into Duhok, and others went to Erbil. Two types of social class ended up in two kinds of situations: those from the upper working class, like doctors and engineers and so on, went into rented housing or relatives' houses in Duhok; while those from the working class and the poor, who lost their houses and their jobs, ended up in camps.

Mostly the movement happened from the centre of cities, avoiding bombing and shelling, and headed towards the outskirts of the city. This movement was reversed during the ISIS attacks in 2014, bringing with it a different type of demographic into the centre of the city, from the villages and countryside. The type of displacement meant that farming became scarce, and people who left their villages found other jobs inside the city.

In 2014, Mosul was attacked by ISIS from the west to the east of the city, during which the city witnessed displacement of people that moved in the same direction. We live in the eastern part of the city, I remember my brother came to stay with us, to leave his house empty for relatives who had to leave their homes in the western part of the city. I remember huge waves of people walked towards our part of the city. Lots of families shared their homes with relatives and other relations. We provided others with food, especially those who had to stay in tents in public spaces and parks. Others stayed in deserted buildings, empty houses, schools, local clinics and mosques. To this day, there is a half-built school that was squatted at the time, and the displacees are still living there – they have nowhere to go.

The east side of Mosul, which was seen as the safe part of the city, struggles to this day with lack of housing and public services, as well as regular violations of agricultural land for housing purposes. People are against rebuilding their houses in the west side of the city and, instead, a few have bought houses in Duhok, all due to continued fear and the instability in the country.

(Sultan 2022)

Only two of Basra's city districts are Sunni-dominant areas, Abu Al-Khaseeb and Al-Zubayr. Despite the large dominance of Sunnis in these two areas, they still failed to protect themselves. We did not have violence in our neighbourhood because we lived in a Shia-dominant area. Next door to us was a well-known Sabian Mandaean family who had lived there for years and were part of the community. At the start of the sectarian violence they received death threats and, overnight, they were gone. There are similar stories across the city, especially in the two Sunni-dominated areas like Abu Al-Khaseeb for example, where I know Sunni families who left for Mosul and others who left for Syria.

There was a lot of mobility and movements of people who were displaced from one part of Basra into another, or from other parts of the south of Iraq. For example, our neighbourhood was not as dense as it is now. There were hardly any houses when we first moved here ten years ago or so. Now, there are lots of informal houses [*ashwaiyat*] all over the residential neighbourhood, which is close to the Shu'aiba Road. These informal houses are usually small, single-storey buildings with tin roofs. Iraqis displaced from the south of the country came in irregular waves and built on any piece of land without approval for buildings, nor proper paperwork for land ownership. Basra authorities tried to evict people who built without approvals, but this is not a solution to the problem of displacement – there was no alternative.

There was a large building complex (Muwafaqiya complex) designated for Iraqi Army officers and their families during the Saddam era. These were medium-size flats that were deserted after the fall of Baghdad. These flats were squatted by displacees from other parts of Iraq into Basra. They are still living there now. Mosques and churches were squatted too, but only for a few months, especially during the few weeks of the invasion.

(Wadi 2022)

> Displaced people ended up everywhere in the city. I feel now that the original Basrawis do not exceed twenty per cent of the population of the city. The majority left the country, especially Christians (where we live, which is called the Armenian district was full of Christian Armenians), and the rest left for other cities.
>
> (Sabah 2022)

Despite the diverse spatial possibilities that the concept of 'informality' in housing (Roy 2005) can engender, the term 'informal' continues to carry negative connotations, overlooking the everyday spatial creativity it can facilitate. This negativity is inherently colonial and in the case of Iraq, is also influenced by social class distinctions. Clearly, both social status and religious belonging played significant roles in the mobility of Iraqis, determining their routes and destinations. The different accounts from interviewees highlight this chasm of difference between certain communities. Below, Qasha tells of the story of many Christians who were in the north of Iraq during the ISIS attacks; Ibrahim and Sameer speak of a different, violent story of escape from Sinjar; while Mohammed-Amin reflects on the Kurdish region's response to the exodus of people from across the Nineveh Plain and elsewhere into Kurdish cities.

> During Daesh or ISIS, Alqosh was the only Christian village that was not taken. As you are heading north of Mosul, before you enter Alqosh, there are two main roads: both lead into the main international route between Turkey and Duhok, and then Erbil, heading towards Iran (the Ibrahim Al-Khalil route). This route feeds all trade coming from and heading towards Turkey and Iran through the Iraqi Kurdish region. In 2014, all the families in Alqosh left their homes, leaving one member of each family, usually men, behind to protect their properties, although my mother stayed in our house in order to cook for the remaining men in the family. The majority of families headed towards Duhok or Ankawa [a suburb in Erbil]; both are part of the Kurdish region in Iraq. All of a sudden, my mother and brothers who stayed in Alqosh heard that Daesh [ISIS] are on their way to the town and are advancing. By that time, Daesh was about 2 kilometres away from Alqosh, and a massive exodus towards the north of the Kurdistan region in Iraq began. My brother and sister and their families loaded their cars with several relatives and headed up north. A few young men, mainly those who are communists from Alqosh, decided to bear arms and head towards the mountain to protect the village, and only a handful of men remained in the village itself, a couple of whom were religious figures in the community – the abbot of the monastery and the church priest. This situation continued for about two weeks. This was the first time in history where the church bell did not ring. We are talking here about one of the earliest Christian communities in the history of humanity.

One of my brothers has his in-laws in Ankawa, and my parents, sisters and another brother, with their families and an aunt and an uncle, all ended up in a relative's empty property in Duhok. Our relation has left for Germany and has a flat in the north of Iraq that remained empty. My brothers used to go back and forth to pick up a few things from the house. Other families all went to their relatives' and relations' houses, but those who did not have anyone, they camped in churches, especially in Dohuk. I feel that Iraqi Christians of the north did not witness the worst brunt of displacement like the Yazidis, although several families were relocated abroad with the help of humanitarian organizations (one of which was French). They all belong to our Archdiocese, which is based in Alqosh.

(Qasha 2022)

After walking for three consecutive days, we reached the mountain on the morning of the 3rd of August 2014. We did not know what to do – we even thought of returning. We even received news that ISIS, occupying Sinjar, were not there to kill the locals but to bring down the government. Yet on the same eve, we heard that ISIS committed a massacre in the north of Sinjar, where mass graves still exist to this day. So we abandoned any thoughts of return and we waded deep into the mountain instead towards Syria. We heard that the Iraqi planes were coming towards us to drop food parcels and help rescue and relocate us, but they never materialized. A week later, we reached the border of the Kurdish region. That last leg of the journey we had cars come for our rescue that took us from the Syrian-Iraqi border to the border of the Kurdish region in Iraq. These cars were provided by Syrian Arab tribes, who had organized help for us. We were surprised to see the number of international organizations who were deployed there to help in Kurdistan. Rescued Yazidis were looking for their relatives and we were overwhelmed by the sheer number of people who came to help. That was the moment when I felt, we are safe now. We were not the first to arrive: others who took the route to the border with the Kurdish region instead of going towards Syria arrived before us. People who lived to the south of the mountain had a much more difficult time in their routes of escape than those who lived to the north of the mountain.

When we reached the Kurdish region, there were no camps, and international organizations had poured their efforts into making safe routes and passages to transport Yazidis to safety, but there was no clear organized effort for providing housing. We ended up taking refuge in abandoned structures and buildings such as schools, churches and mosques; others camped in local parks and public spaces. Two months later, camps were provided and people went into these camps and remained there until this day, including me and my family. Eight years on and we still live in the same makeshift camps. Some are made of tents and others are made of metal cabins, but the quality of life remains as basic as it ever has been in these camps.

(Sameer 2022)

The Iraqi forces and YBS [Sinjar Resistance Units, a militia affiliated with the Kurdistan Workers Party (PKK) forces] tried to open the way for people who were living in the mountain. We then came down from the mountain and it was safer for us to go to the Kurdistan region in Iraq through Syria. Then we stayed in Kurdistan in the camps for five years .... Then we returned to Sinjar only last year.

We returned to our village, but not to the same house, as most of the houses were destroyed. But we are living now in our relatives' house, who have migrated to Germany.

(A. Ibrahim 2022)

The Kurds responded to the waves of displacement towards Kurdistan with mixed feelings, especially at the height of the ISIS attacks across Iraq. I was living outside the country at the time, but my mother developed strong friendships with the displaced Iraqis renting in our neighbourhood, from the middle and everywhere, some of whom are still friends to this day. A lot of people felt it was basic human decency to welcome people in your city who have escaped violence and are seeking refuge. But there were other people who were complaining about pressures on resources, on housing, etc.

Basically, there were two types of displaced people who were coming from other parts of the country. The wealthier kind managed to rent, and that was available to them. The poorer kind had no resources and were placed in IDP camps. This was happening around 2014, when the Kurdistan region's economy was terrible at the time, both from the steep oil price drop and the Kurdistan region's budget, cut by the federal government over oil extraction and exporting disputes with the Kurdistan Regional Government. From what I heard, this fuelled resentment, where locals were struggling to buy their basic needs, meanwhile the wealthier displacees had better lives. Yet other locals felt that if it had not been for the wealthy displacees, our economy would have been in a worse place, from a dead local market.

At the heightened times of ISIS, when they were in Sinjar and approaching the Kurdistan region, I heard that many people in Erbil evacuated their homes and city. But the impact of ISIS stayed at the borders and did not reach into the Kurdistan region. In terms of displacement of Iraqis, Sulaimani had much fewer IDPs than both Duhok and Erbil. These cities are both much closer to the border [the hard border with Turkey and the soft Iraqi border for the Kurdistan region, with Mosul and the affected area] and therefore witnessed higher numbers of people fleeing ISIS.

(Mohammed-Amin 2022)

Although it involves being uprooted from the familiar and a state of transition, it is possible to see displacement as an active, yet protractedly nonlinear, form of domesticity and refuge-making. While the concepts, processes and meanings of 'displacement' and 'domesticity' might appear to contradict one another, the act of placing these two terms together provides a way of understanding different forms of spatial practices (Singh et al. 2020). As displacement becomes entangled with causes, roots and routes of mobility, it starts to change the social and spatial make-up of cities, villages and borders, blurring the boundaries between instability, on the one hand, and refuge, on the other. This continuous negotiation between processes that fall between uprootedness and homing practices forms the main threads of the visual maps that accompany each of the interviews presented in the following section.

Creative negotiations of spatiality between trauma and violence

I have already addressed the palimpsestic method of deep mapping in earlier chapters. This method is crucial to understanding how to visualize the negotiated spatiality between memory, imagination and trauma experienced by Iraqis between 2003 and 2023, if we want to avoid falling into the 'mimetic/representational' trap (Rugo 2023). Maps can be considered frames in which traumas are critically and iteratively captured in order to disrupt the ways in which trauma and memory are understood in space and time. Through the affective layering of identity, belonging and memory-work, these maps help to conceptualize the spatial storytelling of the Iraqis who are sharing their lived and felt experiences of war and violence. They capture moments of temporary meaning, however stretched these moments may be, and yet they are able to convey dense descriptions of trauma that are always in the making – memories remembered, relived and retold – highlighting their performativity (Della Dora 2009). I intend for these maps to produce, along the way, deeper insights into Iraqis' experiences of trauma in a way that documents and articulates topological frames of knowledge concerning the historicity, geopolitics and socio-spatiality of trauma.

Sarah De Nardi (2021: 3) uses similar methods of deep mapping in their own research, and describes their process in *Visualising Place, Memory and the Imagined* as 'boundless' and 'open-ended' resembling life experiences and their processes, 'and reflects, multiple affectual linkages, experiential assemblages and imaginaries'. De Nardi (2021: 3) characterizes the maps produced through these cognitive counter-cartographic methods as being materially transient, 'vulnerable', 'objectionable' and 'more-than-textual' visual forms of storytelling that possess 'affectual textures'. The maps produced during the *Rupturing Architecture* project appear to emphasize this point, situated as they are between the cognitive, textual and counter-cartographic elements of map-making, and the thick, contextual, conceptual, material and socio-spatial fragments of events, memories and presence lived and imagined through oral histories and storytelling. This is because they are conceptualized through a processual rather than a representational understanding of mapping (Kitchin, Gleeson and Dodge 2013). Tim Cole (2015: 33) defines 'double distance' as a concept within oral history interviews, which taps into past spatial strategies of retelling difficult stories, whereby 'double' refers to 'both the chronological gap between then and now and the geographical distance between there and here as they tell of events'. Cole (2015: 49) further emphasizes how spaces and places within oral narratives are embodied, at which point oral histories become 'oral (historical) geographies'. He explains the importance of the 'microgeographies within the stories people tell', as follows:

> In oral history interviews, people remake the past not simply as a series of events chronologically placed into – generally speaking – a linear order. They also remake past place (as well as past time), positioning themselves and others closer and further from the action and each other. Where people place (and re-place) themselves and others in the past is … potentially significant and a way to uncover the meanings given to past events.
>
> (Cole 2015: 49)

Borrowing the term from Cole, we can see that this 'double distance' is fundamental to the conceptual understanding of the maps in this section, as we uncover the 'microgeographies' of memories, events and people's lived and imagined spaces. Combining this understanding with the concept of 'rupture' within the detours of mobility (Ratnam and Drozdzewski 2020: 670) – the lifelines of many Iraqis – emphasizes the confluence of different scales of rupture over time, for example in the conceptual and emotional, the material and the geospatial forms of trauma and violence. As for the technical aspects of the maps, these followed the iterative processes of thematic analysis: studying the oral interviews, highlighting a significant moment within an event chosen by the interviewee, and matching it with their shared photographs and objects. Each map, therefore, contains the following: collapsed geographies of mobilities within and between cities, villages or borders; three-dimensional depictions (in the style of a pop-up book) created from the oral interviews of their major traumatic event; a photomontage of the material objects of trauma shared; and quotes from the interviews relating to those events.

These multimodal maps facilitated the creation of the microgeographies of memories and events at three different performative and transdisciplinary scales: the conceptual, the material and the geospatial. The conceptual transcends the lived experience through the imagination, as interviewees retold their memories of their most traumatic events. The material is temporally connected to the conceptual and geospatial. The geospatial reflects the rootedness of memories within spatial locations, while simultaneously traversing different spaces through mobility. Each element of each map has been composed not only to visualize the oral histories under discussion but also to capture moments lost in the chaos of trauma and violence that had never before been documented in this way. Interviewees often expressed the fact that they regretted not having documented more, whether through films or photographs, the traumatic events that were unfolding before their eyes. These counter-maps form part of a cathartic process of capturing visually these stories before they flee from people's memories. What follows are fifteen deep maps, each with a short accompanying description, which serve as vignettes of journeys of rupture across many parts of Iraq. The maps were produced using open-source software whenever possible, such as OpenStreetMap, Snazzymaps.com, OpenAI and Google Earth. These were further designed, manipulated and collaged (physically and digitally) through several iterative processes of development, and the interviewees' stories and photographs were placed within the composition. They further include collages of photographs taken by the interviewees of their memories.

Before the fifteen maps are presented, I include here a geopolitical map of Iraq that traverses time (Figure 3.1). This demonstrates the layers of history that have shaped the land since the making of modern Iraq from the earlier Mesopotamian region. Figure 3.1 also shows the rivers Tigris and Euphrates, as well as the internal divisions within the land, including the soft borders mentioned in earlier sections, which cut through the Nineveh Plains, driving a wedge of contested territories, origins and belongings into the history of the region. Lastly, it shows the locations of all fifteen deep maps shared by the Iraqi interviewees, highlighting the locations of geotrauma and places of mobility across the country.

1. Rawaa Qasha's map

Dr Rawaa Qasha is an Assistant Professor and Director of Scholarships and Cultural Relations at the University of Mosul. As mentioned in the previous sections, she is a Christian from Alqosh, north of Mosul. Qasha's map (Figure 3.2) attempts to preserve the heritage, identity and geography of the Christian village of Alqosh. Her family and ancestors have strong connections to the mountainous landscape, the monastery and the ancient traditions passed through the generations here (Figure 3.3). From thousands of kilometres away in Newcastle, UK, Qasha agonized for weeks over the fate of her family, her village and their history as ISIS were progressing towards Alqosh in 2014.

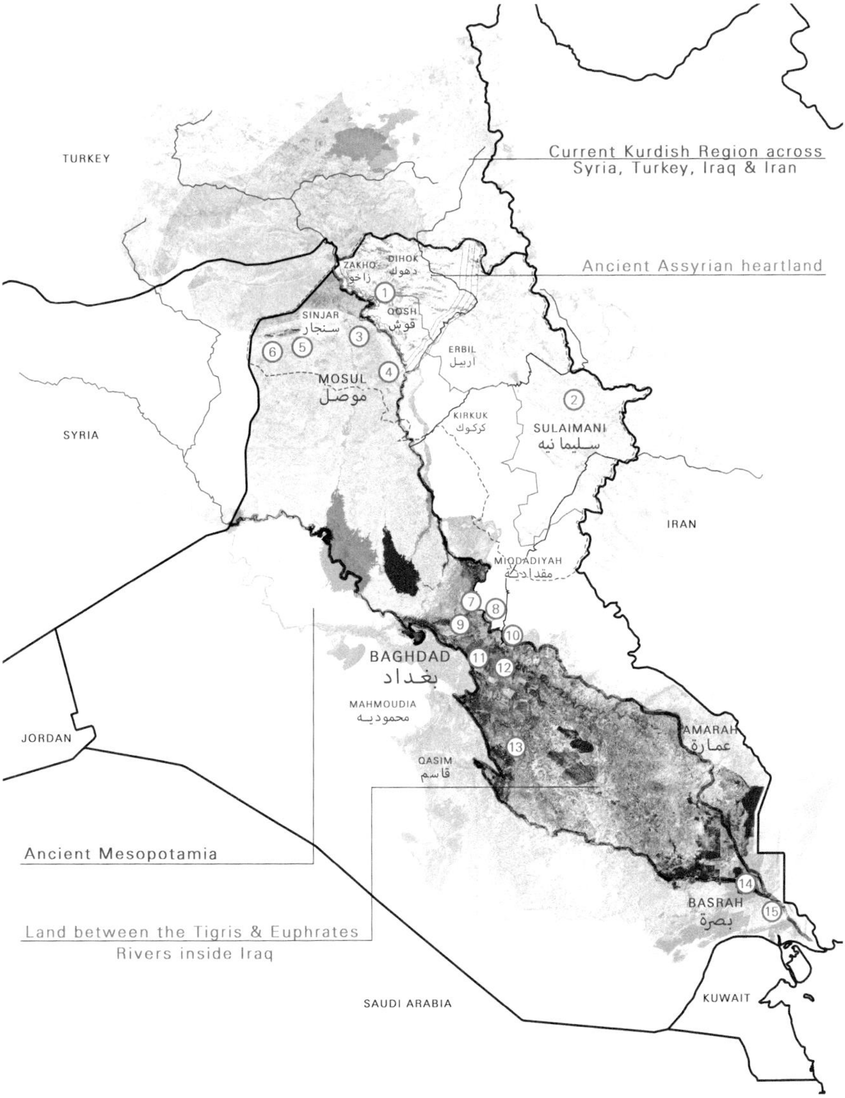

FIGURE 3.1 A geopolitical map of Iraq.
Courtesy Sana Murrani

FIGURE 3.2 Qasha's map.
Courtesy Sana Murrani and Rawaa Qasha

FIGURE 3.3 Qasha's trauma, showing the monastery nestled into the mountain. Courtesy Sana Murrani and Rawaa Qasha

Qasha (2022) recalls:

> At that time, I was in the UK doing my PhD at Newcastle University, watching everything on my phone and weeping. The entire university heard about what was going on. There was a lot of empathy and support around me, but all I was thinking of was my family back home. A few weeks later, the Peshmerga [Kurdish military forces] returned to their positions. People started returning to their homes in Alqosh and, within two months, the entire village returned to their homes, despite the fact that, 15 kilometres away, Telskuf [another Chaldean village north of Mosul] was already occupied by ISIS. I returned home from the UK in spring 2015 (eight months after these events occurred).
>
> After making sure my family were safe, the first thing I checked when I returned home was my grandfather's sculpting and calligraphy tools [which were found safe], because they were left behind in the house when my parents left for Duhok during the events. These are heirlooms that I would have felt incredibly upset about if we had lost. They remind me of our roots in this place and also our heritage, as my grandfather's books have reached as far as India and Europe.

2. Rozhen Kamal Mohammed-Amin's map

A Kurd from Sulaimani, Dr Rozhen Kamal Mohammed-Amin is the Director of the Digital Cultural Heritage Research Centre (DCH) and Lecturer at the City Planning Engineering Department, Sulaimani Polytechnic University (SPU). As she was telling her story, Mohammed-Amin pictured an image that collided

FIGURE 3.4 Mohammed-Amin's map.
Courtesy Sana Murrani and Rozhen Kamal Mohammed-Amin

FIGURE 3.5 Mohammed-Amin's trauma, showing the eeriness of the homemade chemical masks made from coal wrapped in cotton fabric.
Courtesy Sana Murrani and Rozhen Kamal Mohammed-Amin

with a distant memory of the Kurdish uprising in 1991, where bullets hit her mother's bedroom door in Sulaimani (Figure 3.4). This was the same room that the family took refuge in at the start of the 2003 invasion of Iraq. What is evident in Mohammed-Amin's map is the fact that her trauma traverses time more than it does spatiality (Figure 3.5).

Mohammed-Amin (2022) remembers:

> I feel that we already had our fair share of civil war in Kurdistan, between the PDK [Kurdistan Democratic Party, also known as KDP] and PUK [Patriotic Union of Kurdistan] in 1996, leading to 2003. Even though the two parties reconciled, you are still able to distinguish between the PDK Green Zone and PUK Yellow Zone. Still, the Kurdistan region has been and is still enjoying relatively much higher stability and order. I think that has to do with having fewer variables in comparison to the more complex equation in the rest of Iraq. Yet all of this did not shield us from the fear of the unknown, especially after the fall of Baghdad in 2003.
>
> Images and memories in my head that will never be forgotten – of my mother's bedroom, the television, the homemade masks (made from coal wrapped in cotton cloth, in case of a chemical attack by Saddam's regime) – bring back floods of memories of violence of the Halabja massacre in 1988. Seven of us [six sisters and their mother] spent a long, stressful time in that

room. In this heightened sense of distress, there was a sense of intimacy. We were all huddled together.

I am looking at the bullets on the door [now repaired] of my mother's room in the house we evacuated in April 1991, and my memory takes me to the many items stolen from our house, and a bloody army jacket that was left in our living room by an intruder. The worst thing I and my family discovered when we returned to our evacuated and intruded house was that many of the clothes of my deceased father [who died on duty a month earlier during the 1991 uprising], that we were keeping in his memory, were stolen too.

Despite the trauma caused by the Iraqi Army soldiers, I have a strong image and pleasing memory of how, when the second Kurdish uprising happened later in 1991 [which was then protected by the UN Security Council's no-fly zone], my mother helped a fleeing wounded Iraqi soldier passing by our neighbourhood with a first aid kit, food and water, despite strong objections and condemnation by many of our neighbours.

3. Ali Al-Baroodi's map

Ali Al-Baroodi, from Mosul, is a photojournalist and expert on Mosul, as well as a translator and an academic at the Department of Translation, Mosul University. His map (Figure 3.6) is a homage to home, a home lost and refound after it had endured multiple traumas, materially and conceptually, during the Battle for Mosul in 2014. The map shows the moment shrapnel entered the window of Al-Baroodi's room (Figure 3.7), marking the beginning of multiple traumas over the months of ISIS attacks.

Al-Baroodi (2022) recalls:

On the day of the bombing, the first house we moved into was my aunt's house. It was in the same neighbourhood and not that far from my house, but we had that trauma of the day of the bombing. We had to leave. There was a very small room, which was only 3 by 3 metres, and we were sixteen people living in that room for five to six days. We were all together, we lost our privacy, we slept on the floor on mattresses. There was only one narrow bed, which we left for my injured brother, and we used the couch for my old father. When you sleep in a certain position, you can never move, and when you wake up, your hands and legs are numb. We spent five days like this.

Then, when we were evacuated, we were received by my cousin [in a different neighbourhood] and we stayed in his house for forty-five days. This time, we chose a small room, a specific place that is in the middle of the house [like a sitting room] that had no windows out to the streets. Still, when there was bombing, some of the windows across the rest of the house shattered. Our survival code was to stay in the middle of the house and on the ground floor only.

FIGURE 3.6 Al-Baroodi's map.
Courtesy Sana Murrani and Ali Al-Baroodi

FIGURE 3.7 Al-Baroodi's trauma, showing a broken window, a disturbed bed and scorched walls.
Courtesy Sana Murrani and Ali Al-Baroodi

Then, in January 2017, Mosul was liberated from ISIS. My mother wanted to go back to our house straight away, but I said we needed to wait for three more days or so, because even though Mosul was liberated, we needed the Iraqi Army to secure the areas that had become safe.

Four days later, I went back to check the house. I had to cross over the rubble of the bridge that was hit over the Khosr River. I came to the house and I could not recognize it. It was not hit directly, but ISIS had occupied it, and in our culture it is a taboo to enter people's houses without permission. All the windows of the house were broken. All the doors were shattered. I could not see a single thing that had not been messed with. The house needed work. I went back to my mother and said, 'You will have to stay where you are, and I will go back to the house and fix it. I will make it liveable.' It was the only time when I stayed in the house on my own for two months.

Mosul was liberated, but rockets and mortars were still hitting parts of the neighbourhoods. I changed where I spent the time inside the house from my bedroom, beside the window that was hit, to another, safer room. I fixed the house with the help of tradesmen to make the house liveable again. The family returned to it, and it was once again a lively place.

After the liberation of Mosul, emotionally we felt safe, because we kept saying to ourselves, 'ISIS is gone.' But we cannot forget about ISIS atrocities, who knows what ISIS had left behind? Their legacy has continued to occupy our minds for years. We still have neighbourhoods destroyed and you never know what is beneath the rubble. There are bombs probably covered with rubble that have not exploded.

Wars are easy to stop and people think that they end at a certain cost, but urban wars in particular will live with us for generations to come.

4. Raad Sultan's map

Raad Sultan, originally from Mosul, is an architect, a faculty member of the School of Architecture at Mosul University, and a PhD researcher at the University of Plymouth, UK. His experience highlights the fact that, the more responsibilities people had, the more varied were the scales of violence they had to endure. Sultan's map (Figure 3.8) illustrates routes across several parts of the north of Iraq, both to and from Mosul during the ISIS offences. These crossed neighbourhoods as well as different natural terrains and landscapes, encountering soft and hard borders at the edges of cities, and culminating in the destruction of the main bridge that connected Mosul from east to west (Figure 3.9).

Sultan (2022) recalls:

> I left Mosul twice: once at the beginning of the ISIS offences in 2014, but I could not make it; and then again two months later, knowing the dangers around me were closing in. I took the road towards Hawija – I had to walk some of the way when I could not use a car – I then crossed the bridge [the main bridge in Mosul over the Khosr River] and, by the time I got in a taxi, the bridge had been hit with a missile. I then reached my in-laws in Kirkuk, then moved into a one-room and then a house, and remained there for three years. Throughout my entire stay in Kirkuk, I witnessed so many painful stories from Iraqi students who had been displaced several times during their education. On my way back, I spent hours in the desert. In the first year, I was myself a master's student. I had to defend my viva voce in person in Duhok, where most academics from the University of Mosul had fled to. I had to go through so many checkpoints to cross from Kirkuk through Erbil, and then into Duhok. Then I returned to Kirkuk and took up a management role as part of the university's mobile site.
>
> As an architect, the material association that I have with the darkest times is the moment when the Hadba' Minaret [meaning 'hunchback' minaret] was destroyed by ISIS. I felt the city's identity was lost then. I feel that most Mosulis felt that they had lost the most precious icon that represents Mosul.
>
> I found a sense of refuge in helping students across the years of violence through their university years. I worked so hard, seven days a week over three

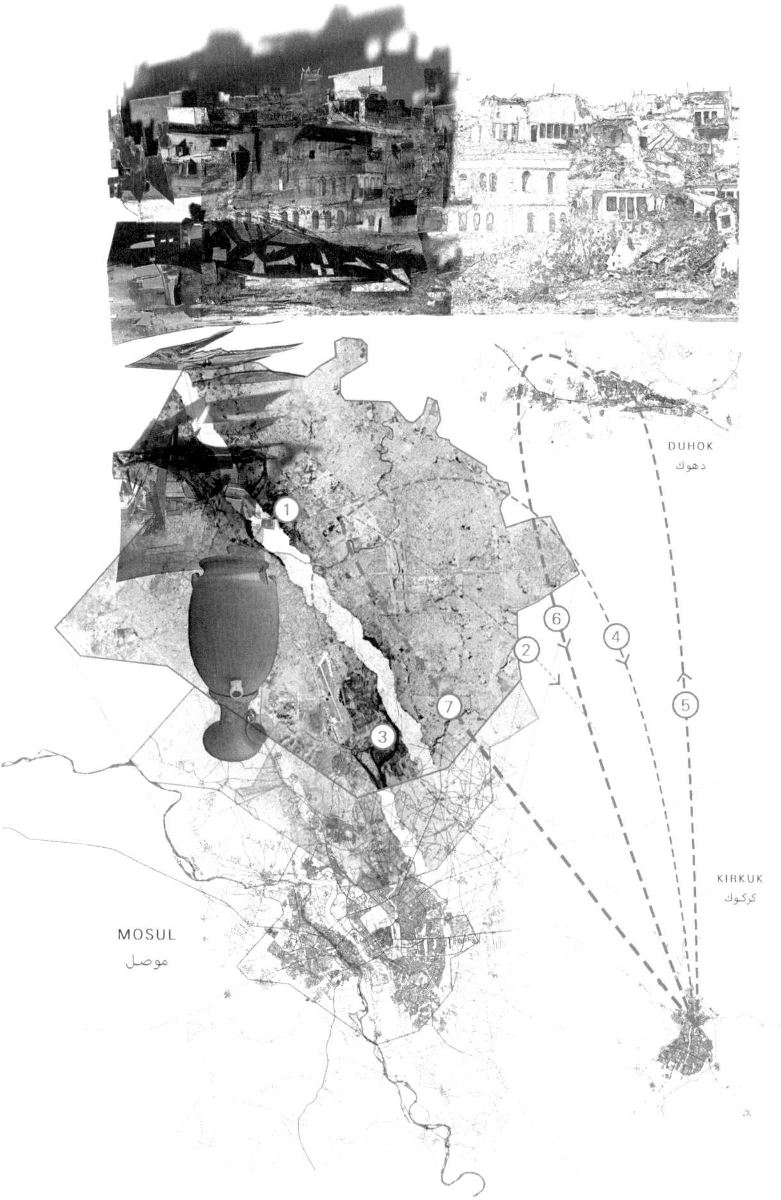

FIGURE 3.8 Sultan's map.
Courtesy Sana Murrani and Raad Sultan

FIGURE 3.9 Sultan's trauma, showing the broken bridge over the Khosr River, which connects eastern and western Mosul.
Courtesy Sana Murrani and Raad Sultan

> shifts a day, to help as many of them as I could. It was a way for me to keep busy and escape the trauma.

5. Amera Ibrahim's map

Amera Ibrahim is a biologist who, at the time of interview, was working as an associate for Sinjar Academy (a charity supporting the education of Yazidis in Iraq). Born shortly before 2003 in the north of Sinjar, Ibrahim's encounter with violence and trauma was at the hands of ISIS in 2014. Her map (Figure 3.10) charts multiple journeys of displacement between camps in the north of Iraq, moving from tents to cabins, until she returned, against all odds, to Sinjar (Figure 3.11).

Ibrahim (2022) recalls:

> There was no time to discuss anything. There was chaos. We went along with another five families, who were relatives, who together decided to get out of Sinjar and head towards the mountain. Adults were in charge as they knew the shortcuts and routes through the mountain that would be difficult for ISIS to trace, and we, the children, just followed.
>
> When we arrived at the camp, Bersivi, in Zakho, we were only given tents. After a while, international organizations tried to help us with some equipment (cooking, cleaning, etc.). After that, people started improvising and improving their tents, so, for example, we created gardens to grow trees between tents. We had more tent material and made extra spaces or partitions inside. After two years, we moved to Rwanga camp and lived there for three years, as it was safer than others. The gardens were the only places that resembled life back in Sinjar before ISIS.

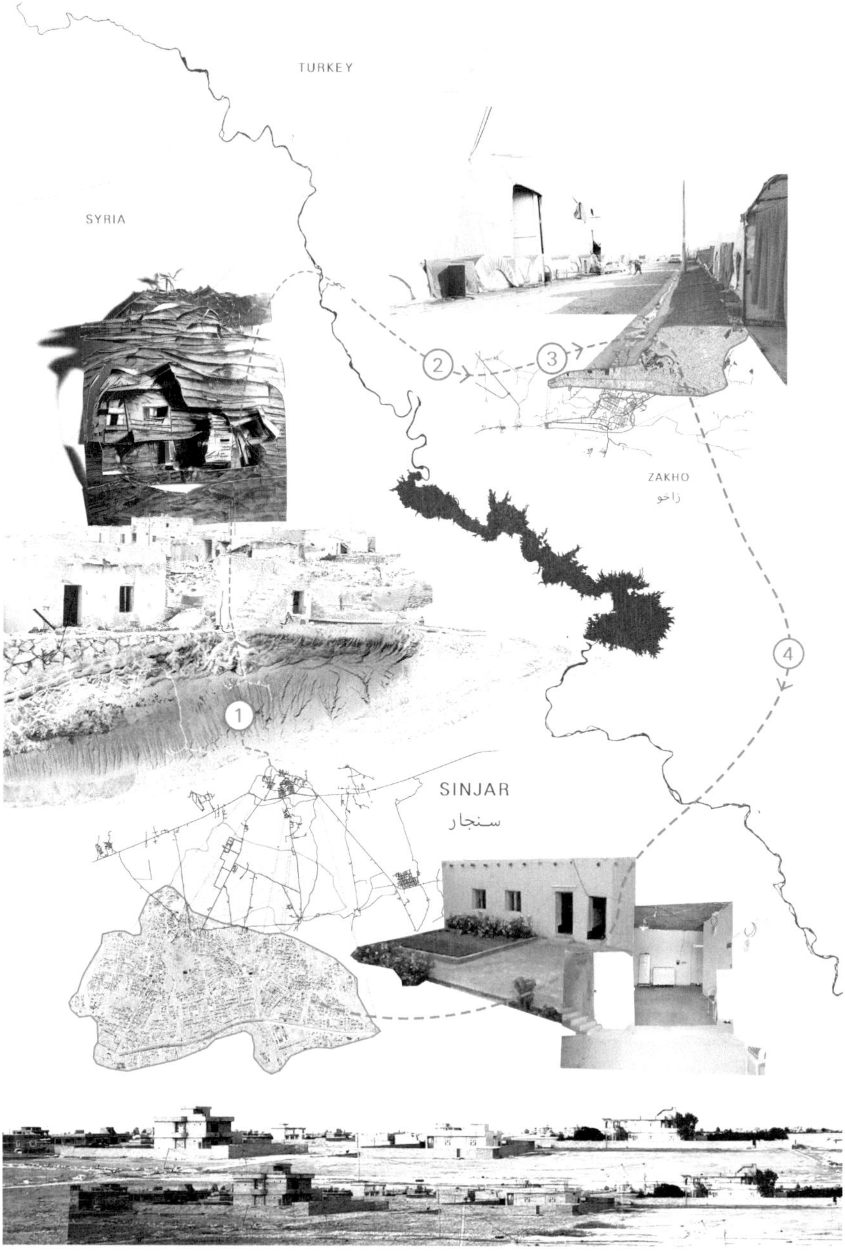

FIGURE 3.10 Ibrahim's map.
Courtesy Sana Murrani and Amera Ibrahim

FIGURE 3.11 Ibrahim's trauma, showing a home collapsing under layers of rubble. Courtesy Sana Murrani and Amera Ibrahim

We completed school inside the camp and, after that, we went to the university. Then we were able to go out and come back to the camp. It was very difficult at the beginning, but after a while we adapted to the new life in the camp. People who lived outside the camp in the Kurdistan region also adapted with time.

The government needs to help rebuild Sinjar, even if this means building a small house for each family. Camps are not safe places for living. Fires have burned so many tents and we lost so many people to accidents like these. That is why we decided to leave the camps and return to Sinjar.

6. Shahab Sameer's map

Originally from the south of Sinjar, Shahab Sameer is a writer and member of the Union for the Literaries and Writers in Iraq. His map represents the trauma of thousands of Yazidis from Sinjar who were brutally uprooted from their village by ISIS attacks in 2014. In Sameer's map (Figure 3.12), through the material objects of Yazidi traditional clothing, the concept of identity becomes anchored to the trauma of the mountainous landscape that saved many people who fled the village. The map charts the journey of Sameer and his family from the south of Sinjar to a safe place that was only ever supposed to be temporary – the camps in the Kurdistani area of Iraq. Eight years on, however, Sameer and his family and thousands of others are still internally displaced, with only a few managing to return to Sinjar (Figure 3.13).

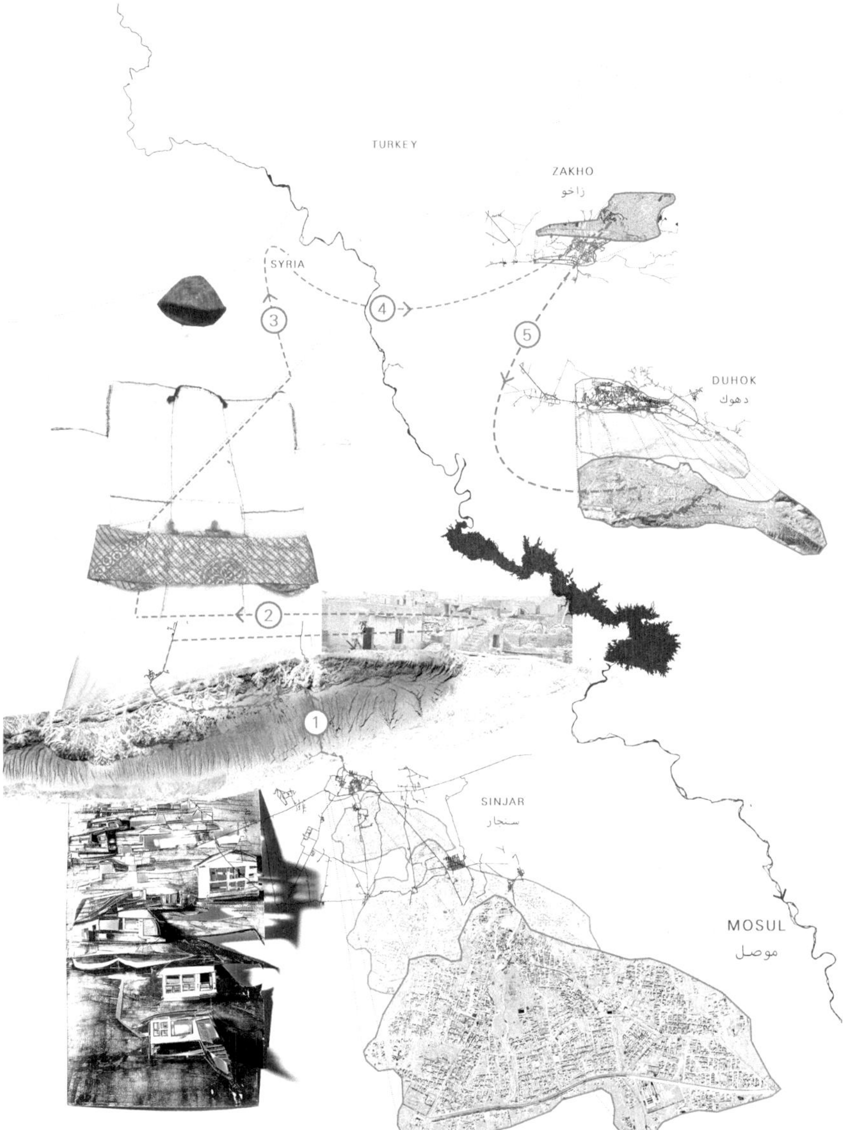

FIGURE 3.12 Sameer's map.
Courtesy Sana Murrani and Shahab Sameer

FIGURE 3.13 Sameer's trauma, showing the destruction of mud houses in Sinjar. Courtesy Sana Murrani and Shahab Sameer

Sameer (2022) recalls:

> I was only thinking of saving my family. We had no cars, I had to look after my heavily pregnant wife and small daughter and my brother had his daughter too. We joined the rest of the family when we reached the mountain, then we headed to Syria and back into Iraq, through the Kurdish region. Two days after we arrived in the Kurdistani region in Iraq, my wife gave birth. We rescued our traditional costume clothing, which is distinctive to Yazidis. We each have one – it strengthens our identity.
>
> Now, we have a metal cabin in Camp Sheikhan that belongs to Mosul, which is officially part of Nineveh province, but the camp is controlled by the Kurdish authorities. Over the years, we developed our cabin a little and brought in a few pieces of furniture. We can freely leave the camp to go to work or university, but our longing for a return to Sinjar remains as strong as our love of Lalish Temple.

7. Basma Al-Azzawi's map

Basma Al-Azzawi is a ceramicist from the highly dense, mixed neighbourhood of Adhamiyah in Baghdad. Both her marriage and her social life were affected by the violence on the streets of Baghdad, forcing her to leave the country with her young daughter via risky and treacherous routes. Al-Azzawi and her daughter are now living and seeking asylum in the UK. Her map (Figure 3.14) records their multiple attempts to escape violence, both domestic and urban, as they crossed

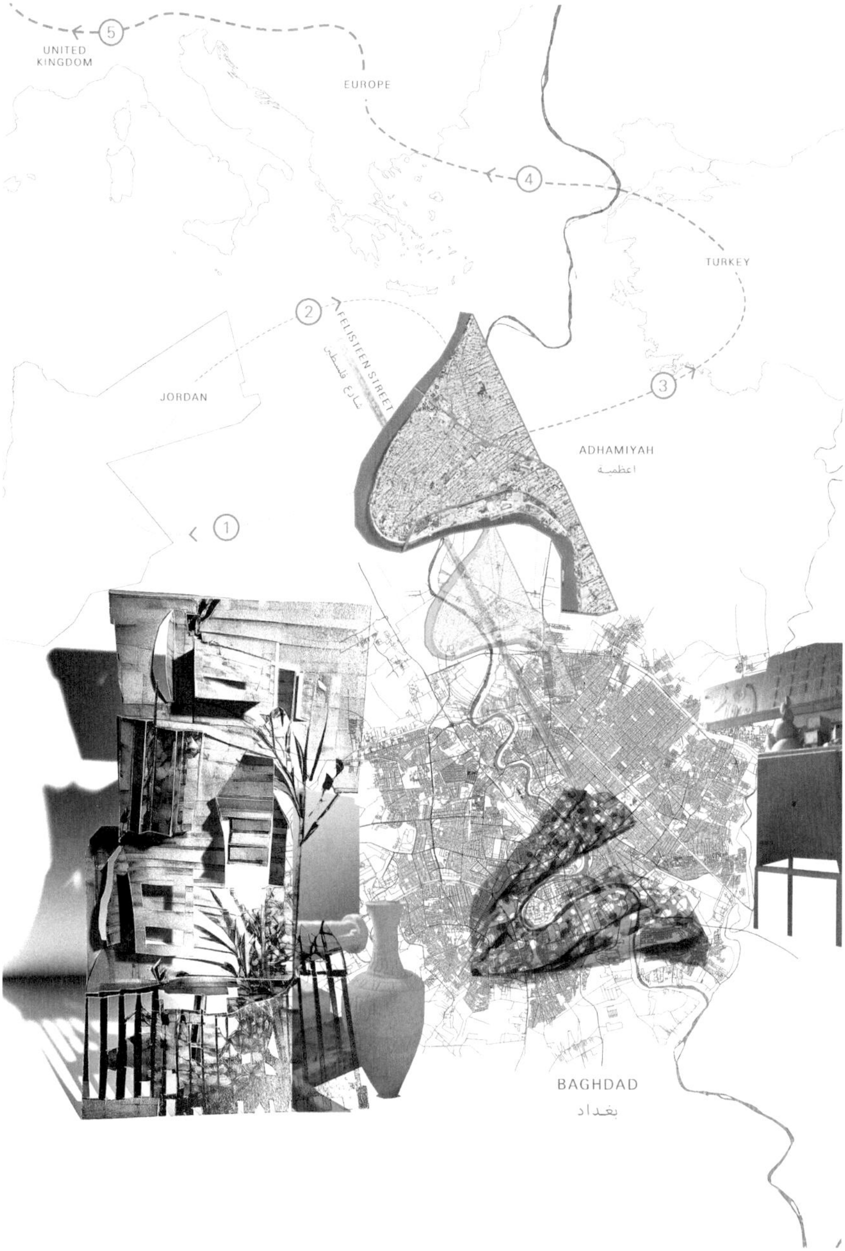

FIGURE 3.14 Al-Azzawi's map.
Courtesy Sana Murrani and Basma Al-Azzawi

FIGURE 3.15 Al-Azzawi's trauma, showing the stairs to the third-floor apartment that provided refuge for Al-Azzawi and her daughter.
Courtesy Sana Murrani and Basma Al-Azzawi

national and international, soft and hard borders, leaving behind her last place of refuge (her apartment in Baghdad) and a career in pottery and a social life that she still misses hugely (Figure 3.15).

Al-Azzawi (2022) explains:

> The trigger was when my daughter reached fifteen years of age and her father wanted to have her marry. He used to come around the house and assault me, trying to force me to hand her over, but my neighbours and friends protected me. That was the moment that I thought, 'Neither she nor I are safe here anymore.' I had to escape. In 2018, I managed to obtain a passport for her, and I had mine, and in a day and night, I decided to leave for Amman, Jordan, where my parents are. In Amman, I applied and was rejected three times for a British visa. I could not stay in Amman, so I went back to Baghdad, sold all the contents of my third-floor apartment in Felisteen Street in central Baghdad, and packed a backpack and decided to take the difficult route into Europe through Turkey.
>
> I find refuge in the scarf that I wore when I escaped through Turkey, but I hate the black *abaya* that women were forced to wear during the years of sectarian violence, and the taped windows on houses. The minute I see these two anywhere, even here [in the UK], bad memories flood back.

8. Zeinab Shuker's map

Dr Zeinab Shuker is an Assistant Professor of Sociology of Political Economy and Climate Change in Iraq and the MENA region at Sam Houston State University,

Texas. Originally from Baghdad, Shuker recalls the sense of refuge and homing she felt when returning to Baghdad fifteen years after her encounter with a militant in the street. Her map (Figure 3.16) oscillates between senses of refuge and trauma as her life was constantly threatened by violence as a result of her father's activism. He was a well-known radiologist in one of Baghdad's main hospitals, Yarmouk, and, as an active member of the Communist Party, refused to join the Ba'ath Party. Over the years, her father's work took the family across Iraq, from south to north, and as they experienced violence at the hands of different groups with different allegiances during this time, Shuker took refuge in writing and her father's library. Before having to flee the country at the height of sectarian violence, Shuker faced what seemed to her to be an Afghan (Sunni) militant running through their Shia neighbourhood in Baghdad, holding a machine gun. He saw her peeking through the gate, but nevertheless chose to spare her the bullet (Figure 3.17).

Shuker (2022) recalls:

> Pre-2003 era, social connections either kept people alive or handed them over to authorities, so it was a matter of pure luck if you happened to be surrounded by people who saw value in you, who respected your work and supported you. I see the 2003 war, which I feel very conflicted about, as the moment we felt freed from this constant unsettling feeling of lack of refuge. I had no sense of home. I felt that I was betrayed by my home. It was not until recently, through my scholarship, that I felt a sense of connection with home. I was terrified to come back because I was afraid that I was building that feeling over unrealistic nostalgia. I was petrified of what I would see to be the truth. You try to hold on to a sense of home or a sense of belonging or refuge, or identity, but it never existed here. This is a place that never accepted me, or accepted us as a family for who we are. I feel it is a laborious process to try to build a refuge now, after all those years, and to sort of reconnect with a place that I never belonged to in the first place.
>
> I resented the entire Arab world, not just Baghdad, for fifteen years. Years during which I hated speaking Arabic, saying my name, and explaining where I am from. I just hated the constant strangeness of me in a place where you are constantly reminded that you are not a member of that community or that locality. And I blamed Baghdad and Iraq, I blamed the Middle East for it. I felt angry that I was let down, I felt that my country should have been better, instead of letting me down. It should have been better so that I could return when I wanted to. But it is not better. Yet the chaos of the city and the stray cats and dogs and garbage everywhere did not feel strange. Iraq's political economic disaster still felt familiar. Yet I now feel angry for Baghdad, for the hurt and abuse she has endured, instead of angry with her or because of her. Now, through my research, I am reconnecting back to the city, knowing that professionally it is difficult to change its structural issues, yet I cannot help

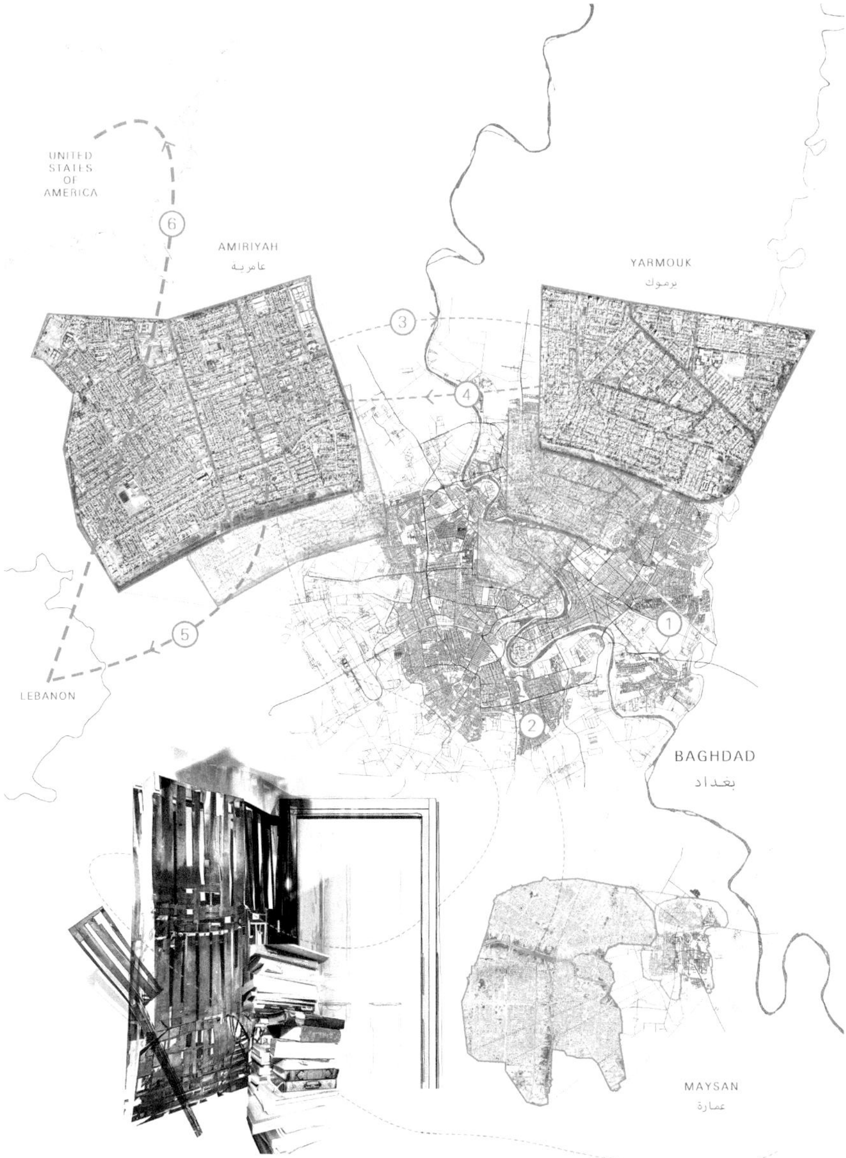

FIGURE 3.16 Shuker's map.
Courtesy Sana Murrani and Zeinab Shuker

FIGURE 3.17 Shuker's trauma, showing the iron door that saved her when she came face to face with an armed militant during the years of sectarian violence.
Courtesy Sana Murrani and Zeinab Shuker

> myself having this sense of hope that I can help her [Baghdad] overcome this disaster that is unfolding. After years of anger and rage, I am back to talk to her again. I am no longer mad at her anymore. I can now separate her from the Saddam regime, from the horrors of checkpoints, from the car bombs.

9. Farah Murrani and Sana Murrani's map

This piece is a joint autoethnographic map of the seemingly fleeting, yet deeply traumatic few months that followed the night Baghdad was struck in March 2003. Farah and I lived in Baghdad within 2 kilometres of each other, and our friendship was strengthened by a shared fear of violence, as well as through our family ties. We were both recent university graduates: I had just completed my master's degree a week before the invasion of Iraq, and Dr Farah Murrani had recently graduated from Baghdad University Veterinary School. Our map (Figure 3.18) traverses material and spatial refuge-seeking quests, from the makeshift corner in my house, near the built-in cupboard in the living room, to Farah's dining room table, which was large enough for my family of four to nest underneath it (Figure 3.19). An item as mundane as an old blanket now holds such significant and varied memories: of childhood, of warmth, of stopping shattered glass from hitting our bodies and of hiding money in its seams as I fled the country a few months later. After my departure, Farah was able to make a major contribution to her field, veterinary medicine, by finding refuge for all the animals in Baghdad Zoo just before leaving Iraq herself. Neither of us has since returned.

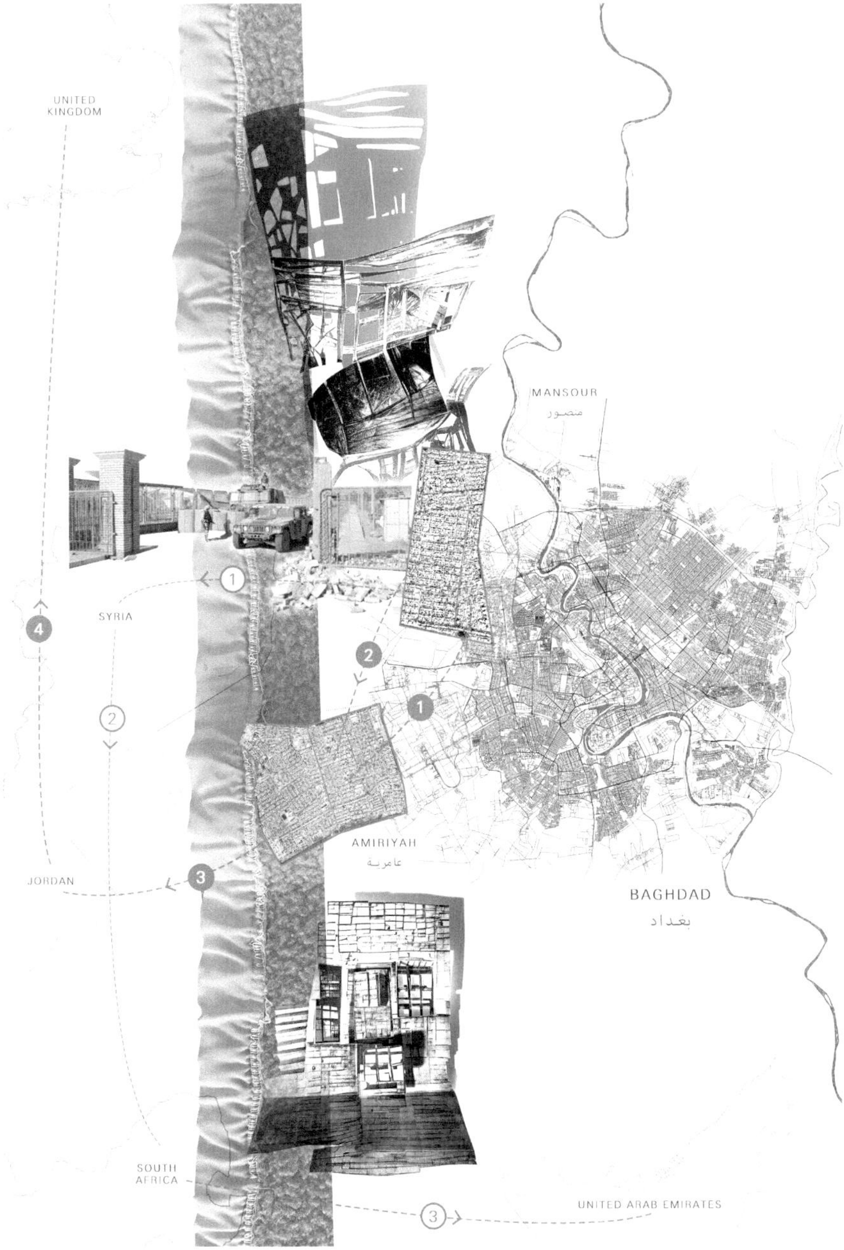

FIGURE 3.18 Farah Murrani and Sana Murrani's map.
Courtesy Sana Murrani and Farah Murrani

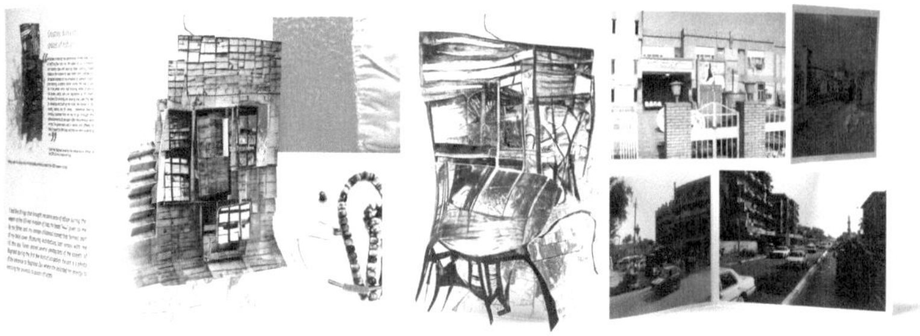

FIGURE 3.19 Farah Murrani and Sana Murrani's trauma, showing the process of making a hiding place under the dining table and barricading windows ahead of the 2003 invasion of Iraq.
Courtesy Sana Murrani and Farah Murrani

Farah Murrani (2022) comments:

> Years later, when I saw on television what was happening on the streets of Baghdad when the sectarian violence kicked in, my heart broke, because I knew that, once upon a time, none of this mattered to Iraqis. It was that same neighbourhood that stuck together: Sunni, Shia, Christians and so on.
>
> I do not associate home with Baghdad. It is a place that I love but it is not home anymore. I do not have anything that ties me to it anymore. The people have changed, the way of life has changed. I do not recognize it anymore. I do not know it.
>
> South Africa became home just by default – that was my first place of refuge after leaving Baghdad that I felt a sense of home in.

10. Ula Merie's map

Dr Ula Merie is a Lecturer in Architecture in the Faculty of Engineering, Department of Architecture, at the University of Babylon, and is originally from Baghdad. The sectarian violence in Baghdad between the years of 2006 and 2008 tore part of Merie's house to pieces (Figure 3.20), displacing her and her family at multiple times into different neighbourhoods, over the river Tigris, and across national and international borders. Her spaces of refuge included the comfort of her parents' bedroom (Figure 3.21), other homes in her area (Dora), a rented property on the other side of the city and even water tanks on the rooftops of houses. These were used during specific threats and attacks against women during the sectarian violence.

FIGURE 3.20 Merie's map.
Courtesy Sana Murrani and Ula Merie

FIGURE 3.21 Merie's trauma, showing the destruction of part of a home. Courtesy Sana Murrani and Ula Merie

Merie (2022) recalls:

After that missile destroyed part of our house, we had to leave. At that time, the Sunni areas were being attacked by different groups. We ended up in a rented house in Felisteen Street, with my uncle who, at the time, had received death threats for being an academic professor in the university. This is where I finished my last year, studying at the University of Baghdad, Department of Architecture. The journey to the university was always traumatizing – you'd see so many young bodies and corpses on the streets.

On top of that was the mess that mixed families endured. I am from a mixed family. I do not consider myself a Shia or Sunni. I hate this division. I consider myself a Muslim. My father is from a Shia family and my mother is Sunni. Most Baghdadi communities are mixed too, for example, Felisteen Street that we stayed in was a mixed area. Concrete walls were everywhere around neighbourhoods littered with checkpoints. Inside our house we have water tanks on the flat roof of the house, which is where we thought we – women – could hide to protect ourselves from the rumours that were going on of specifically kidnapping women and girls. The day I finished my last exam, I travelled to Syria, where my father came from Amman to pick me up to join the family in Jordan.

Before I fled to Syria, I went back once to the house in Dora to pick up a few things. I found it looted – some rugs and clothes were missing – and I found

> a message left for us written in Arabic saying: 'Sorry we had to take stuff from your house, we will bring them back.' But that was the last time I set foot in that house.

11. Dhirgham Alobaydi's map

Dr Dhirgham Alobaydi, from Baghdad, is the Chair of the Department of Architecture Engineering, College of Engineering, at the University of Baghdad. Alobaydi's map (Figure 3.22) follows several lines of mobility as he and his family sought refuge through connections with work and family. Their journeys took them across both national and international borders, though back alleys and other difficult routes between city and countryside. Alobaydi is originally from New Baghdad, a highly dense, urban area of Baghdad, east of the river Tigris, situated near the Army Canal highway that divides several similar neighbourhoods such as Sadr City (Figure 3.23). As well as seeking refuge across distances, Alobaydi found more immediate refuge in certain material objects, which in turn, sometimes represented the face of violence.

Alobaydi (2022) states:

> In 2003 we boarded up all the windows with sheets of wood and we kept only one door. This was a risky move, because if a house gets bombed or if an accident happens inside, then there is only one way out. But we had to do what we did to protect all entrances into our property. We stayed in our home in a Shia-majority neighbourhood, and everyone knew one another. That is how we lived together under the rule of Ba'athists for over eighteen years.
>
> During the years of sectarian violence in 2006 and 2007, I faced problems moving across the city between my home and workplace because of my surname, which is predominantly a Sunni surname, but there are a few Shia with that name too. My parents worried about me and so I had to leave the area or leave Iraq altogether. At that time, I was fortunate to have a one-year contract to work in Muscat, Oman, so I left.
>
> To this day, wooden boards remind me of both war and refuge. They were heavily used during the war to protect us. The other object is the prayer rug [known as *sijade* in Arabic], as well as the holy book of Koran, both of which are objects of refuge for me wherever I go.

12. Sanar Hasan's map

Sanar Hasan is an award-winning journalist and feminist. She grew up in the highly conservative and traditional Mahmudiyah area, south of Baghdad, where

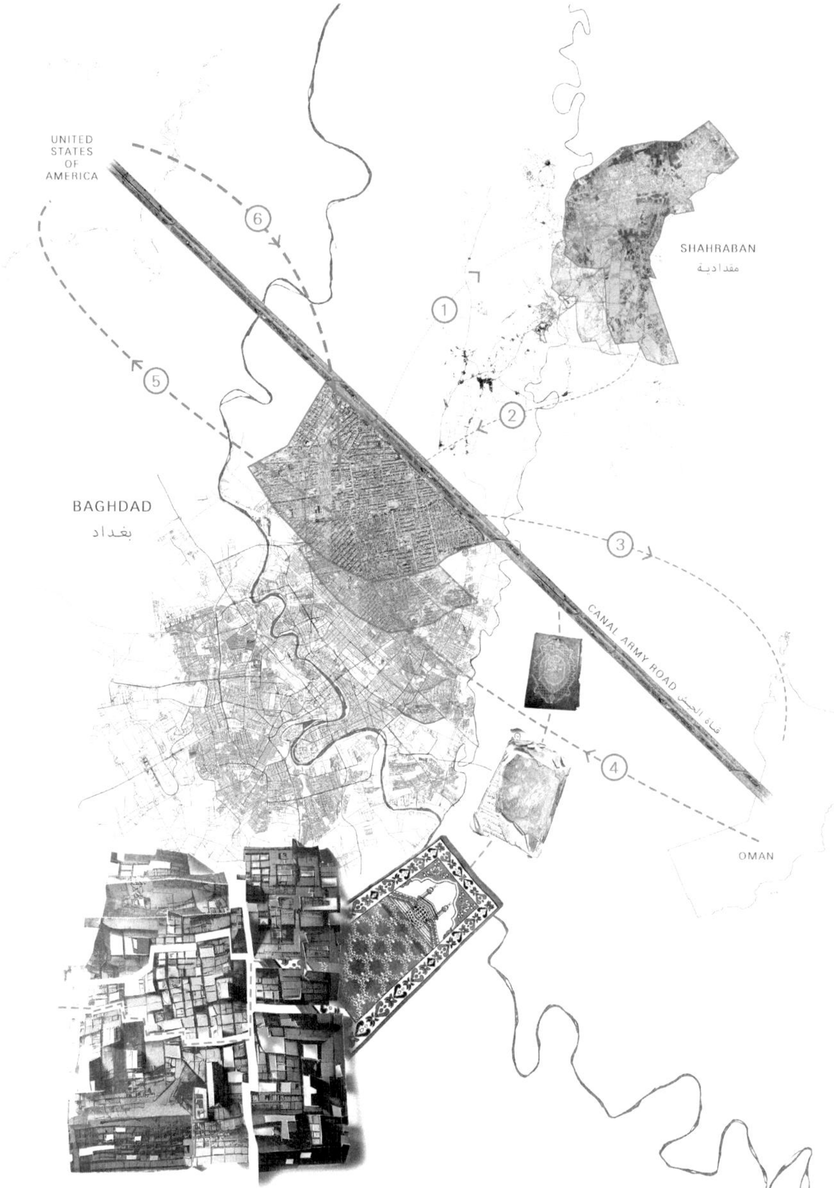

FIGURE 3.22 Alobaydi's map.
Courtesy Sana Murrani and Dhirgham Alobaydi

FIGURE 3.23 Alobaydi's trauma, showing the possibilities of escape within the complex historic Baghdadi urban grain.
Courtesy Sana Murrani and Dhirgham Alobaydi

the lines were blurred between urban and rural, as well as freedom and oppression (Figure 3.24). The only female teenager in her family, Hasan was overly protected in her early life, despite her ambitions. Her activism came to the fore during the 2019 Iraqi revolution (Tishreen Movement) as she participated in and documented the events unfolding in Baghdad's Tahrir Square. Soon after the revolution, she fled her home alone (Figure 3.25) and sought a safer, freer place in the UK.

Hasan (2022) recalls:

> In 2003 I was a child, only 13 years old. At that age, all I wanted to do was to be close to my family. It is difficult to contemplate now telling another child what we went through, because we would be traumatizing them just by telling them our stories. To this day, even though I am now in a relatively safe place by comparison, I still jump whenever there is a loud bang or if a car skids on the road. Or the fireworks – the sound of the fireworks is unbearable. It takes me a few seconds to remember I am no longer in a war zone.
>
> In times of war, my writing was my world of freedom and refuge. Even though I was a teenager who had not perfected her critical writing skills, I wrote about everything and the details of every day. Every day I would wake up finding that the electricity was out. I used to ask myself: 'What will tomorrow look like?'
>
> I also had toys, like soft toys, that I used to speak with and pretend they were real characters in my life. I still have these toys, back home in Iraq. I did

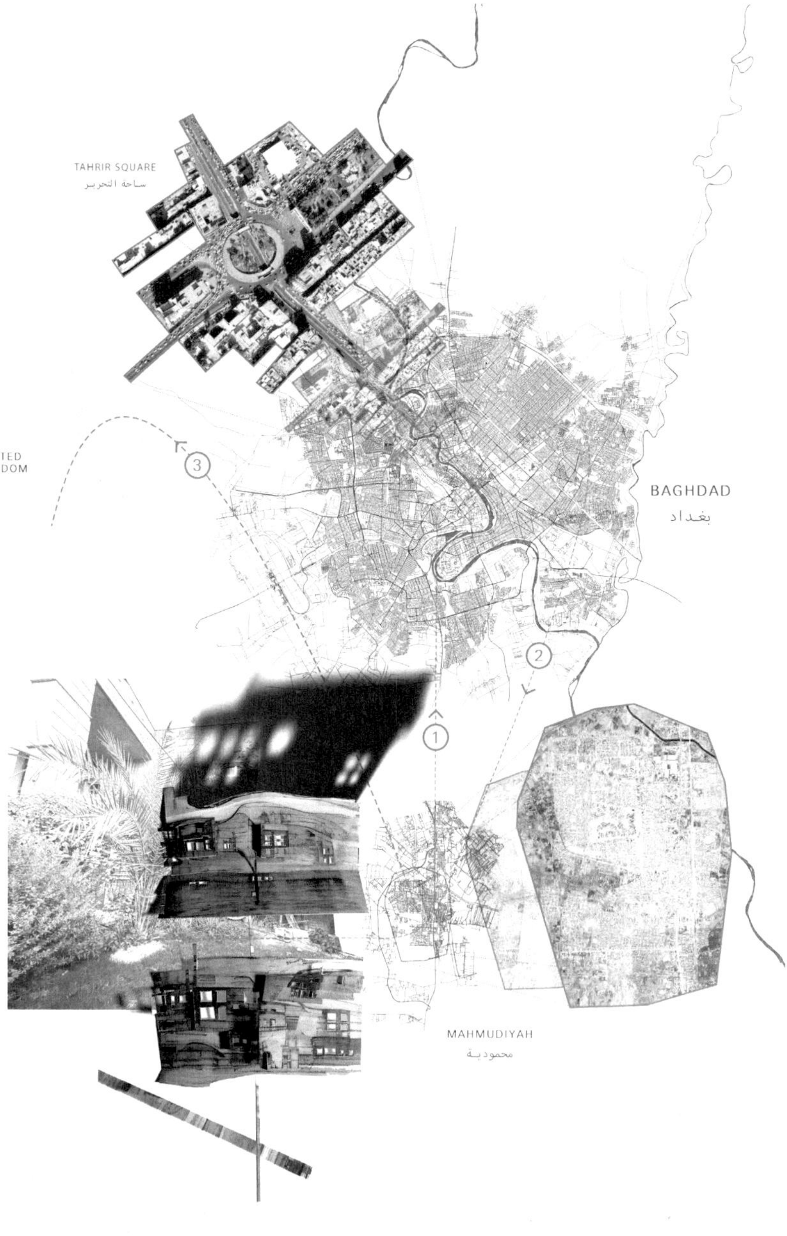

FIGURE 3.24 Hasan's map.
Courtesy Sana Murrani and Sanar Hasan

FIGURE 3.25 Hasan's trauma, showing the routes into the violated homes in cities and the countryside.
Courtesy Sana Murrani and Sanar Hasan

> not feel the need to bring them here [to the UK] with me because here I have real people to talk to. These toys were my friends, I shared my dreams and the details of my life with them. I used to imagine they lived in a place far away from the reality of my life. It might sound strange saying this now, especially since I had these imaginary friends well into my university years.

13. Jaafar Jotheri's map

Professor Jaafar Jotheri is a geo-archaeologist at the University of Qadisiyah. He is originally from Babylon, but in 2003, he was studying for his master's degree in geology at the University of Baghdad. Jotheri's map (Figure 3.26) reveals the traces of refuge-making in its continuous charting of routes of mobility: from city to village, from mud houses to marshland (Figure 3.27), and from the material (the old family *chawen* as it is known in colloquial Iraqi Arabic, which is a wooden tool that has similar function to a pestle and mortar) and geographical (the marshes) to the digital, in the pursuit of preservation.

With a voice filled with emotion and trauma, Jotheri (2022) recalls:

> I was doing my second year of my master's at the time in 2003, in the Department of Geology at Baghdad University, and my mother insisted that I go back to Babylon because Baghdad was too dangerous. I left half of my luggage, books, and everything else in the student hostel and then I got a ride from Baghdad to Babylon. I stayed in the countryside. We followed the news about what was happening in the south and in Baghdad, and when the coalition forces came near Babylon, we started to see more military presence. We stayed in the

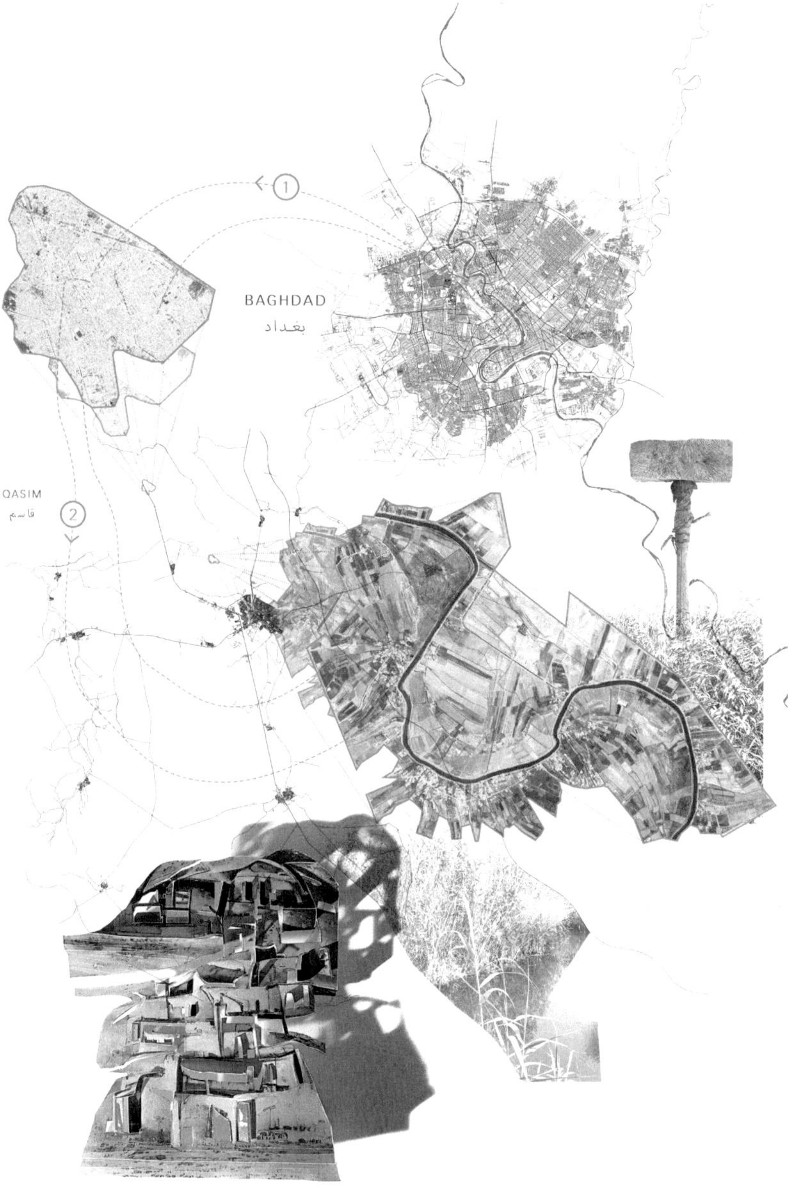

FIGURE 3.26 Jotheri's map.
Courtesy Sana Murrani and Jaafar Jotheri

FIGURE 3.27 Jotheri's trauma, showing the mud houses built into the folds and creases of the marshes.
Courtesy Sana Murrani and Jaafar Jotheri

> countryside because it was safe and closer to the marshes if we needed to take refuge. Only cities were dangerous at that time, but I saw lots of people coming from cities, staying in schools or mosques and even staying in abandoned houses, which are made from mud in the countryside.

Jotheri (2022) then goes on to describe his efforts to preserve his family story:

> I digitized everything. I have three copies of hard drives to protect our memories and my family's memories. This is a coping strategy when you live in an unsustainable and unpredictable way of life in Iraq. I learned it the hard way after a friend in Mosul lost all their memories when their house burned down during the ISIS offences. Suddenly they were left with nothing.
>
> So you see, we are preparing to move at any time, to be attacked at any time, so we have to be agile in our thinking about preserving our heritage and history all the time. This is what living through a continuous trauma looks like.

14. Abrar Wadi's map

Born and bred in Basra, Abrar Wadi is a civil engineer and a feminist activist. Wadi takes pride in both her heritage and activism, which come into regular friction with each other, owing to patriarchal societal traditions and taboos. Born during the years of UN sanctions, she was a child in 2003 during the scarcity of food amongst other essentials, and subsequently became attached to Iraqi flatbread (*khubez*). Her map (Figure 3.28) crosses uncomfortable borders between the two houses that belonged to her family and that of her father's second wife (Figure 3.29), and her activism formed part of the feminist Tishreen Movement in Basra in 2019 and 2020.

On making the Tishreen Movement in 2019 truly female, Wadi (2022) recalls:

> To begin with, we saw male colleagues from the university dominating the revolution. Even the rights they were calling for were patriarchal and masculine and would have served men more than women. We organized more than one march in the centre of Basra, in an area called Jubaiyla, specifically in the main square [Bahriya Square], led by female activists. Even the slogans we were carrying were calling for female equal rights. I felt this was a kind of a mutation in our way of life. We endured a lot of abuse and harassment from men in the city. Culturally, what we were doing was not acceptable of course, but we did it anyway. All girls and women who were students in high schools or university would leave their houses in the morning, telling their parents they would be going to study, but they ended up in the square protesting.

15. Nawrast Sabah's map

Originally from Basra, Dr Nawrast Sabah studied geology in Mosul for her master's and PhD between 2003 and 2013. Her map (Figure 3.30) engages with the different materiality and geographies of multiple cities across her seasonal commute from the north to the south of Iraq and back. Over the span of ten years, Sabah frequently had to traverse through the country between these two cities and her research location in the archaeological sites in Sinjar, alongside the river Tigris (Figure 3.31). Both cities were undergoing massive urban, social and political change, so while she was experiencing the violence in Basra where she lived, she was forever thinking about the trauma being inflicted in Mosul, too.

Sabah (2022) recalls:

> In 2003 I was in the middle of my master's degree in the Department of Geology in Mosul University, but at the start of the war I returned home to Basra. The looting happening simultaneously across the country meant that, at the same time Basra was being looted, my room in the students' accommodation in Mosul was being looted. I had a sack in the geology department at the university full of sample rocks from Sinjar mountain – these were lost in the chaos. Six months after the fall of Baghdad, I returned to Mosul to complete my studies.
>
> I completed my master's in 2005 from Mosul and returned to Basra, started working at the University of Basra, and in 2008 returned to Mosul to start my PhD, and completed it in 2013, a year before Daesh attacked Mosul. During the time sectarianism was at its peak [early 2007], I remember one day I was

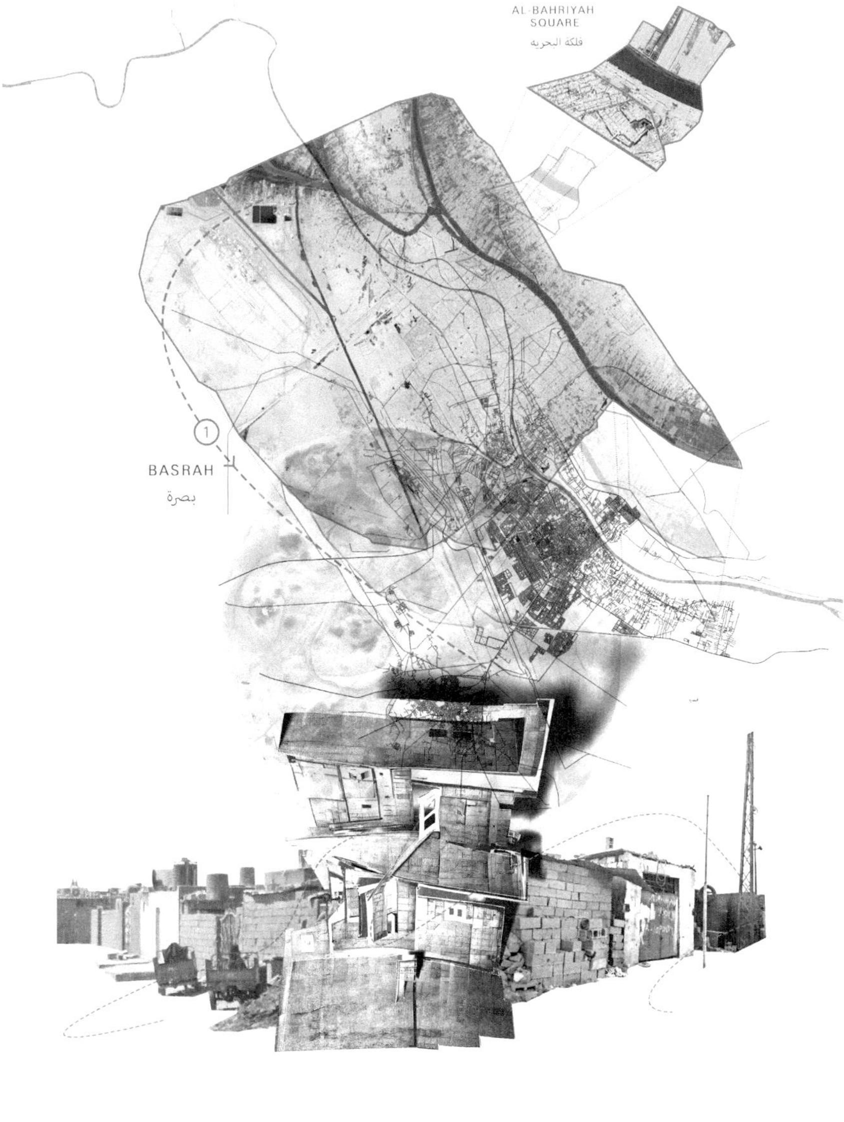

FIGURE 3.28 Wadi's map.
Courtesy Sana Murrani and Abrar Wadi

FIGURE 3.29 Wadi's trauma, showing the deliberate cutting through of internal walls to allow safe passage.
Courtesy Sana Murrani and Abrar Wadi

> heading from Mosul down to Baghdad and I had my family on the phone several times, warning me about Baghdad. On that day, thirty-five car bombs exploded across Baghdad.
>
> In 2013, when I returned to Basra from Mosul, I witnessed a massive change in the city. Local residential areas were all turned into multi-storey commercial buildings. Even the original traditional houses of Basra are endangered now, because all people want to do is turn land into multi-storey commercial buildings. If I want to describe Basra now, I can only think of one word that represents it: alienation. I feel it is alien to its old self and to Basrawis too.

Collectively, these fifteen maps capture instances of violence in their unfolding narratives. But they also illustrate people's creative ingenuity in coping with trauma and making spaces of refuge, and work together to form a living archive of spatiality. These maps expand the meaning of ordinary and everyday spatiality, as the stories they narrate are steeped in the trauma of past experiences, present realities and future imaginings. To use Dillon's (2007) formulation, this creative process has a 'palimpsestuous' quality, offering insights that exceed what can initially be gleaned from the interviews alone. The maps trace numerous scales and distances across time and space, while the three-dimensional pop-up books, and their accompanying photographs, shed light on the intensity of specific traumas. Through acts of drawing, layering, folding, pushing, pulling, cutting and tracing, these visual compositions can engage varied audiences both

FIGURE 3.30 Sabah's map.
Courtesy Sana Murrani and Nawrast Sabah

FIGURE 3.31 Sabah's trauma, showing her imagined shuttling between Basra and Mosul on a traditional narrow canoe (known as *mashoof* in colloquial Iraqi Arabic). Courtesy Sana Murrani and Nawrast Sabah

performatively and iteratively. At the same time, the quoted texts from interviews serve to further support this engagement, coupling together the meaning and the process of creation behind these novel forms of knowledge.

The images and words combined in this dual approach foster the synthesis of meaning and the generation of fresh perspectives. In doing so, they traverse diverse Iraqi geographies, each imbued with unique socio-cultural and political significance. And yet, they are united by a common thread – the ceaseless search for refuge across multiple dimensions of space and time, spanning past and present realities as well as future imaginaries. Importantly for this project, the work contained in this book does not offer graphic depictions of violence. Rather, it views violence not as a separate entity or a mere portrayal of reality, but as an integral part of the creative process of forging new understanding, assigning meaning and instigating disruption.

Also addressing the synthesis of image and reality through a non-representational approach, Rugo (2023) confirms the intention behind the processes of visibility and visuality in creative practices: the former disassembles, while the latter constructs new interpretations and significance in context. This dynamic process allows for different meanings to permeate through the evanescent layers of the maps, thereby constructing a novel lineage of refuge spatiality.

As I began this research, I noted the emergence of a significant query: how can we scrutinize the spatial possibilities that emerge from the architectural ruptures caused by trauma, specifically in terms of disrupted spaces of refuge? The aim of this exploration is to shape future spatial practices, particularly through facilitating a space within the field of architecture that acknowledges indigenous design responses to the trauma of war. These kinds of spatial practices display remarkable characteristics, defined by resilience, creative resourcefulness and adaptability, and they serve as fluid cartographies of negotiated agency and power. We can see that, amid persistent trauma, our diverse participants recall oscillating dynamics between various forms of actions, including resistance, negotiation, agency and power. This rich manifestation offers a fluid spatial map of resilience in action that can be defined by the following characteristics:

1 *Spatial reclamations: The adaptive appropriation of place (site and building)*
The spaces we inhabit become more than extensions of our lives and stories. Our creative and adaptive appropriation of sites and buildings – abandoned, damaged or otherwise – becomes an essential strategy for survival, place-making and remaking.

2 *Negotiations of terrain: Undulating landscapes*
Landscapes, like the conditions of life, are not always smooth. Through spatial practices, we who endure continuous trauma manage ingeniously to negotiate its highs and lows, adapting to the undulating terrains of both literal and metaphorical change.

3 *Material alchemy: Deconstructing and reconstructing objects*
An act seemingly as simple as the creative repurposing of an object – through disassembly and reassembly – can take on profound significance. This kind of material alchemy, the reimagining of the ordinary into the extraordinary, can become a tangible reflection of our resilience and adaptation.

4 *Routes of mobility: Creative cartography under stress*
In times of trauma, we are tasked with mapping routes for survival and escape under extreme duress. This kind of chaos and uncertainty can lead us to produce innovative wayfinding strategies.

5 *Scale transitions: From the intimate to the geopolitical, and everything in between*
The range of our spatial experiences can shift drastically, from the very intimate to the geopolitical. Such transitions demand skilful navigation and adaptability from us.

6 *Memory-driven futures: Reimagining worlds through history and trauma*
As we carry our history and memories along, they form the foundations for our ability to reimagine worlds in stark contrast to our own. Our ability to recall, retell and reinvent is testament to the enduring power of human creativity, even in the face of adversity.

4 ARCHITECTURAL STRUCTURES AND DISRUPTED MEMORY OF REFUGE IN RELATION TO TIME

Time plays a significant role in architectural structures as they assume, change into and embody different uses and functions amid rupture. This is the focus of this chapter, which takes a sectional view of six spatial case studies and analyses how they have been shaped through geotrauma (Pain 2021), displacement and temporality. They are not presented chronologically, but rather thematically within the following three categories: sudden rupture; ruptures of mobility and movement within cities and soft and hard borders; and temporal rupture – the nature of negotiated refuge. In times of war and violence, both social and spatial structures are affected alike. All six case studies manifested different spatial responses to time – both sudden and protracted – by actively and reactively altering their purpose, use and legacy.

The chapter unravels deep connections between space, time and memory through the socio-spatial relations that emerge and construct meanings within sites and buildings. In these explorations, time and space are held to be dynamic concepts that are constructed through, and continue to impact, multiple social actions. I discuss both violent and peaceful social actions in relation to the diverse spatial practices that emerge from them. In their work on planning theory, specifically city planning, Stephen Graham and Patsy Healey (1999: 628) describe the synergies between the concepts and effects of time and place, stating: 'Just as time is non-linear and multiple, so socially-constructed places are non-contiguous, diverse, dynamic and superimposed'. They further acknowledge Doreen Massey's (1993) concept of 'power geometry', which is inscribed into the multiplicities of space-time, whereby actions in space and time manifest as a form of power: 'power over space, time, social processes, and people' (Graham and Healey 1999: 629). This form of power plays a fundamental part in the following case studies and the way they are shaped, and have in turn shaped Iraq's recent history.

The previous chapter unpacked violence as it moved through various spatial hierarchies, from the intimate to the geopolitical. This chapter asserts a more dynamic understanding of the collapse of spatial scales, and does so within the framing of 'intimacy-geopolitics' and 'complex of violence' put forward in Rachel Pain's (2015: 72) 'Intimate War'. Pain (2015: 64) states:

> Military strategy is also-intimate: domestic violence is also-political. In both cases, these dynamics are made and lived. Wound into everyday lives, they are perpetrated, negotiated and resisted by individuals and groups of people in specific ways. They intersect with and frequently feed off obligations and customs of care, emotion, and social relations with others. And they are framed through gender, race and class, and refracted through the histories of places, nations and citizenship.

Through these six Iraqi case studies, which focus on events between 2003 and 2023, this chapter calls attention to the dynamic relationships woven through time, space and memory, crossing boundaries between the intimate and the global. Furthermore, the chapter engages in a form of place-making (Gieryn 2000) by examining how different scales of violence, whether intimate or geopolitical, are just as political as they are social. The six case studies have been carefully chosen to convey this dynamic complexity, showing how temporality and protractedness of trauma and violence can impact political and social action and manifest themselves in spatial structures. Depending on the type of violence and its impact, these structures fluctuate irregularly and uncharacteristically, from spaces of refuge and resistance to spaces of violence and aggression.

As described above, these are organized thematically into three categories, each covering two case studies: sudden ruptures, ruptures of mobility and displacement, and temporal ruptures. The first section, 'Sudden ruptures', discusses the abrupt change in function of certain architectural structures as a result of a sudden force or an event. The section takes two buildings that had a ripple effect into social and spatial, local and geopolitical areas within their cities and the country as a whole: the Amiriyah shelter in Baghdad, and Mosul's National Insurance Company building. The two case studies trigger a new method of place-making through negotiated relationships with violence across time and memory. The second section, 'Ruptures of mobility and displacement', describes a series of events across time, and how these changed what were once structures of refuge into other kinds of structures: the Yazidi Internally Displaced

Persons' (IDP) camps and the fate of Sinjar, and the rise of informal housing in Basra, amongst other housing projects elsewhere. These case studies reveal a newly negotiated relationship with attachment to place through identity, memory and loss. The 'Temporal ruptures' section focuses on structures that change and disappear, and their impact on city navigation and refuge. These include the blast walls in Baghdad during the years of sectarian violence, and the temporary appearance of structures of refuge through social activism and resistance (Kiddey 2020), for example Tahrir Square in Baghdad during the Tishreen Movement in 2019. These two case studies situate difference, power and resistance within emergent temporal spaces. Discussed in this chapter are theories of memory – both individual and collective (Wertsch and Roediger 2008) – and processes of remembering and forgetting (Middleton and Brown 2005). The chapter demonstrates that these are woven together within the historicity and imaginary of place-making for the purpose of creating spatial knowledge, not only of the past, but of the future too.

Sudden ruptures

The two case studies discussed in this section share several characteristics. Some are built-in similarities, while others were acquired after these buildings experienced a sudden moment of rupture. The first case study, the Amiriyah shelter (Figure 4.1), situated in western Baghdad, has received international attention and still is the most well-known, purpose-built bomb shelter in Iraq for all the wrong reasons. While, technically, the time of its sudden rupture occurred outside the period of study for this book, its lingering impact on Iraq's social, cultural and collective memory has caused Iraqis to avoid all thirty purpose-built shelters across the country, most of which are located in Baghdad. At dawn on 13 February 1991, during the First Gulf War, the public shelter was hit twice by a US so-called 'smart missile' without prior warning – a legal requirement imposed by international law concerning civilian buildings (Human Right Watch 1991). The first missile cut through its reinforced roof and the second also entered the building, before they detonated their combined almost 1,000 kg (*c.* 2,000 lb) weight, killing over 400 civilians. As an example of how difficult it is to account for such ruptures within the socio-spatial history of war and violence in Iraq, there was a discrepancy in the numbers reported from different sources. The Iraqis declared 300 casualties – a number the White House (2003) contested, meanwhile more recently Iraqis reported over 400 dead (Antoon 2023), whereas other studies suggest a much higher figure of 750 casualties (Dyregrov, Gjestad and Raundalen 2002). The capacity of the shelter was 1,500, and a few sources described it as having been at full capacity at the time, with only a few survivors. This single attack marked the highest number of casualties during the first Gulf War, or 'Operation Desert Storm' as it is known to the American troops.

FIGURE 4.1 Amiriyah shelter. a) Exterior photograph, 1991. Independent Picture Service/Universal Images Group via Getty Images. b) Interior photograph, 1997. Scott Peterson/Hulton Archive via Getty Images.

The shelter was originally built in 1984 as part of a campaign led by the Iraqi Interior Ministry during the Iraq–Iran eight-year war. Also known as No. 25, the Amiriyah shelter was an unassuming box-like shape, occupying an area of 500 square metres. Typically designed as two-story buildings with one floor submerged underground, the walls of these structures were 1.5 metres thick and ceilings of 3 metre thickness, and made from reinforced concrete and steel rods. Two firms led the construction of the shelter scheme: a Finnish civil engineering company called Perusyhtymä (which later became part of YIT Oyj) and a Swedish firm called Armerad Betong Vägförförningar (ABV; now part of NCC Aktiebolag). Both original firms had extensive experience in the design and construction of reinforced bomb shelters, and were part of a team of contractors who worked on Iraq's thirty shelters. Amiriyah district had two civilian shelters that were 4 kilometres apart, and both were equidistant to my family home. Both were full of families, mostly women and children. My family left the other shelter when it got too crowded, deciding to return home just three days before Amiriyah was struck by the two missiles. I remember the flakes of black soot flying in the sky and the strong smell of burning flesh that lingered for days afterwards. That day marked the moment when Iraqis would never set foot in a bomb shelter ever again, yet these shelters remained as unattended, derelict buildings, eyesores nestled between houses and neighbourhoods across Baghdad. Their purpose had changed forever; they were no longer seen as spaces of refuge, but rather triggers of the trauma of war and loss. The Amiriyah shelter itself became a spatial memorial, a museum of the tragedy, and was cared for by a mother who lost all eight of her children, but it was later taken by the Iraqi Army and turned into a military station. The site is now closed to the public, who remain the victims of a tragedy and the propaganda of two sides: one fuelled by the Saddam regime and the other led by the Pentagon and the White House.

This symbol of refuge, which became a metaphor for trauma, is not the only building in the country whose function became the opposite of its original intention. Iraqis navigated these buildings over three decades of war and violence, during which time such shelters went from being spaces of safety to spaces of aggression. For example, they were used as human shields by the Saddam regime, as male-only gymnasiums and bodybuilding spaces, as weapon and artillery storage spaces, and as military stations. Iraqis had no agency in the decision-making when it came to such public buildings, supposedly intended for civilian use. Although these buildings are wedged in the heart of neighbourhoods, their use, or change of use, was never up for public consultation. They were either monopolized by the Saddam regime or targeted by the occupying forces. The sudden event described above that ruptured and shattered the function of civilian shelters in Iraq in 1991 served to change the course of these buildings forever. As a result, Iraqis had no option but to adapt their own homes into shelters or seek shelter elsewhere at relatives' houses, in mosques and churches, in schools, in parks and other public spaces.

In my conversations with the fifteen Iraqi interviewees, I asked specifically whether any of them, or anyone they knew, had sought refuge in these purpose-built shelters between 2003 and 2023, and the answer was a resounding 'no'. Besides the fears of the safety of the buildings themselves after Amiriyah, and the fear that the United States might use nuclear weapons, they also feared contamination from uranium already within the buildings, since most of these shelters were used by the Saddam regime to store weapons and ammunition (Cigar 2014: 277). Moreover, they were afraid to leave their houses alone, to be subject to the vandalism and looting that occurred in the weeks following the 'carefully orchestrated media event' of the toppling of Saddam's statue in Baghdad on 9 April 2003 (Bevan 2016: 121). In his book, *The Destruction of Memory* (2016), Robert Bevan asserts that this kind of political targeting of architecture takes on a 'totemic quality', playing on the meanings and memories attached to a community's presence and future. When these public shelters are attacked, it is seen as the destruction of a particular building typology, in this case public safety, effectively erasing its history, function, memory and identity (Bevan 2016: 18).

The second case study represents the epitome of such an erasure of histories, memories and identities, in a deliberate act of violence involving the weaponization of architecture. In 2014, the National Insurance Company building was used as a theatre of horror by ISIS, who accused young men of either being gay or of not following their strict Islamic law, and executed them by throwing them from the roof of the seven-storey building. Built in 1966 and designed by Rifat Chadirji, Iraq's pioneer of modern architecture, the National Insurance Company building was the tallest building in downtown Mosul, and considered to be one of the finest pieces of modern architecture in the country. Chadirji's celebrated designs were inspired by historic Baghdadi houses, whose courtyards and arched balconies he recessed into and extruded out from the space of the building in the form of the traditional *shanasheel* (a structural element usually made from highly crafted wood, extruding from the façades of buildings) (Warren and Fethi 1982). Chadirji's building was iconic, part of the heritage of the city and highly valued by locals as an exemplar of Iraqi local talent in its design, material and craftmanship (Al-Ta'ai and Al-Ali 2022).

ISIS ravaged the city of Mosul between 2014 and 2017, and as a result of battles waged to defeat the group, the building came under several assaults to its structure. What once was a symbol of development and pride in the city quickly became a haunting site of violence and grief for the young men who had been killed. It was rendered to rubble in 2017, after five of its seven storeys were destroyed during the battle to remove ISIS from Mosul. The building resembled a wreck, with its fractured concrete and debris hanging off the curled, torn steel rods that once held it together. The direct violence being caused by ISIS was stopped in 2017, yet sadly the memories of their violence live on. By then, Mosul had lost a significant number of its UNESCO World Heritage Sites and other important buildings, yet Chadirji's National Insurance Company building was the most haunting and traumatizing for the collective memory (Boyer 2001) of the city. It had also received international attention after footage appeared on social media showing the ISIS fighters throwing the men from its rooftop. It was one of many sites that ISIS had weaponized by changing their relevance, meaning and purpose in Mosul for good.

In 2018, the Iraqi conductor and cellist Karim Wasfi organized a memorial concert as a sign of resistance and hope after the violence the city had experienced at the hands of ISIS (Figure 4.2). Mosul debated the possibility of restoring the building as part of its rebuilding efforts, which began soon after its liberation, but several foreign experts, local architects, residents and historians could not agree on the fate and the future of the building ('Mosul Destroys Iconic Building' 2019). In an International Organization for Migration (IOM) report, Frazer Macdonald Hay (2019: 27) states that 'like all features of public memory, this building and its notoriety has become politically and socially significant'. By saying this, Hay implies that public memory is complex, and that it reflects the level of healing and resilience – or the absence of it – within local communities. Hay establishes these points through a series of interviews conducted with locals about the fate of the building, among other sites. In these, he highlights a clear divide: there are those who have a positive association with the building, who are reminded of the defeat of ISIS in Mosul, and believe the building should become a museum so that people will never forget the group's brutality; and there are those who see it as 'a negative symbol of cruelty and a method to help dehumanise ISIL and those affiliated to the group, while reinforcing victimhood and social suspicion' (Hay 2019: 27). The report findings highlight a significant 'shortage of advice and awareness material aimed at educating the government, public, NGOs and the staff of international organizations' in relation to the way violence is memorialized, specifically in their role in establishing 'successful and sustainable peacebuilding processes' (Hay 2019: 51).

Gruia Bădescu (2022: 194) speaks of the complexity of such debates in her work on key violated buildings in Belgrade, stating that making sense of such ruined buildings 'often implicates multiple, sometimes conflicting threads, of collective memory'. In the case of Belgrade, this process involves the weaving together of several political histories and belongings to different pasts, including socialist Yugoslavia, the Second World War, NATO and the famous architectural legacy behind these buildings (Bădescu 2022: 194). These debates can reveal huge tensions between geopolitical and spatial memories of a place. As Rosie Bsheer asserts in her piece 'Heritage as War' (2017), the process of reconstruction can be seen as an act of violence in itself, just as the process of destruction was. Bsheer (2017: 729) discusses how heritage sites, buildings and architecture can come to

FIGURE 4.2 Iraqi conductor and cellist Karim Wasfi's concert in front of the remains of the National Insurance Company building, Mosul 2018.
Courtesy Ali Al-Baroodi.

represent causes for celebration and causes for injury to people, where, 'In times of peace as in war, they are terrains of symbolic and material contestation whose creative destruction can be deployed as political spectacles and projections of power'. Looking critically at similar sites and their meanings in relation to violence, Andrew Herscher proposes that there is a temporality to such acts of violence in the way that they can inflict new meanings onto architecture, rather than violently destroying a fixed meaning and identity that these buildings might have (Weizman and Herscher 2011). Herscher postulates that 'violence transforms the meaning and identity of architecture in the very process of destroying it' (Weizman and Herscher 2011: 114).

The act of collective remembering, which also implies collective forgetting as it involves both loss and preservation of memory, falls directly between two philosophical thoughts on socially constructed memory and individual experience (Middleton and Brown 2005). These debates have been explored at length (Wertsch and Roediger 2008) in terms of where we might situate collective memory conceptually and theoretically, as it overlaps and opposes history studies, collective remembering and individual memory. The development of collective memory as a methodological framework begins with early writings on the social construction of memory by Maurice Halbwachs (1992), and shifts into concepts of continuous evolution of memory through past and present time, particularly in relation to the theory of duration (*durée* in French), as championed by Henri Bergson (1992). This entanglement between memory and time has a profound effect on place-making, particularly in relation to sudden-impact events, such as the ones discussed in the case studies above. There is certainly a sense of the fleetingness of collective acts of remembering and forgetting embodied in the temporality and spatiality of such trauma and violence.

Unlike the first case study of the Amiriyah shelter, the site of Chadirji's building retained a different kind of presence, not only in the collective memory of the city and its people, but also in the form of an archive. While Amiriyah remains an important memory in Iraqis' collective traumatic history, the shelter as a building, despite its continued physical existence, has no documented presence in the architectural sense. Meanwhile, Chadirji's entire design work was donated in 2017 to the Aga Khan Documentation Centre at MIT. The collection's archivist, Betsy Baldwin (2019), published this work after the building's destruction, and it contains a wealth of documents, maps, photographs and working plans spanning five decades. Such open availability and access to these kinds of documents is not the case with the bomb shelters. In my own attempts to research their history, I have contacted both the Finnish and Swedish construction firms that worked on the scheme in Iraq in the 1980s. In 2012, the YIT Finnish construction company published a book about the firm's work and growth over the past 100 years. The book explains its long history and expansion into the Middle East and elsewhere, especially in Iraq, and its work on large-scale projects such as oil refineries and water supply systems (e.g. in Karbala in 1958 [Herranen 2012: 22]), yet it only contains a passing mention of the company's involvement in the construction of the bomb shelters in Iraq.

At the beginning of the 1980s, Iraq became one of the main destinations for Finnish construction exports. Between the late 1960s and mid-1980s, Iraq had twelve different Finnish companies working on major projects across the country. In particular, Iraq's oil money allowed for a surge in building and construction across the country, chiefly in Baghdad. The YIT group started several projects, including the prestigious Baghdad Congress Palace, however the threat of war with Iran slowed work in the centre of the country. Though they relocated the Finnish construction workers to Mosul in the north, these companies still found themselves back in Baghdad, working on a scheme for shelters across the city. Intentionally designed to be used for many different functions, the shelters that were constructed by the Finnish Perasto group (now part of the YIT firm) were completed in the mid-1980s (Herranen 2012: 64). After that time, the war with Iran and the drain it had on Iraq's finances meant that Finnish work diminished in the country. Sadly, after the fall of the regime in April 2003, any other archives holding further information on the shelter scheme were either destroyed amid a wave of looting and systemic erasure of heritage, educational and public sectors in Iraq, or confiscated by the Americans and their allies.

As we have seen, these unassuming bomb shelters across Iraq became 'place-sensitive' after the strike of 1991, and their locality, their material form and meaning (whether intended or acquired) began to further define their spatiality and existence (Gieryn 2000: 466). In his seminal article, 'A Space for Place in Sociology', Thomas F. Gieryn (2000: 471) asserts that places are continuously made, not only by the influence of the powerful or the input of design professionals, but also by ordinary people as they 'extract from continuous and abstract space a bounded, identified, meaningful, named, and significant place'. This form of extraction occurs when space becomes place-sensitive. It also arises when a place suddenly becomes remarkable, through the 'unwindable spiral of material form and interpretative understandings or experiences' (Gieryn 2000: 471). This bounded and co-dependent relationship between place and people is the same, whether in times of war and violence or times of peace and refuge. The performative characteristic of this relationship follows a discursive, practical and iterative process of production and imagining between people and places, inscribing meanings and experiences both at the same time. The nonlinear interplay between time, memory, and place-making and remaking intricately shapes the evolving meanings and their diverse forms of spatial representation.

Said (2000: 176) reminds us that, as 'Memory and its representations touch very significantly upon questions of identity, of nationalism, of power and authority', it is simultaneously subject to people's own experiences and therefore at risk of being misused by those who have control over the narrative. Said (2000: 185) further asserts that 'collective memory is not an inert and passive thing, but a field of activity in which past events are selected, reconstructed, maintained, modified, and endowed with political meaning'. With this in mind, we should view the case studies in this section as places that have a complicated relationship with people and their memories, past and present, where both memory and invention have shaped their existing narratives. This relationship is of a sudden rupturing, both spatially and socially, which lacks negotiation yet remains in the collective memory of the city for generations. The recollected memories within the two case studies serve to anchor their sites in a 'symbolic construction', which is situated between recalled images and memories about those places, and their imagined spatiality (Hornstein 2011: 3). Regardless of their material existence – or loss of it through destruction – the critical geographies of memory and place (Hoelscher and Alderman 2004) cannot be separated from the frames of temporal spatiality that are found between those memory- and place-making processes. In this way, Bădescu (2022: 183) describes architecture that has been annihilated as a 'mnemonic device for memories of political violence'. Collective memory is therefore not only held within different groups of people but also embodied within these sites of violence – making memory a truly spatial and political phenomenon.

The following section engages with this palimpsestic relationship between memory and place in sites that have been drenched in violence – violence inflicted on people and imposed upon the urban and rural environment – rupturing their fundamental characteristics of material and mental place-making.

Ruptures of mobility and displacement

This section covers three types of 'place-wounding', a term coined by Amanda Kearney (2016), who described 'place, cultural and environmental wounding' – the moment when violence and harm have been inflicted on a place, affecting its relationship with its local ecological environment. These three types of place-wounding are demonstrated through two case studies that feature several ruptures of mobility and displacement. First, we encounter acts of genocide and domicide in the form of ISIS atrocities in Sinjar and the Yazidi community in the north-west of Iraq. Furthermore, it examines the forced displacement of survivors of the Yazidi community from Sinjar into the north of Iraq (the Kurdistan region). In the second case study, from Basra, we observe the displacement and mobility within a certain class of poorer Iraqis who have moved from rural parts of the country into urban centres with the rise of the so-called informal housing sector. These three types of place-wounding reveal different qualities of place and place-making as they negotiate memory, place-attachment, identity, loss, return, uprooting and regrounding.

This first case study, then, delves deeply into the place-wounding of Sinjar and the forced displacement of the Yazidi people native to the north-west of Iraq. Sinjar is a semi-desert town of approximately half a million people, predominantly Yazidis, located in the north-west of Iraq in the Nineveh Plains. The town is about 5 kilometres from Mount Sinjar, close to the border between Iraq and Syria. Although the town is located in Nineveh province, which is under central governmental rule, it has struggled with a history of political tension between Baghdad and the Kurdish government. From the 1990s to the aftermath of the 2003 US-led invasion of Iraq, the town and its people suffered dramatically under fifteen years of UN sanctions, which were further impacted by a lack of resources or financial support for investment in the area. The people of Sinjar essentially lived in poverty, working as seasonal farmers and shepherds for half of the year, and otherwise living hand-to-mouth. With this simple way of life came a scarcity of opportunities for education. The relationship between the people and their place was built entirely on their fragile yet deep connection to the land, the mountain and the mud houses that are at one with the landscape of that part of Iraq. Our next interviewee, Murad Ismael, is President and Founder of Sinjar Academy, as well as the Founder and former Executive Director of the Yazda Foundation. He describes the harsh reality of life in Sinjar prior to 2003:

> Most of those who lived in Sinjar were seasonal workers coming and working in the Arab areas, particularly in Rabiya subdistrict. Many families, including mine, lived this way for many years, spending spring through fall at the farm and winter in their homes in Sinjar. Some years, people would have earnings of ten or twenty US dollars a year for the whole family. One year, I remember my family came back and all the money we made was enough to buy one bag of flour. At the same time, farming provided the Yazidi community with livestock, which enabled families to feed themselves.
>
> This agricultural way of living prevented starvation, yet it impacted the community, especially in terms of access to education and in terms of health as well, where malaria and other diseases impacted the community so much. Many children had to drop out of school to take care of the sheep and the farm. I was the only one among my siblings who had the privilege to go to school and continued education.
>
> Our homes were built from mud, with nothing more than mattresses and covers that are handmade from sheepskin and wool, and maybe one wooden cabinet in the corner. People lived a bare life, but they had peace of mind and routine, which together made the quality of life acceptable.
>
> (Ismael 2022)

Ismael (2022) continues to describe the change that took place after 2003 and the strategic locality of Sinjar, which also led to its obliteration by ISIS in 2014:

> This very distinctive way of living changed dramatically in 2003. Yazidi Areas under Iraqi authority control changed hands to the Kurdistan Regional Government [KRG]. This was the case for both Sinjar and Bashiqa. Political change also changed people's way of life, as KRG brought a lot of money to the region. With its strong political position in Baghdad, it was able to do so. For example, in 2006 and 2007, Article 140 of the Constitution allowed many Yazidi families to receive almost 10 million Iraqi dinars' compensation [roughly US$ 7,000] for the repression that was enforced on Yazidis, causing displacements from their villages in 1979. On the whole, the Kurds invested in the region, especially during the times of high oil prices. There was a lot of spending, which shifted lifestyles from an agricultural society to a more urban one. These were in a way political expansions for the Kurds in the north of Iraq [which happened in Christian areas of Nineveh and Kurdish-majority areas of Kirkuk as well]. This expansion in fact benefited the Yazidis economically. A large number of Yazidis worked in the security sector for the Kurds and wages were as high as 1 million dinars (a big difference to $10 a year of earnings). Political parties brought money to the region too, for example, the Kurdistan Democratic Party [KDP] was funding probably 15,000 families, and so did the Patriotic Union of Kurdistan [PUK].

The Yazidi territories in Iraq are arbitrarily divided, or, per the current constitution, are disputed, and territories are geographically within different geopolitical and cultural regions, so, for example, communities in Sinjar lived a slightly different life to those living in Bashiqa and Shekhan. While Sinjar and Bashiqa were often under the Iraqi central government rule, Shekhan was under Kurdistan region's rule since 1991.

The tensions between these political soft borders and the territorialization of the region's geography were exacerbated by the hostility the Yazidis received towards their religion and practices. As mentioned in earlier sections, the Yazidis are one of Iraq's ethno-religious minority groups. They are indigenous to the north of Iraq, but also have a small historic presence in Syria, Turkey and Iran. Violence has been a part of Yazidi experience for a long time, especially during the sectarian trouble that erupted throughout the country in the form of terrorist car bombs and similar attacks, yet in the summer of 2014, ISIS committed a genocide on a scale not seen before, using religion as justification. As a result, 300,000 Yazidis were internally displaced, and over 100,000 displaced outside the country (Tezcür 2022: 44). As for those who did not escape, it is thought that twenty-five in every thousand Yazidis were either killed or kidnapped by ISIS (Cetorelli et al. 2017). Ismael (2022) comments:

> One very clear reason for the persecution of the Yazidis or any other minority is that a large percentage of Muslims did not see the Yazidi as a legitimate faith. The radical ones even see persecution of Yazidis as justifiable, and whenever they have the opportunity and the capacity, they will hit the Yazidis whether it is this year, eight years ago or in the future. This was a major factor, and that fear is in the back of every Yazidi's mind, even today. But there were other factors, for example, when the Kurds took over control in Sinjar [after 2003], they limited access to it for the Arabs, although Sinjar's mayor before the Kurds were in power was a Sunni Arab. The Arabs often felt they were mistreated, and this created tensions with them and fuelled their sense of emotional response, coupled with terrorism that surged with ISIS. Remember, the Yazidis also supported the US military and that also accumulated more hate toward them.

Ismael's life and the lives of all Yazidis changed on 3 August 2014, when ISIS attacked Sinjar and its people. He continues:

> 2014 changed life for me, but also for my entire Yazidi community. The genocide reshaped who we are as individuals and reshaped our personal and collective thinking, whether we were outside or inside Iraq. That was the moment when I got involved with advocacy, which eventually became a permanent activism

for me on behalf of the Yazidi community. Being in the USA, and being able to speak English, I was able to help the cause in many different ways.

Post the attack on Sinjar on August the 3rd, 2014, I was involved in organizing demonstrations before the White House, and then we had meetings with the State Department, and then we created the Sinjar Crisis Management team. The team provided information to the US to conduct airstrikes against ISIS positions around the besieged district of Sinjar. We helped mobilize the distribution of food parcels to people stranded on the mountain, and mapped locations of Yazidis who were held captive. The Sinjar Crisis Management Team became Yazda [an NGO organization] and I and my colleagues in Yazda then worked with Nadia Murad [Nobel Peace Prize Laureate and human rights activist]. The Yazidi case between 2014 and 2019 was almost exclusively my full-time job. Currently, I am writing a guide on how to respond to genocide. My writing helped the Yazidi case. I always thought I would be a writer, though I never imagined I would be writing advocacy reports for the Yazidi cause.

(Ismael 2022)

Ismael and his team were instrumental to the survival of Yazidis, who fled Sinjar through Mount Sinjar. Some walked for days and crossed international borders with Syria, then crossed back into the Kurdish region of Iraq. In his interview, Ismael shared some key GIS maps (Geographic Information System) that he generated after communicating with Yazidis who were fleeing ISIS. They were able to provide geographical locations of ISIS cells, snipers and captured routes, which are identified in thick black lines on the maps in Figure 4.3. These maps also provided safe locations and routes for the US troops to drop food and water from the air to the Yazidis who had managed to escape through the mountain. Of particular interest for this study is the fact that agility in collective mapping saves lives; spaces of refuge do not have to be static localities, but can instead embrace action, mobility and change across borders and different time zones. The maps further assert the strong connection between place-making (as an active action of refuge-seeking) and place-attachment (in the form of memory and identity within the landscape) as a dual ecology that has helped Yazidis and similar minorities survive centuries of hostility and discrimination in their own lands. The ISIS fighters had encircled Mount Sinjar, trapping thousands of Yazidis in Iraq's hottest month of the year (up to 50°C), leaving people without water and food for days (Cetorelli et al. 2017). While many perished, Ismael's ability to respond to information and alter his maps at pace played a huge part in identifying the right moments to rescue survivors.

The ISIS attacks against Yazidis have been recognized as an act of genocide by several United Nations organizations, including the European Union. Unfortunately, despite Ismael's work and the efforts of others like him, the Yazidi community in Iraq have endured and continue to endure a great deal of anguish,

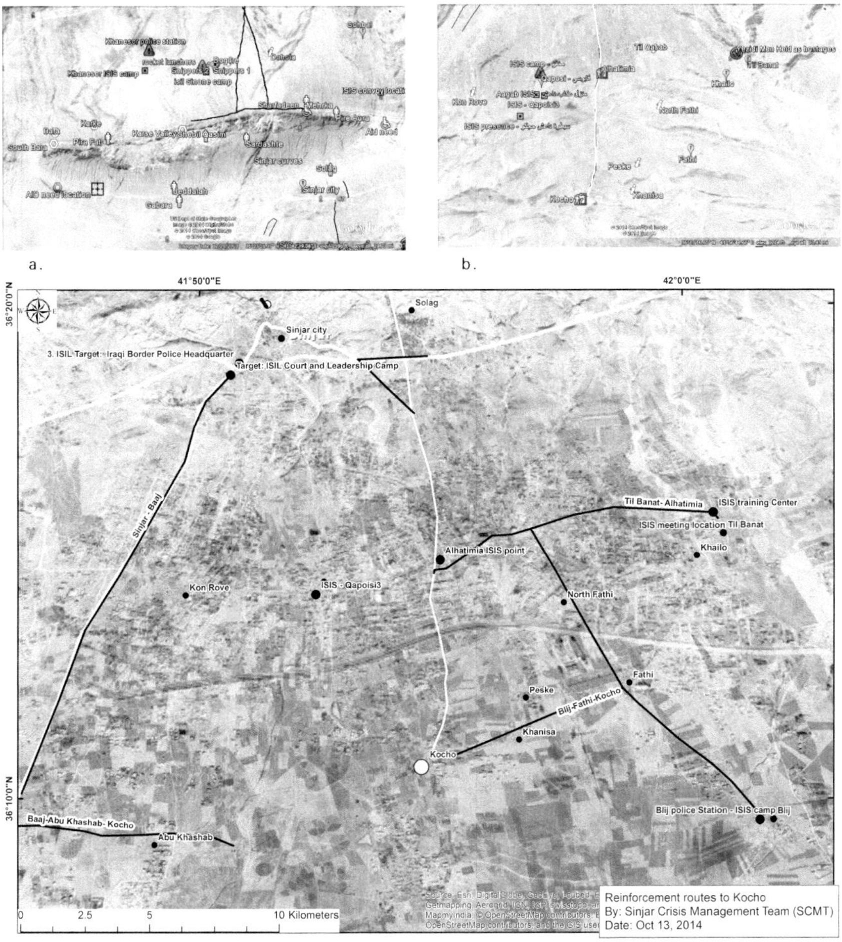

FIGURE 4.3 Ismael's maps of the Sinjar Crisis Management Team's efforts to help Yazidis into places of safety, 2014. a) Map of the routes north of Sinjar. b) Map of the south of Sinjar, showing the village of Kocho. c) Map showing the entire operation of the Sinjar Crisis Management Team, 2014.
Courtesy Murad Ismael.

loss and abuse at the hands of ISIS fighters, Sunni insurgents and the current Iraqi government. Their towns and villages have been annihilated; their shrines, religious buildings and mud houses have been burned and destroyed (Figure 4.4); their elders and children have been killed; and their women and children have been kidnapped and sex trafficked, abused and sold in Iraq, Turkey and Syria, with nearly 3,000 still missing (Tezcür 2022: 44). Since the defeat of ISIS in 2017, over eighty mass graves have been exhumed as of 2019 (Tezcür 2022: 45), and Yazidis have made several attempts to reach out to international communities for support and recognition. One of the most powerful messages that has emerged from Yazidi experience has been Nadia Murad's (2017) memoir of captivity by ISIS. Since her escape, the Nobel Prize awardee, who lost most of her family in the village of Kocho, south Sinjar, has been actively working to end sexual violence as a weapon of war.

The place-wounding that took place in Sinjar has been a protracted and a repetitive form of violence, affecting people, their homes and their neighbourhoods – extending to genocide and domicide. This trauma then led to another type of place-wounding: the forced displacement of Yazidis in the Kurdish region of Iraq. Most of these displaced Yazidis now take refuge in one of the twenty-six camp sites across Nineveh province and the Kurdish region, while others still reside in derelict, unfinished building sites and other informal camps. At the beginning of the ISIS assault on Sinjar, survivors who fled through the mountain, into Syria and back into the Kurdish region of Iraq took temporary refuge in parks, schools and other public buildings, as well as derelict buildings. Nearly a decade later, the Kurdish government's camp sites that were set up shortly afterwards are still in use. This

FIGURE 4.4 Sinjar after ISIS offences, showing the level of destruction, 2022. Courtesy Shahab Sameer.

is because, after the destruction of Sinjar in 2014, very few families returned due to a wholescale lack of government support for returnees, investment in building and infrastructure, demining efforts, and interest in rebuilding neighbourhoods. Yazidis have identified other factors in their reluctance to return (Travers 2021), including fear of discrimination, lack of security protection and lack of independent financial means for return. As a result, the camp sites have grown over the past decade and started to resemble their own urban neighbourhoods, with basic services and, more importantly, protection.

While these IDPs are still residing in camp sites, in tents, in metal cabins and makeshift shelters (Figure 4.5), the complexity of the issue of return deepens with each passing year. As we have seen from our interviews, the issue of mobility and forced displacement has been a problem for Iraq for the past two decades. The case for Yazidis and Sinjar is particularly compounded, however, by the ill-treatment and discrimination inflicted upon them by local host communities and society at large, as well as the lack of educational and clear political systems in that region of Iraq. While several reports (Hay 2017: 46), technical documents (Shelter Cluster and UN-Habitat 2021) and studies (Sabie et al. 2019) on the issue of return and the current state of housing post-ISIS have reported a strong desire to return to a sense

FIGURE 4.5 Yazidi camps in Kabarto, Dahuk, 2022.
Courtesy Shahab Sameer.

of home, community and a normal way of life, these studies have also found that IDPs fear a lack of security and the threat of exposure to intimidation by militia groups. The practicality of any kind of return is tied to several complex factors:

1. The state of property, land and infrastructure, which can require anything from complete rebuilding to structural repair, to façade damage of walls, windows and doors.
2. The state of security in the region, as well as the capacity for trust between local communities, IDPs and police or militia, who tend to stop and search men in particular, taking their documents and in some cases detaining them (Hay 2017: 6).
3. The availability of resources and opportunities, including finance, health (physical and mental), education and employment.
4. Changes in the environment and climate crisis impacting the country at an accelerated rate, including deforestation (through change of land use), desertification (through climate change, including rapid drought), over-urbanization and densification (through rising populations) and the shift from rural areas to urban centres (redistribution of the poor towards urban centres).
5. The country's uncertain political landscape, specifically in the north, owing to the push-and-pull factors between the central Baghdadi government and the Kurdish government. This is further complicated by Turkey's sporadic aerial attacks on this part of Iraq (Kadhum 2023), as well as the fact that the Kurdistan region has been supporting IDPs (Iraqis, Syrians and others) for two decades and is reaching 'hosting fatigue syndrome'.

Collectively, these conditions contribute to a protracted place-wounding caused by complex patterns of displacement, which are further compounded by a lack of initiatives for supporting return.

The Operation Data Portal for the United Nations High Commissioner for Refugees (UNHCR) and the ReliefWeb repository of the United Nations Office for the Coordination of Humanitarian Affairs (OCHA) provide humanitarian information with detailed data on each IDP camp in Iraq. Using maps and statistics, they reveal the location, spread, numbers and demographics of displaced peoples within these camps across Iraq. As of December 2022, there were over 1 million Iraqis registered as internally displaced persons (OCHA ReliefWeb 2022). Further to this, there are an estimated 4 million displaced persons unaccounted for because they reside in informal settlements across the country. Around half of these are considered to be people who have returned to the region from which they were first displaced, but have not returned to their homes. The 2022 map shows that IDP camps tend to congregate and intensify around urban centres across the country, particularly in and around Baghdad, the Kurdish region (Nineveh), the west and east, and Basra and other cities in the south (UNHCR 2020). Apart from the twenty-six camps managed by the Kurds, the official and unofficial camp sites dotted across several other maps have mostly been marked for closure by the Iraqi government (UNHCR 2021). The five factors listed above apply to nearly all of the sites across the country, with the added pressure of discrimination against the poorer, less educated sections of society who have moved from rural to urban centres.

This brings us to the rise of so-called informal housing settlements in the country, with the case study of Basra. Basra is home to the second largest number of informal settlements after Baghdad (UN-Habitat 2017), although it is not alone in being overwhelmed owing to the mobility and forced displacement that occurred especially during the post-2003 years of ethnic cleansing and sectarian violence. Before delving into this case study, it is pertinent to explain the background to this third type of place-wounding, which takes the form of the rising informal housing sector in Iraq. This is where informality wounds spatiality rather than fostering creative everyday practices. Despite this wounding, it is crucial to acknowledge the abundance of 'difference making' (Stanley 2009: 1004) and the various scales of power dynamics that such informal settlements have given rise to, which contributed to the emergence of different yet spatially relational patterns of displacement across the country.

In his book, *The Iraqi Refugee*, Joseph Sassoon addresses the significant change to the patterns of displacement that took place, both inside and outside Iraq, before and after the 2003 invasion and occupation of the country. He states, 'Under Saddam Hussein, expulsion of people from their homes was a state policy intended to punish recalcitrant populations' (Sassoon 2011: 9). Prior to 2003, displacement patterns came in waves, which took place across the country in the north (mainly against the Kurds) and in the south (against the Marsh Arabs and Shia, who were targeted by the regime) (Sassoon 2011: 10). This type of displacement led to further, external displacement within neighbouring countries and further afield. After 2003, Sassoon (2011: 14) adds that, 'Once the state had collapsed and its institutions, which were run mainly by a secular urban cadre, had disintegrated, ethnicity and tribalism took over', further noting, 'when the state stopped functioning and violence began to rise, people turned to their communities and ethnic groups for help and protection'.

During and immediately after the bombing campaign in 2003, a growing number of people fled their homes, seeking refuge in the countryside and other remote locations. Most of these were temporary displacements, lasting only a few weeks. The previous chapter brought forward several such stories from across Iraq, where mobility and movement was at its highest. Soon after the collapse of the regime and the occupation, a different mode of displacement practice emerged. This involved movement between urban centres and neighbourhoods following ethnic and religious tensions, which were further met by returning refugees and exiled Iraqis, mainly returning to the country from Iran (Sassoon 2011: 11). As in the Battle for Fallujah in 2004, entire cities were often besieged after residents called for the Americans to leave and began to organize their own army against the occupation. In this particular case, almost the entire city of Fallujah was wiped out, hundreds of thousands of people lost their lives, and it was estimated that the same number of people fled to other cities including Baghdad. Civil unrest began to ripple through most of the eighteen Iraqi governorates: against the occupation, between ethnic tribes and against ethnic minorities. This period, particularly between 2006 and 2008, saw a new pattern of displacement that changed, and continues to change, the social demographics and spatial urban contexts of Iraqi cities. The unrest led to protracted displacement that dissected cities spatially from their 'previously mixed sectarian and ethnic populations', rendering 'internal displacement a semi-feature within Iraq' (Chatty and Mansour 2011: 51). In return, this protracted displacement further contributed to the sense of 'nation-destroying' of which Oula Kadhum speaks in her piece on emigration and displacement and Iraqi nationhood after 2003. In particular, Kadhum (2023: 1) highlights the impact of war and violence on the 'gradual disappearance of many non-Muslim Iraqi minorities' from Iraq through ethnic cleansing and intimidation.

As well as having a 'nation-destroying' effect, these three complex waves and patterns of displacement that ripped across Iraq before and after 2003 also caused a new kind of place-wounding – the rise of informal housing settlements. These settlements continue to blur the boundaries between the urban and the rural – redefining peripheries, borders and edges (both soft and hard) – and they modify cities pushing for gentrification and over-urbanization supported by the lack of planning policies, security and financial support for displacees. Despite each Iraqi government having stated its intention to close all IDP camps and allow more than 4 million Iraqis to return to their homes, the IOM continues to record that the number of internally displaced Iraqis (officially over 1 million), has not decreased with time (Wing 2023). As mentioned above, this figure includes only those registered and residing in official IDP camps across the country, and does not include the ethnically cleansed neighbourhoods across Iraq that remain segregated, nor does it include places that have been abandoned by a portion of their residents where they were once populated with mixed ethnic backgrounds and religions. The informal housing sector in Iraq has only grown since 2003, and continues to expand the edges between neighbourhoods, stretch the borders of cities and claim empty land, public areas and even agricultural land. Between the Iraqi Ministry of Migration and Displacement's figure of 1.2 million IDPs, and the Ministry of Planning's figure of 3.2 million residing in informal settlements (also known as 'encroachment areas'), housing is one of the biggest crises in Iraq. Usually, these encroachments also tend to occupy public land, abandoned public buildings (especially those associated with the Ba'ath Party), disused military bases and grounds, squatters' land and abandoned agricultural land. These encroachment areas, technically known in colloquial Iraqi Arabic as *ashwaiaat*, are also known as *hawasim* by locals 'in a sarcastic reference to Saddam Hussein's naming of the last battle of Baghdad the "Battle of Al-Hawasim" ("The Decisive Battle") [which] led to the occupation of Iraq in one month's time, while Saddam's propaganda insisted that the invasion would lead the US forces to commit suicide at the gates of Baghdad' (Al-Jaffal 2022). In fact, *hawasim* became the phrase used after 2003 referring to any act of looting or what is being looted from the state.

After Baghdad, Basra is home to the second largest number of informal housing settlements in the country. These settlements lack planning and basic infrastructure in the form of sanitation, electricity, health services and so on, yet they continue sporadically to increase their space in tandem with a sharp increase in population sizes. There is a stark contrast here between the high expectations of a city that, thanks to its oil, should be one of the richest in the world and its reality, in which an estimated 20 per cent of the city's population reside in some of the largest informal settlements in the country (Al-Kaabi 2019). This fact is what brings Basra forward in this section as a particularly pertinent case study. Not only is Basra oil rich, but it is also rich in cultural heritage: Old Basra boasts one of Iraq's first canal systems, complete with lagoons, gondolas and footpaths. The 'Venice of the East' also boasts traditional *shanasheel* buildings and houses with balconies and carved wooden-screened windows. However, much of the Old Basra has deteriorated over the years and has been passed over in favour of under-resourced modern developments (Mumtaz and Thung 2020: 42). Just as Baghdad has undergone waves of master planning strategies within the housing sector in the 1950s and 1970s, with the likes of Frank Lloyd Wright and Doxiadis (Pyla 2008), so too has Basra undergone changes under PolServis (Mumtaz and Thung 2020: 16). Much of the urban growth of cities across Iraq since then has followed similar initial plans. Basra grew into generous plots of land from the south of Shatt Al-Arab up towards the north, confined between the Tigris and Euphrates. These were later expanded further, west of the two rivers and north of Shatt Al-Arab, situating the old part of the city in the heart of Basra.

A UN-Habitat report on the urban profiling of Basra reveals that the rise of informal settlements in the city from 2003 onwards has surfaced owing to several conditions. These are predominantly connected with: the 'relative success of the city', incentivizing people to move in from poorer areas; unreliable legal planning systems and building legislation; the failure of construction industries to adequately plan and respond to supply and demand for housing; and lastly the 'willingness and ability of lower-income households to invest in housing and other amenities even under threat of expulsion and demolition' (Mumtaz and Thung 2020: 30). As well as being the largest and most advanced city in the south of the country, attracting incomers for economic reasons, Basra's location also affects its already stretched resources and requirements for housing. The city has had to deal with several waves of displacement and exodus from other parts of the south, from inside Basra itself and from Iraqis returning from nearby Iran. The settlements appeared everywhere: on empty public and private land, in between existing neighbourhoods with generous plot sizes, and in agricultural lands to the west and north of the city that had been abandoned owing to drought, deforestation and desertification (Figure 4.6). In the following interviews with two native Basrawis, we learn of the overwhelming numbers of new residents, the change in demographics after the ethnic cleansing between 2004 and 2008, the deterioration of public services (Merkel et al. 2021: 142), and, as Sabah (2022) puts it, 'the absence of cleanliness from the city'. Sabah notes that this lack of cleanliness is actually one of the more painful visible manifestations of the disruption in the city. She recalls the quick succession of land grabs that followed the fall of the regime in 2003:

> We live very close to the University of Basra students' accommodation. We saw how these buildings were emptied out of poor students' possessions. People we have never seen before went in and stripped the entire building. To this day, this building is squatted by people not only poor and displaced, but by people who are profiting and potentially renting their homes while squatting elsewhere in the city. *Hawasim* became the term used to describe governmental and public buildings that people have squatted in since 2003. Other parts of the city that were empty lands – people came and built quick one-storey block buildings and populated the areas. These are also called *Hawasim*.
>
> (Sabah 2022)

Iraqis had been grappling with housing scarcity for decades before 2003, but this shortage was certainly exacerbated by the invasion, its consequences and the complex patterns of displacement that followed. It would be misleading to suggest that the Iraqi government have had no plans to deal with the situation, but those plans have been largely unsuccessful, owing to a lack of appreciation of the full, complex picture and an inability to form partnerships across multiple sectors (private, public and NGOs). Further to this, governmental bodies often make seemingly small decisions that are not well thought through, or express knee-jerk reactions to novel situations, all of which have unseen repercussions. Add this to the fact that Iraq has had eight different governments and seven prime ministers between 2003 and 2023 (Hadad 2022), and thus plans are often abandoned, altered or affected by corruption. Alongside the various pledges and unrealistic time frames that have been proposed over the years by different governments (Moussa 2022), there have also been plans to provide financial incentives for returnees, and to expand cities by building on and outside their green belts. In her interview, Professor Ghada Alslik presents one of the major problems facing the architecture profession, situated as it is between three entangled conditions: internal displacement, shortage of housing and expansion of cities. She states:

FIGURE 4.6 Informal housing settlement in Basra, 2022.
Courtesy Abrar Wadi.

Iraq faced a big housing problem with internally displaced people, and to solve that problem we built camps. Yet we were then faced with the question of time and the eventuality of these camps. As people started to return to their cities, we started thinking of alternative functions for these camps, instead of neglect or demolitions. People returned to their cities and found their homes destroyed or severely damaged, so we had to come up with a plan that first assesses the damage of people's homes and then provides solutions for them accordingly. Our research used a traffic-light system that responded to the level of damage in cities and people's housing. This was, for example, used in Mosul, where the green light was designated for the buildings with little damage, the yellow was for considerable damage and red was for dangerous damage. People who were found to be in red coded buildings were designated new housing in alternative districts on the outskirts of cities, which allowed for flexible growth. Some of the camps nearer to cities were suggested to become part of the urban fabric, designated for low-income housing. Some were suggested to become tourist cabins. But also public and cultural buildings and complexes, such as Baghdad University campus, temporarily hosted internally displaced people, especially from Fallujah during the Battle of Fallujah in 2004.

Another side of the response was in the form of informal settlements [*ashwaiaat*]. These are different to the camps that the state built or the temporary camps that popped up in and around public spaces and buildings. These were people's own responses to providing housing for themselves after their homes were destroyed or there were cities and villages they could not return to, for example, the ex-Rasheed camp or ex-military sites, and also the old Baghdadi houses on the front of the riverside in Abu Nouas. The latter were expensive houses, which were abandoned by their owners, who fled the country. Later they were occupied by displaced people, who settled inside. These were all solutions that had a major impact on the urban life inside cities and changed the ways cities in Iraq looked to this day.

There is no national housing strategy in the country, even though we have desperately needed one since 2003. The estimated shortage of 3 million units has driven people to build on agricultural land or dissect and divide a building or an area of a district into smaller houses, which is also illegal, just like the *Ashwaiaat* are considered illegal. Once people manage to link these self-built houses to electricity and water, they settle in the area for longer periods of time. The problem with shortage and self-built housing is that, as professional bodies or governments, you cannot provide for them otherwise. So, the only way forward is to allow them to stay by changing the land use into housing to be able to provide them with better services, schools and health care. Obviously, this was one of the solutions which improved the lives of people, yet with further expansions of housing into the green belt around Baghdad, this has aggravated the climate and contributed to the increase of the dust storms that we are seeing now.

In short, there is no big overarching strategy. Each municipality is dealing with it in their own way and doing what they can to provide for the people. We in the main committee in the municipality of Baghdad have also encouraged the multi-storey housing projects, which have been seen as not the right type of living for Iraqis, but that is not true – these housing projects are now providing people with flats and places of dwelling. Potentially, these housing projects can be a solution to stop the grabbing of land and changing its use from agricultural into housing. Eventually, this solution will not solve the problem completely but it will certainly help bring down the house prices and plug a hole in the estimated housing shortage across the country.

The municipality also introduced satellite cities like the Bismayah, to the south-east of Baghdad, as new cities adjacent to large cities. The problem with these new development cities is that they need centres – commercial, industrial or a university – in order for the people who work there to settle there. Now, people from Baghdad who have bought flats there are suffering from the lack of transportation links. But there are solutions, so, for example, if Baghdad could speed up the work on the tram or metro line systems, this issue could be resolved. However, when I was consulted on this issue by the Ministry of Housing, I suggested that instead of going ahead with building satellite cities as

> part of the research study called 'New Cities' [continuing a project that began in the 1970s], I suggested developing and investing in the villages and countryside areas instead. These have their own way of life, history and people, who already need attention.
>
> (Alslik 2022)

The Ministry of Planning has approved seventeen new residential cities across the country. Some, like Bismaya, are located at the edges of cities, with others such as Al-Rafeel infringing onto agricultural land; nevertheless, these sites contribute very little to the overwhelming housing crisis in Iraq (H. Ibrahim 2022). Over the two decades since 2003, the Iraqi National Investment Commission has invested billions of dollars in multiple housing projects, some of which have stalled for various reasons, while others have resumed development in phases. Most of these developments are thought of as stand-alone, independent city-like spaces, with little thought having gone into their connectivity with main city centres, where higher education and other public sector institutions are located. This is compounded by the issue of rising house prices, which means that the poor are again priced out of renting or buying in these new cities. Moreover, Iraqis are reluctant to uproot and move themselves and their families to these new structures because they lack employment opportunities, adequate planning and foresight in terms of their intended demographic (Al-Jawari et al. 2020: 4). Another hazard to consider is the issue that regular electricity blackouts, one of the major continuing problems in the country, despite its backup generators, would trap elderly and disabled people living in multi-storey buildings. From a socio-spatial perspective, these cities not only are designed as stand-alones but also are built to house people without regard for their place in society and desired lifestyle, which usually requires large families to live near to one another. This is a planning oversight that could potentially deepen feelings of resentment and encourage sectarianism. Kearney (2016: 2–3) reminds us that there are three different actors that emerge from 'wounding events': 'the perpetrators of violence, recipients of harm and those who witness the events and their calamitous fallout'. This is certainly articulated with clarity in this section's first case study, concerning the Yazidi genocide. In the case of informal settlements, however, this is less plain to see. The latter type of place-wounding is far more complex an issue to untangle, and these new cities only add to that complexity. In these cases, the place-wounding and violence that occurs is protracted in a palimpsestic way and inflicted onto place – both rural and urban.

The new cities across the country therefore only add to the place-wounding triggered by the different waves of displacement across time. These cities clash with, and are in complete contrast to, the informal settlements that sprout from the centres and edges of cities. Their presence creates even more soft borders of blurred spatiality between rural–urban structures, and disrupts the social make-up of neighbourhoods, creating wedges and cracks between the rich and the poor, between ethnicities and between people's histories and imaginaries. In the absence of a national urban strategy and policy, the Kurdish region has invested in its own studies so that it may better understand the complexity of urban growth in the north and be able to respond at a local level (Jarah et al. 2019). They have also learned from research on urban sprawl and the definition of 'new forms of rurality' in a Mediterranean context (Salvia et al. 2018) and elsewhere in the region (Alnsour 2016). This kind of nuanced and dialogic approach to the ways in which informal settlements are sprouting, developing and expanding could yield a more sensitive set of strategies for the future – strategies that can be led by local actors through everyday urban–rural imaginaries. These imaginaries are 'cognitive and somatic' images that people carry within them concerning the places they inhabit and their everyday lives (Huyssen 2008: 3).

Craig Larkin's (2010) work describes the urban imaginary as a methodological tool for urban development in the context of Beirut's post-traumatic landscape, after it witnessed colonization, civil war and economic disaster. Larkin (2010: 416) connects urban imaginaries to memory and space, stating that analysis of this type of context 'must take account of the city's immaterial sites, spaces, and absences, which shape the territory of the imagination and mediate daily urban encounters'. In this sense, sites of memory, whether traumatic or nostalgic, and their protracted history that overlaps with their presence, whether material or immaterial, constitute real collective fragments of the everyday. These memories and their imaginaries are engaged in a constant process of healing and harming the place-wounded sites and contexts. They do this through acts of place-(re)making, whether in the form of constructing or rebuilding the so-called informal settlements, or via other acts of resistance and mobility as people seek refuge after forced displacement.

Temporal ruptures

The final section in this chapter uses two case studies to explore how the temporalities involved in negotiating refuge through rupture have impacted both the spatial and social structures within cities. The first case study examines the impact of the concrete blast walls that were installed around the Green Zone and some parts of the Red Zone during the sectarian violence that peaked between 2006 and 2008. The second sheds light onto the 2019 October (Tishreen) revolution, focusing on Tahrir Square in Baghdad. Taken together, these are both protracted yet pivotal events in the recent history of the country, and they remain in the collective memory of Iraqis, demonstrating two very different structures of power dynamics. In the case of the blast walls, the power structure embodies religious and ethnic divides, where trauma is inflicted through sectarian and ethnic divisions, changing the urban make-up of Iraqi cities (particularly Baghdad) forever. In the Tishreen Movement, the power structure is one of people's resistance to oppressive forms of power and their championing of secular justice and creative agency. This movement came with a big promise of hope for a changing, secular Iraq, presenting real Iraqi imaginaries for a better life, but it was soon crushed by violent government retaliation and the outbreak of the deadly Covid-19 pandemic. In both case studies, the focus here is on the difference in temporality between the short-lived events and the protracted spatial ruptures that resulted from them. They furthermore assert Till's (2012) proposition that the geographies of power and oppression continue to influence the everyday urban and social structures and relations within cities.

For four decades prior to 2003, Iraq was governed by a centralized power structure within Baghdad, which functioned as a top-down dictatorship. In an arrangement not dissimilar to this, the US-led Coalition Provisional Authority (CPA), which the UN Security Council pronounced to be the occupier of Iraq on 22 May 2003, also centralized the locality of its power (Al-Ali 2014). The Saddam regime's former insulated base of power thus became the new CPA base, and with that the Green Zone in the centre of Baghdad was born. Prior to 2003, ordinary Iraqis were prevented from entering the area that housed the main presidential palace, as well as other governmental and parliament buildings. Habituated to this lack of access, physical or visible, into this secluded area in Baghdad, Iraqis did not feel any differently about the hostility of the place when it became the CPA base, also known as the Green Zone. Iraqi interviewees for this book recall feeling a sense of familiarity with the types of violence and fear that emerged after the fall of the Saddam regime. Shuker (2022) recalls:

> Trauma is in the memories of the incidents and their places. But if I was to choose something or a place that reminds me of trauma, that would be my grandparents' house, which is very close to Zaitoon Street, very close to Zawraa Park and Sahat Al-Ihtfalat [Sahat Al-Ihtfalat means Celebrations Square in Arabic]. It is also where politicians had their mansions. I remember that, after the fall of the regime and the period of looting, lots of these houses were looted. My father, uncle and I walked across the road to see inside, after the looting. I remember that, for a very long time – these houses no one could walk past, let alone see inside –they were fortified, yet they were so close, like neighbours. To see these hateful places destroyed and empty was an ugly sight that made me feel sick. Now, just looking at these houses from the outside brings back that memory and makes me nauseous. It symbolizes the cycle of violence that the country has witnessed, of people rising to the top, abusing all that power, and then falling and being ripped apart by others, who then repeated that same cycle.

This cycle of violence was even more pronounced after the appearance of concrete T-blast walls, which insulated 9 square kilometres of central Baghdad around the Green Zone. Construction companies such as the Erbil-based Company 77 in the Kurdish region, were manufacturing 300 to 400 units a day to send to Baghdad (Ahmed 2018). In the years between 2004 and 2007, after the expulsion of Al-Qaeda operations across the country, Company 77 reported that demand for these T-blast units outstripped supply. Soon after the instalment of these around the Green Zone, further T-shaped concrete blast walls sprouted around other governmental buildings, hospitals and, later, residential neighbourhoods. While ostensibly, these walls were introduced for security reasons, they in fact served to fuel divisions and sectarianism within the country, which developed alongside the CPA's ongoing policies, including 'de-Baathification', demobilization (dismantling the police and the Iraqi Army) (Pfiffner 2010), and alienating Sunnis from the decision table. These policies opened up historic wounds between certain Sunni and Shia communities that, soon after, led to a full-blown civil war between 2003 and 2008 that changed the social and urban structures of cities, particularly Baghdad (Damluji 2010). Only five years after the 2003 invasion, tens of thousands of civilians had lost their lives and over 4 million people had been displaced by the urban warfare and ethnic cleansing that took place between neighbourhoods (Amnesty International 2008). Neighbourhoods that had been mixed in the past were all cleared in favour of Sunni or Shia dominance, which further compounded the internal displacement, putting pressures on land and resources. The acts of informal land-grabbing and dissection of existing plots that happened in Sadr city became widespread during this time, and continue to this day on a larger scale across Baghdad.

Iraqis received these blast walls with resentment, seeing them as methods of occupation and colonization similar to those used in the historic Sykes–Picot Agreement imposed on the region by the French and the British after the First World War. These military tactics work on the principle of 'divide and conquer', and are the first glaring signs of occupation. Toby Dodge suggests that this same strategy was used by ISIS later on in their own military advancement throughout Iraq. He notes that, 'Within the Arab political discourse, "Sykes-Picot" refers to both the conquest of the Middle East by Britain during the war and the covert attempts to retain control over Arab lands in the aftermath of the conflict through the division of the region into separate states' (Dodge 2014: 7). The warfare practice of installing blast walls across Baghdad thus quickly became a symbol of foreign conquest, control and occupation, triggering a series of systemic failures in the country that allowed lawlessness and sectarianism to take over society's structures. During this time, multiple checkpoints and security guards were placed at intersections of main roads, enabling the troops to secure and navigate the city, and blocking access between neighbouring areas outside the Green Zone. More blast walls continued to appear in the centre of Baghdad in response to retaliation and organized attacks against the US troops. This created a chasm between the so-called Green Zone and anything outside it in Baghdad, hence it being known as the Red Zone. By the end of 2003, the centre of Baghdad had been completely dissected by barriers, concrete walls of all shapes and sizes, and checkpoints that debilitated Iraqis' everyday movements, further deepening their negative feeling towards their occupiers (Rashid and Alobaydi 2015). The occupying forces were required to operate from within the boundaries of these walls, ultimately creating a city-within-a-city complete with uninterrupted electricity, a hospital, restaurants, leisure facilities, housing (previously belonging to the Saddam regime's ministers, etc.), taxi drivers, cleaners, cooks and so on. This constituted a fully functioning urban environment for the troops and the international community associated with them, such as journalists and UN personnel.

As the Green Zone grew in radius, its walls created a political, socio-spatial wedge between those who were protected inside, and those living under lawlessness outside. Furthermore, these walls provided urban localities with spaces and opportunities for waves of violence, demonstrations, protests, and religious and social events to emerge (Chandrasekaran 2008). In other words, they became simultaneously places of violence and refuge. Contrary to the luxury lifestyle inside the Green Zone, Baghdad's Red Zone faced a lack of electricity, unmaintained sewage systems, interrupted journeys, dissected urban spaces, and pavements congested with large generators and litter (Al-Naimi 2020). In 2016, I published an article about the complex and sudden manoeuvring of these walls for security reasons, and how Iraqis responded to these daily disruptions through equally complex and creative negotiations and interventions (Murrani 2016). The article visually mapped the walling strategy across thirteen neighbourhoods in Baghdad on both sides of the river Tigris – Karkh and Rusafa – revealing the residents' ingenious and creative ways of coping as they utilized these walls as a method of resistance (Murrani 2016: 191).

As these walls were only ever intended to be used as a temporary measure, a large number of them were taken down across Baghdad after the sectarian violence in 2017 tapered off. The walls around the Green Zone, however, still remain, twenty years after the 2003 invasion. Just as the Baghdadi urban and planning structures have continued to affect Iraqis negatively, so too have the traces of the walls within Baghdad's neighbourhoods had a lasting and damaging impact on the society and its fragile structures of ethnic diversity. In their work on the political geographies of walls, Karen Till and colleagues address the lasting impact of these kinds of violent infrastructures beyond their material and physical presence. With examples from Jerusalem, Berlin, Belfast, Nicosia and the US–Mexican border, they discuss state power in relation to place-based sovereignty, where 'creating divisions between people is a walling strategy' (Till et al. 2013: 54). In the context of Baghdad, specifically, Bret Windhauser (2022) analyses how the walling strategy and the presence of manned checkpoints assisted in allowing counter-occupiers and other non-state powers to surface, who in turn made use of the placelessness these walls and checkpoints created, which later led to the divisions within Baghdadi neighbourhoods that culminated in civil war between 2006 and 2008. In the following quote, from the perspective of a US war veteran who experienced the war and occupation of Iraq in 2003, we can see that the shadows cast by these walls reached further than the urban structures of the city:

> As walls go up around the world, between rich and poor, between military and civilian, between Americans and everyone else, what we face isn't merely a division of space, but a division in the mind, a deepening segregation of the world into Us and Them that will only increase violence, tension and strife, especially in the face of mounting resource depletion and environmental crises; as in Baghdad, the drive for immediate security brings long-term insecurity, and separation breeds alienation.
>
> (Scranton 2007: 291)

The lack of accurate and definitive geographical maps that trace the walling strategy in Baghdad between 2003 and the present day is evidence of their intended temporality. This, in itself, played an important part in developing what Yi-Fu Tuan (1979) terms 'Landscapes of Fear'. The landscapes of fear, in this case, were sprouting from different corners in different neighbourhoods, main streets and footpaths (Figure 4.7). The temporality of these walls and checkpoints brought with it high tensions and intimidation – something that was clearly marked by the ethnic and religious cracks that deepened in Iraqi society, particularly between Sunni and Shia powers, both historical and emergent. The interviewees from Baghdad recall how this sense of temporality paralysed the city during the years of sectarian violence between 2006 and 2008. Shuker (2022) remembers a moment from 2007 in which she casts these structures of violence as a continuing existential threat that overwhelmed the city's social and urban contexts. The city was segregated into enclaves, separating Sunni from Shia Iraqis. At checkpoints, Iraqis had to undergo ID checks so that guards could establish their religious background, and those who did not conform or belong to the identity of the overtaken neighbourhood were shot dead. Shuker (2022) explains:

> We were in a taxi, and about to approach a checkpoint. We did not know whether it was an army, militia or police checkpoint, because they are intentionally ambiguous, so we did not know whether it was a Sunni or Shia checkpoint. Regardless of the fact that I am an atheist, and so is my father, and my mother was barely religious, our surname is the ultimate Shia name. I remember my mother holding my hand. I was completely calm, ready for it to end, just no emotional reaction whatsoever. At the checkpoint, they asked for our IDs. We

FIGURE 4.7 The walling strategy in Baghdad. a) Blast walls segregating neighbourhoods in the centre, 2009. ALI YUSSEF/AFP via Getty Images. b) Blast walls around a market, 2010.
AHMAD AL-RUBAYE/AFP via Getty Images.

> just had to be honest, because you cannot really predict what their religious allegiance will be. It was, as it happens, a Shia checkpoint.

These moments shook the lives of so many Iraqis. Hasan (2022) recalls:

> 2006 and 2007 were the darkest years I have ever witnessed in Iraq. Our area, Al-Mahmoudiya [south of Baghdad], was a mixed neighbourhood. It got dominated by the Shia and the ethnic cleansing reached our next-door neighbours, who were Sunnis. Overnight, a street next to another street in the same neighbourhood started heavy shelling and rocket attacks on each other. We lived in a battleground of blood, forced displacement and looting. I am from a mixed background myself: my mother is Sunni and my father is Shia.
>
> Violence took different forms in the neighbourhood, not only kidnappings of young men who just happened to be from an opposite ethnic background to the Shia militia in control at the time, but also in the form of stealing cars that belonged to Sunnis and selling them. Our neighbourhood also was close to one of Saddam's weapons factories. These were looted during the early days after the fall of the regime, so the militia was fully equipped. During that time, a militant walking in the street fully equipped with weapons was a common scene.

The temporality of the landscapes of violence and fear drawn by these walls continued to create deeper wedges between ordinary Iraqis and the subsequent Iraqi governments and ruling classes in the country. These violent landscapes transcended material geographies and, twenty years on, have become ingrained in Iraqis' minds, fuelling anger and dismay. Generations who were born in the late 1990s and early 2000s have seen nothing but brutal violence and the deterioration of basic standards of living in the country. In what she calls 'ethnosectarian separation', Ali (2023: 4) emphasizes the spatial, material and social impact that the blast walls have had on poorer neighbourhoods in Baghdad in terms of class and political divisions, limited access to wealth and public areas in the centre to a network of people with close ties to the ruling government who held special badges. Both the fortified Green Zone and the corniche on one side of the river Tigris were two such privatized and limited areas.

This brings us to the second and final case study of this chapter, the protracted violence that led to the 2019 Tishreen Movement that was eventually crushed by Iraqi riot police and later muted by the Covid-19 pandemic. This revolution was led by frustrated, poor and unemployed youth who had witnessed, for too long, families and individuals struggling under corruption and the exploitation of Iraq's depleting resources. Alongside the protesters in Lebanon and Sudan, Iraqi youth joined the struggle against their government, calling for better employment opportunities, public sector services (particularly health and education), and an end to sectarian and foreign involvement in Iraqi politics. What makes the Tishreen Movement of 2019 a unique case study in this book is the fact that it constitutes the ultimate spatial manifestation of counter-violent forms of resistance, creativity and agency. The protest began peacefully and creatively on 1 October 2019, with participants marching towards Tahrir Square (tahrir means 'liberty' in Arabic) reading and singing poems and songs by Iraqi youth, who were calling for liberation from oppression, for a better life and for a homeland (Alkhudary 2022).

To begin with, the youth that initiated the movement were mainly young men from low-income Shia neighbourhoods in Baghdad, including street vendors and tuk-tuk drivers. Soon, however, they were joined by Iraqis from all walks of society, from different ethnicities and backgrounds, including union members, students and advocacy groups (Ali 2023). The complex geographies that unfolded in and around Tahrir Square in the centre of Baghdad in October 2019 were triggered by years of ethnosectarian and class separation. The youth was in revolt against this imposed socio-spatial separation, and they responded by showing the ruling government that the people yearned for a unified country beyond its manipulated religious and political divisions. In terms of strategy, it made sense for the first initial protest to take place in clear sight of the Green Zone. They had learned from failed attempts before, however (between 2011 and 2018), that being too close to the Green Zone's blast walls would not help the revolution, owing to the difficulties in penetrating the high walls and their exposure to snipers ordered to subdue any uprising. In 2019, then, the October protesters chose to march towards the iconic Tahrir Square for its symbolic value as a place of liberation, and went on to occupy the derelict, fourteen-storey Turkish Restaurant building, which overlooks the Green Zone across the river Tigris. Hasan (2022), one of the interviewees for this book, recalls the initial starting point of the revolution:

> These protesters were young men in their late teens and early twenties, who have had to live a compromised life for their entire being in this world. Calling for employment opportunities, healthcare services and basic living needs, topped their agenda. I remember even my brothers used to go there for the entertainment – there was music and poetry, art in all its forms, acting and performances. Young women and girls were not allowed to go there by their parents (because they were worried about their safety) but they did, and their voices were equal to men's voices.

Built in 1983, the Turkish Restaurant building was originally intended for premium office space, with parking at the ground and basement levels, and a restaurant on the top floor. One of the tallest buildings in the centre of the city, it was bombed in the First Gulf War in 1991 and then again in 2003 during the

US-led invasion of Iraq. From then onwards, the building remained derelict, being used over the years by Iraqi snipers and security forces. The significance of the building therefore lies in its history, as it had previously been used to take down protesters during, for example, the 2011 uprising (Mousa 2022). In October 2019, then, the building was still being used tactically, but this time in a peaceful way. As it was situated opposite Tahrir Square, the building had an unusual perspective overlooking both the Green Zone and the bridges that connected it to the Karkh bank of the river and the rest of Baghdad on the Rusafa bank. The location of this building and its occupation by the protesting youth made it the centre of the revolution, allowing it to connect and respond to what was happening on the ground, both in and around the square (Alkhudary 2022). In a matter of days, its occupiers had extended electricity throughout the building, established running water through a pulley system and filled it with cultural expression through murals, events, exhibitions, poetry readings, music, singing and dancing. There remains a dedicated archive titled 'Baghdad Tahrir Art', supported by Germany's Federal Ministry of Foreign Affairs, containing videos, murals and posters that were created in the square during the days of the movement (Saad, Rady and Zohdi 2019). The protesters also covered the building with an Iraqi flag – another symbol of the revolution that became a contested commodity, as it was associated closely with protesters and those who supported the Tishreen Movement. Hasan (2022) recalls: 'The first thing that went over the building was a large Iraqi flag. This sent a message for a united, civil Iraq, calling for Iran to stop meddling in Iraq's politics. Protesters were banned from carrying the Iraqi flag. In fact, they were targeted by the authority if seen carrying the Iraqi flag. Cynically, the Iraqi flag was associated with the revolution.'

In addition to this architectural symbol of the revolution, the Tishreen Movement embraced multiple material spatialities of refuge and imaginaries of a better, more unified Iraq (Figure 4.8). Just beneath the building, tents appeared on the periphery of the square with stalls selling water, Coca Cola (used to wash the tear gas from protesters' eyes during clashes with the authorities), ice cream and food. As days went by, the mothers of several protesters turned up with large cooking pots and washing buckets, helping with the protesters' basic needs. Charities and individuals also arrived on the square to donate blankets and clothes, junior doctors and nurses tended to the wounded, and tuk-tuk drivers (another symbol of the revolution) ferried wounded protestors back to the square from the front line on the Jamahiriya Bridge (connecting the Green Zone to Tahrir Square). These tuk-tuk drivers were predominantly young men from poorer backgrounds, born after the 2003 invasion. They were usually uneducated and, unable to afford a taxi, had opted for the cheaper option of owning a tuk-tuk to help support their families. Commenting on these tuk-tuk drivers during the days of the revolution, Hasan (2022) states: 'These young men grew up learning that women are a different species, have no voice, get to serve their families, but

FIGURE 4.8 The 2019 Tishreen (October) Movement, Baghdad 2019. a) The Turkish Restaurant building in Tahrir Square. SABAH ARAR/AFP via Getty Images. b) The Tahrir Square murals and the iconic tuk-tuk.
Erin Trieb/Getty Images News via Getty Images.

this changed on the square and these young men accepted this freedom and equal rights across all genders and groups.' During these 2019 protests, we can see Till's (2012) 'place-based ethics of care' manifesting itself in urban centres as a form of social ecology between place, time and affect that protesters negotiated, lived and imagined.

Tahrir Square in Baghdad was witness to over a million heroes and heroines, participating on an equal footing, from the brave protesters on the front line to the people in the square supporting them, to the tuk-tuk drivers manoeuvring nimbly through narrow spaces peppered with rubber bullets and gas canisters. Among the thousands wounded (Alkhudary 2023: 8) was a young activist and poet, Safaa Al Sarai, who died when a gas canister impacted his skull. Safaa became an icon of the revolution, and his death mobilized Iraqis inside and outside Iraq to call for a unified, free country with the famous slogan, '*Nreed watten*' ('We want a country/homeland') (Alkhudary 2022). Although the main protest started in Baghdad, several other southern cities with Shia strongholds followed suit, and also faced the same brutal responses of tear gas and rubber bullets, which killed and wounded thousands. Jotheri (2022) comments on the way the protesters in Hila (Babylon province) managed to create their spaces of refuge:

> They used the main bridge in Hillah. They used Al-Thawra Bridge and the space underneath the bridge, and they halted all traffic around the bridge and claimed that space for the revolution. Concrete walls were brought in, and protesters used them to form a square. They remained there for the duration of the revolution and tribes assisted them with food and clothing as well as tents and shelter. It became a camp for refuge for protesters.

Emerging as the response to, and revolt against, the political and religious partitioning of the country (exacerbated by the blast walls), the 2019 revolution in Iraq produced multiple bodily, material and socio-spatial practices. Ali (2023) eloquently describes this phenomenon as an alternative political imagination for a new social order in Iraq, stating that the narratives and stories that emerged from the revolution:

> … show how in Tahrir Square, people produced a material, discursive and affective space in which they could meet, live together and negotiate an alternative social contract and new codes of conduct, put forward public commons, and experience a different social order. This social order offered an alternative to the militarised, fragmented, privatised and male-dominated social space. It also placed at its centre the most marginalised groups, namely women and the poor, and fostered ways of living a dignified life.

Iraqis continue to negotiate the various temporalities of bodily, material and socio-spatial ruptures that occur within their homes, in different contexts of urban, rural and border spaces. Although the 2019 October Revolution showed that there was a strong appetite among Iraqis for positive change, the full dream did not materialize. Between 2019 and 2021, the movement was slowly paralyzed by 'landscapes of fear' (Tuan 1979) that took the form of imposed curfews, state-organized kidnappings and killings of activists, and brutal public attacks by riot police on the streets of Iraq. Responding to my question about how she feels about the 2019 revolution now, Wadi (2022), a feminist activist from Basra, states:

> This is an existential question; I sometimes wonder whether the revolution can emerge again or not, and my answer would be no. This is for two reasons: the brutality of the state towards the protesters was unparalleled, and people have lost confidence in protesters managing to make a difference. Alone, we will not be able to make a change. A large number of protesters left the country, too. I feel it is difficult now to bring the same energy back.

Accompanying the political and social unrest in Iraq, of course, came the Covid-19 pandemic; yet Iraqis are now also facing one of this planet's most challenging problems – the climate crisis. A recent policy report by Hamzeh Hadad (2023), for the European Council of Foreign Relations, highlights ways in which Europe can support Iraq through economic crisis, corruption, security challenges and climate change. The policy paper suggests that through its history of colonization, imperialism and capitalism, the West has contributed significantly to the deterioration in services, infrastructures and capacities in climate-vulnerable countries such as Iraq, Syria and Yemen. Take, for example, the significant health problems and the rise in young lung cancer patients living around oil refineries, thanks to 'gas flaring in Iraqi oil fields through companies such as BP and Eni' (Hadad 2023).

Different climate crises have the effect of collapsing and overlapping together, causing multiple temporal ruptures across material, geographical and socio-spatial dimensions. They have changed the shape of Iraqi landscapes (through drying up the two rivers and their lakes and marshes), contributed to changes in indigenous practices (through climate displacement within and outside the country) and furthermore put pressures on housing within cities and urban centres. The threat of multiple ruptures from the impact of climate crises onto the country will result in a multiplicity of spatial practices of place-wounding not dissimilar to that produced by war and violence. If we can learn lessons about spatiality from past experiences, this would be instrumental in helping Iraqis to navigate and negotiate future crises. In a brief article, Shuker (2023) identifies how the impact of climate change in Iraq is a gendered one. She highlights that women of all ages are the most affected section of society, stating that: 'no climate understanding or climate action in Iraq is complete without understanding how the climate impacts women's well-being and resource access and without including women in the conversation and the decision-making process' (Shuker 2023). In this section, the concept of place-wounding embraced a temporality of multiple ruptures, which collectively and simultaneously form a series of processes and products of violence and resistance that continue to enact themselves in time. In doing so, these processes negotiate different forms of spatial practices that work towards providing a just spatiality of refuge, agency and place-making in the face of war, violence and climate crises.

CONCLUSION: A MANIFESTO FOR STRUCTURES OF REFUGE IN SPATIAL JUSTICE

Rupturing Architecture delves into the spatial practices in Iraq that emerge amid war and violence, and unravels the architectural transformations that occur at the intimate, domestic, urban and transient spaces of refuge. This exploration moves between fixed sites and mobile spaces, highlighting the unique in-betweenness of mobility as an integral part of the multiplicity of refuge spaces. The book illuminates the many complex, nonlinear narratives that are embedded within each kind of rupture, and captures the acts of place-making, agency and resistance that occur in the face of trauma. Drawing on an array of case studies from Iraq's recent past, and enriched by the memories of the resilient Iraqis who experienced these events, *Rupturing Architecture* offers an academic discourse on the dynamics of spatial practices in times of trauma, underscoring the power of human adaptability and imagination, the everyday creativity, as people seek meaningful refuge amid their protracted struggles and displacements.

To navigate the socio-political terrain of Iraq is to chart a dynamic, constantly changing map marked by colonial, national and international borders and influences. As such, the nation's heterogeneity resists easy categorizations and defies attempts to label it within conventional geographic paradigms. Iraq's identity is woven from multiple, diverse ethnic, cultural and religious threads, placed against a backdrop of historical struggle. Hence, any attempt at delineating or defining Iraq's dimensions should honour its complexity and embrace its diversity. This is a principle that I have attempted to uphold in the grounded locality of the stories and projects discussed in this book. The fluidity of Iraq's map, too, is compounded by a nonlinearity of various spatial scales, perspectives and 'difference making' (Stanley 2009). Equally important to acknowledge are the diverse powers shaped by local and global influences, which situate the spatial practices of these impacts relationally, inviting a critical dialogue on their origin and context. When we traverse the geographical spectrum from north to south, east to west, and back again, we must be aware of how these local and global scales and perspectives interact with the spatial practices in question.

Through its feminist, postcolonial and post-structuralist lens, this book explores complex layers of spatial knowledge in the form of a palimpsest, using textual analysis, storytelling through interviews, case studies, counter-mapping and visual narratives. Such a multimodal approach produces a vivid tapestry of disruption, negotiation and resistance that collectively sheds light on the ruptured spaces of refuge sought and created by Iraqis across the past two decades. The narratives within the work as a whole articulate the transformative potential of humanity's spatial struggle with trauma, emphasizing the indomitable resilience and creativity of Iraqis in the face of war and violence. They further transcend conventional understandings of space, place and built environment, bringing to light the multifaceted potentialities of spatial practice, and help to produce a manifesto for spatial justice. The analysis culminates in a resounding conclusion that underscores the power of place-based research and person-centred approaches to memory-work in shaping spatial imaginaries and future architectural responses to war and violence. The book illuminates the inherent opportunities that lie within ruptured and violated spaces of refuge, and re-envisions these sites as catalysts for producing a manifesto of differentiation, an equitable and just spatiality.

Propelled by empirical fieldwork and a blend of critical reflexive and performative practices, the conceptual explorations in this book serve to expand our understandings within the field of spatial justice (Soja 2010) in architecture, especially within the context of the Middle East. Its insights also reach into other fields, such as human geography and sociology, and work to elucidate the various complexities of home, domesticity, urbanity and their associated geotraumas (Pain 2021). The discussion further illuminates the role of memory-work in post-war and conflict urban studies, critically examining three scales of spatiality and their in-betweenness in relation to time as a fundamental driver of knowledge. By situating the dynamism of rupture at the heart of the process of producing refuge, we can advance a fresh approach to spatial justice, which is both deeply rooted in social realities and projected towards the designing of future refuge structures in post-war and conflict environments. The approach leverages collective memory, as well as people's lived and felt experiences, as they navigate the making and remaking of their lived and imagined environments. Equally, the approach is driven by an ethics of reflexivity, which brings forth a plurality of views (from the ground upwards) into structures of refuge. This place-based research as a practice culminates in a manifesto of spatial justice that seeks to reshape critical architectural discourse in a manner that is just, inclusive and reflective of the multiple layers of lived and felt experience.

This conclusion comprises three salient components: a reconceptualized understanding of architectural trauma; an approach that is performative and methodological, as well as multimodal in its methods; and a manifesto for spatial justice within the field. This exploration stems from an expansive definition of architecture, understood as a process of spatial practice engaging in actions and interventions. In this instance, actions and interventions denote the active and practical expressions of architecture as both political and representational, which, when imagined and appropriated, are negotiated in a dialectic of agency and resistance. A 'politics of scale' (Przybylinski 2023) where scale matters especially in locating 'justice' (Young 2011) through embracing difference within agency. Within the creases of trauma-ridden geographies, the pursuit of refuge morphs into an act of political activism, an embrace of otherness and 'otherwise' (Caruth 1995). This requires us to re-theorize the processes of place-making and remaking within the context of war and violence as making-otherwise. It is in this critical geography that the call for a manifesto for spatial justice becomes analytically important, as it underscores through memory and imagination the urgency of reframing architectural praxis in a manner that is processual, engaging with geographically and spatially induced trauma.

Conceptual findings

In this research, we find various fluid concepts taken from architecture, philosophy, spatial humanities, geography and psychology at work within practices, processes and actions. When spaces are ruptured or wounded, they are affected by a multifaceted divergence and dislocation of power, with implications extending from the intimate and local to broader, global, spatial structures. These factors further oscillate and transition, mutually influencing each other. The notions of *rupturing space* and *place-wounding* actively dissect socio-spatial and temporal structures: they embody spatial trauma, violence and destruction, while concurrently participating in ceaseless dialogues of creativity and imagination in the creation of refuge spaces. These concepts fuse together the processes of annihilation of place, on the one hand, and world-making, on the other. The concept of memory is vital in this work, and it is approached through the triadic lens of lived and felt experiences, events and places. So too is the act of using imagination to encompass history and transform everyday creativity into a meta-model that transcends mere product creation. Acts of remembering, storytelling, rupturing, wounding and place-making frame and embody refuge in their own right, causing it to transition from its usual sense as a noun to that of a verb. As with memory, trauma here is treated not as an isolated incident, but as a multi-layered, interconnected experience that can span diverse places and times, as in the work of Cathy Caruth (1995). When memories are provoked, they can present trauma as an ongoing experience, constantly tethered to its origin, while consistently venturing away. The act of revisiting the site of trauma transforms the original experience, and the process of remembering itself can thus initiate unique traumatic experiences.

Guided by this conceptualization, I present the concept of trauma as being located *elsewhere*: a fluid entity that traverses locales, spaces and time frames, and can be felt relationally across different scales, bodies and emotions. Such a perspective unveils the unstable positioning of trauma as it is both bound and unbound by place, and can thus navigate the realms of spatial and temporal experiences through acts of recollection and repositioning. This conceptualization of trauma validates its origin as a product of varied times and spaces, and further confirms its elusive nature as it resists traditional frameworks that try to situate it in place. Another factor at work in the fluid nature of trauma, within the context of Iraq or any other volatile geography, is temporality: in other words, the protractedness of violence as a recurring phenomenon that can be activated in a nonlinear timeline and in diverse locations through acts of remembering, imagining or returning to spaces and architectures of trauma. This approach underscores a topological interpretation of trauma, characterized by its transformational, mutable spatial attributes, in contrast to a topographical approach, which is characterized by localized, measurable qualities. We can see this being lived out in the context of Iraq's recent past: in the intertwining experiences of Iraqis wrestling with survival, domicide and urbicide; in the lives of those who have been forcibly displaced, who are dealing with loss and the prospect of return; and for those in the diaspora, longing for home. As war and violence have a transformative effect on both cities and their inhabitants, any plans for post-trauma rebuilding must factor in these permanent conceptual alterations, which leave indelible marks on communities, their cities and their spaces of refuge.

Refuge, in this context, is a deeply layered and dynamic process of inhabitation, encompassing a rich tapestry of 'more-than-dwelling' (Boano and Astolfo 2020). It incorporates Paolo Boccagni's (2022) concept of 'homing', moving beyond the idea of a fixed space to embody ideas of mobility, the lived experience of being in place, and the continual making and remaking of worlds. This work also makes use of Colette Daiute's (2017) robust articulation of refuge, which meets at the intersection of political, social, spatial, economic and environmental dimensions, creating a complex matrix of participant interactions. These interactions bind together disparate roles, objectives and resources, and serve to construct a 'complex zone of participation' that extends beyond physical space-time (Daiute 2017). If we are to reframe the narrative of refuge, we must transcend the rhetoric that is concerned only with people's basic necessities and adaptability. This calls for a nuanced understanding of the spatiality of refuge – its negotiated materiality and its inherent involvement with social, material and political performativity. In this understanding, 'homing' becomes a political act, not merely a functional necessity or conceptual tool. The multiplicity of spatial practices and acts of homing presented in this research reflect the politics and negotiations intrinsic to the processes of making refuge in the active act of their materialization (Butler 2009), as well as the boundary-making and discursive practices of human and nonhuman relations (Barad 2003). Refuge-seeking becomes the performativity of agency, an 'intra-action', to borrow Karen Barad's (2003) phrase, of 'practices/doings/actions'. Related to the idea of refuge is the notion of domesticity in this work, which expands beyond the conventional scope of family, dwelling, and gendered spaces and practices associated with the home. Like refuge, the notion of domesticity also contains substantial conceptual depth and methodological rigour. Together, they form powerful instruments for the intricate intertwining of knowledge, working to unveil the multiple layers of intimacy inherent within war and violence.

A fundamental finding that stresses the performativity of refuge as a practice, process and action is the striking plurality of its ontological structure, as revealed throughout this study's fieldwork. In the personal narratives that were shared in interviews, we can see four distinct dimensions of refuge, each illuminated and corroborated by different speakers. The first layer is the *intimate*, which conveys both personal and collective recollections of memories, experiences, material objects and the immaterial connotations of refuge. The next layer concerns aspects of *home and domesticity*, capturing numerous ruptures across varied scales and realms of inhabitation. The third layer exposes *urban* dynamics, illustrating the interplay of vertical and horizontal warfare in 'spherical violence', where violence becomes the unfamiliar familiar in everyday life that continuously reshapes places, shifting their boundaries in, around and between new borders of resistance, power and negotiation. Using topological and topographical landscapes, the fourth and final layer explores *the fluidity of human movement* as its own dynamic site of refuge in the realms of forced displacement and the potential for escape.

A crucial revelation within these interviews that added complexity to multiple refuge experiences was the convoluted nature of time. Interviewees used terms such as 'protracted', 'nonlinear', 'volatile' and 'chronic', amongst others, to depict time, which was seen as fundamentally intertwined with place and, subsequently, memory. The regular addition of suffixes such as *-ing* was also not a mere semantic choice but a necessity for speakers to accurately convey the ever-evolving context this research sought to understand. In this way, we can see that the process of crafting refuge was always ongoing, brought about by aggressive assaults on spaces or by imaginative acts of place-making. The case studies effectively highlight the transitory nature and temporality of space–time vis-à-vis memory, particularly within the context of *durée* theory (Bergson 1992), whereby violence and trauma inscribe fresh meanings onto a place, which over time seep into the collective memory of its community. As it layers on meaning after new meaning, prolonged spatial trauma eventually disrupts a place's existing identities (Weizman and Herscher 2011). In this context, space–time, like the recounted memories throughout this book, is fractured, fragmented and nonlinear. It is vital that we grasp the significance that structural vulnerability has within place, time and memory, as it is pivotal to understanding their performative abilities in the creation of refuge structures. Therefore, this examination into the complexity of time, its interplay with space and memory, and the collective role of all three in forming structures of refuge, allows us to comprehend the nonlinearity and continual evolution inherent in processes of refuge creation.

Methodological findings

The concept of fluidity of spatiality of refuge in this book is anchored in a remote multimodal approach inspired by Linda Tuhiwai Smith's *Decolonizing Methodologies* (2012), involving qualitative fieldwork, autoethnographic activism and memory-work. The combination of fieldnotes, textual analysis and online interviews provided a diverse data pool for the research. Importantly, these techniques amplify unheard indigenous narratives and highlight the spatial responses of Iraqis during key periods (the 2003 invasion, the sectarian violence of 2006–8, the ISIS atrocities of 2014 and the Tishreen Movement of 2019–21). The methodology follows Selina Springett's (2015) idea of palimpsest as a deep-mapping approach, intertwining feminist reflexivity, memory and oral history. More than a method, the performative practice of deep mapping forges knowledge from diverse sources, emphasizes marginalized voices and uncovers hidden potential. Through reflexivity, I used deep maps as an embodying process that reflects the spatial narratives' agency, memory, identity and imagination. Deep mapping intersects various conditions and imaginaries that define a place by transcending simple descriptions. In this book's context, the deep maps that we produce with interviewees penetrate through layers of trauma, amplify muted voices and democratize knowledge production. The narratives presented from the interviews entwine with their accompanying deep maps, reflecting temporality and the precariousness of these refuge spaces within Iraqis' memories of war, violence and displacement. These maps, which were co-created with each Iraqi interviewee, are integral to the indigenization of spatial practice (Rose-Redwood et al. 2020) and negotiate the unpredictable dynamics and ethical weight of research in trauma-ridden geographies. The methodological approach involved in making these maps pivoted on individuals' dynamism, their processual conditions and lived/felt experiences, which necessitated a creative blend of visual, textual and reflexive analysis in order to negotiate and respond to the uncertainty and volatility of such critical geographies.

This research illuminates the transformative potential of map-making, expanding its role from a tool of mere representation to one of knowledge production. It reveals the intricacy of the task of visually capturing the negotiated spatiality that is tethered to memory, imagination and trauma. Importantly, this research finds that the maps produced serve as vital platforms for both encapsulating and expressing the traumatic experiences of Iraqis. Laden with affective layers of identity, belonging and memory-work, these maps capture ephemeral meaning while also providing a dynamic account of trauma in the making – factors that emphasize the performativity of map-making as a practice (Della Dora 2009). The making of these maps functions as a potent practice into the lived experience of trauma, presenting a unique topological frame of knowledge around place-wounding. The study also uncovers the iterative technical composition of the maps, highlighting a profound empathy between diverse geographies across Iraq. This is further reflected in the amalgamation of collapsed geographies and microgeographies of memories and events across three performative scales: the conceptual, the material and the geospatial. As such, these maps serve various purposes: as a cathartic process, a visual documentation of stories at risk of fading from personal and collective memory, and as a method of practising the making of refuge spaces. These findings underscore the disruptive potential of map-making as a means of narrating trauma spatially. The research suggests the potential for a broader application of these methodologies into other critical geographies, contexts and disciplines.

In order to effectively narrate the trauma experienced by Iraqis and to engage with various intended audiences – academics, researchers, policymakers, the media and the general public – it was necessary to adopt many multifaceted modes of practice. These modes included interviews that were transcribed and translated, the thematic coding and analysis of the spatiality described, and the spatially layered moments of trauma that became the core of each map. Other creative forms of representation were also incorporated into the map-making process, such as trauma-focused pop-up books portraying the interviewees' photographs, three-dimensional depictions of the spatiality of these traumas, and postcards. This creative, 'palimpsestuous' (Dillon 2007) approach facilitated the intricate layers of knowledge production through its performative role in the methodology of deep mapping. The reach of this palimpsest of trauma narratives was further extended through an online visual archive (Murrani 2023) as well as an exhibition at the LSE Middle East Centre. These platforms allowed for a diverse range of creative expressions, all offering different perspectives on the narration of spatial trauma. These varied expressions have opened up yet more pathways for this kind of work, including the promotion of self-perceived recovery from trauma and loss, enhancing quality of life through the arts and spatial practice, and improving access to equity and justice. Furthermore, they inform public and political debates that challenge established norms, ways of thinking and modes of practice. The multilayered approach used in this research not only showcases the power and potential of interdisciplinary methods in addressing complex social issues, but also directly contributes a new framework for knowledge-making as a spatial practice in the context of Iraq, culminating in a manifesto for structures of refuge in spatial justice.

Spatial justice manifesto

This spatial justice manifesto is a testament to the resilience and creativity of the Iraqi people amid years of trauma and upheaval. It is also a call to action. It requires us to rethink our understandings of refuge and spatial practices of home, domesticity, urbanity and displacement. It engages deeply with the lived and felt experiences of people in order to propose a spatial justice that is rooted in respect, recognition and the right to refuge. The heart of spatial justice lies in its recognition and validation of the multiple, diverse ways in which people shape, negotiate and transform their built environment. It requires us to acknowledge and respect people's agency in shaping their spatial environment, as well as the deep connections that are always being made between space, identity and belonging. *Rupturing Architecture* closes with a manifesto for spatial justice that presents a critical reassessment of architecture's role within complex, multilayered contexts such as Iraq that are marked by war, domicide, urbicide, displacement, political instability and climate crises. This work initiates a meaningful dialogue about spatial justice by emphasizing the power of place-based research and creative mapping methodologies. As we have seen, these tools cross disciplinary boundaries, crafting an intricate narrative of place that illuminates the intersections of past, present and future within the lived environment. Memory emerges as an intrinsic part of this narrative: neither confined by spatial boundaries nor frozen in time, it shifts and evolves, embodying the dynamic interplay of space, place and human experience. Like refuge, memory expands beyond spatial fixity, and becomes a vehicle for understanding trauma and the way it shapes future spatial imaginaries of structures of refuge.

A spatial justice manifesto for geographies scarred by trauma must contain principles that foster the emergence and development of structures of refuge. This manifesto also addresses a secondary, yet equally vital aspect of this research: the potentialities of place-making practices for a future imbued with equitable spatiality. The manifesto thus serves as a compass for architects, designers, geographers, planners and policymakers. It is an urgent call to action informed by ten fundamental principles that are key to rebuilding and reshaping spatial justice. Each principle recognizes the importance of memory, encourages us to embrace dynamic uncertainties, advocates for deep mapping, champions the plurality of refuge and acknowledges the unique essence of each place. It is through this collective effort, and by adhering to these principles, that we can imagine and realize a just, empathetic and humane spatial future. Spatial justice emerges out of the spatial folds of each of the ten principles, gathered from the synthesis of the series of interviews and map-making with the fifteen Iraqis.

1 *Command memory's presence*
Demand that architecture encapsulates the resilient threads of shared memories and personal histories. Craft spaces that foster healing through preservation, conservation and the protection of trauma narratives.

2 *Examine dynamic flexibility*
Shape spaces that embody resilience and can adapt boldly to the shifting rhythms of change and uncertainty. Acknowledge resistance and negotiation as creative skills in shaping place.

3 *Advocate for deep mapping*
Dig beneath the surface, intertwining the emotional with the material, the past with the present, and culture with place. Craft spaces that belong both in the now and in the imaginary.

4 *Amplify refuge's plurality*
Acknowledge the varied scales and perspectives of refuge-seeking experiences. Infuse this rich diversity into adaptable and versatile designs and spatial practices of human and nonhuman dimensions.

5 *Etch uniqueness into places*
Carve the unique narrative of every place into the practice of its making, weaving threads of local traditions, textures, tales and microgeographies into the fabric of the structures.

6 *Engineer resilience*
Build fortresses of durability through time and space, ensuring that structures of refuge can endure the torrents of adversity and recover with grace, even amid different agencies of power and environment.

7 *Mandate accessibility*
Facilitate structures of refuge that champion inclusivity and intersectionality. Make every corner reachable, make every pathway negotiable and leave no one on the margins.

8 *Demand community participation*
Root equitable dialogue in local soil, incorporating community voices, environment and culture into the core of refuge spaces.

9 *Enforce sustainability*
Choose tools, processes and materials that narrate stories of environmental harmony and longevity, fashioning principles and structures that safeguard the planet.

10 *Champion spatial justice*
Embrace difference making in the role of an activist, defender and educator. Ensure that every space and every story upholds human dignity, security, empathy and empowerment.

This manifesto acknowledges the transformative potential of rupture. It functions as an agent of change, helping to navigate the labyrinth of spatial, temporal and emotional dimensions that constitute domestic, urban and border spaces of refuge. When we frame rupture in this way, as a constructive process rather than a destructive force, we can harness its potential to revolutionize how refuge is conceived, perceived, imagined and practised. The concept of spatial justice proposed here therefore transcends the physical attributes of the built environment. It explores an intricate web of human memories, trauma and displacement, and recognizes its complex layers of lived and felt experiences as integral to the performativity of spatial practices of refuge. With a focus on place-wounding and place-making, this approach to spatial justice highlights the importance of recognizing and nurturing people's resilience. It embraces a palimpsestic approach to spatial practice, and advocates for a reimagining of the *structures of refuge* themselves. These structures, rather than being merely reactive, should be proactively integrated into spatial and urban studies, as well as architectural designs and processes in post-war and conflict areas. Reflecting the dynamic nature of their environments and the resilience of their inhabitants, these spaces offer more than physical shelter – they provide spaces for healing, memory, resistance and reclamation.

This manifesto, therefore, calls for a reorientation of spatial practice. It stresses the need for a plural architecture that transcends spatial fixity by becoming socially, psychologically and culturally conscious. It advocates for a practice that understands, values and engages with the complex interplay between space, memory and justice. In this way, we can imagine an architecture of justice that not only acknowledges the scars of the past but also sows the seeds of hope for a just spatial future. This approach recognizes the complex natures of different places, appreciates the knowledge and histories rooted within them, and promotes participatory and inclusive spatial practices surrounding them. Crucial to this manifesto is an innovative understanding of memory – one that is performative and intrinsically linked to place-based research and creative mapping. In this way, memory becomes a dynamic frame that illuminates the profound relationships of making and remaking that take place between individuals and their environments. This dynamic nature of memory recognizes the influence of past experiences in sculpting present perceptions and charting paths for future actions. In the realm of spatial justice, this view informs approaches that acknowledge historical injustices while striving towards equitable spatial futures.

As we delve into the intricate fabric of refuge and memory, it becomes abundantly clear that place holds an identity interwoven with countless layers of recollections. This book underscores that the methods of place-based research and creative mapping are pivotal in unearthing these layers, facilitating a profound comprehension of spatial justice that resonates with and celebrates these memories. Memories, when shared, evolve into powerful instruments fostering community cohesion and empowerment, enabling certain groups to express their experiences, assert their rights and campaign for spatial justice. In this context, creative mapping can serve as a catalyst, providing a community with a platform for voicing and sharing their collective memories. By integrating the performativity of memory with place-based research and creative mapping, the manifesto encourages us to take several thoughtful and informed actions to redress spatial inequities. In essence, the manifesto presents a dynamic and holistic understanding of space – an understanding that honours the past, cherishes the present and envisions a more equitable and inclusive future.

In conclusion, this book serves as a resounding call to action, culminating in a manifesto for spatial justice in our wounded world. Through the experiences of Iraqis as they navigate, shape and negotiate their built environment under the tremendous pressures of war, conflict and displacement, we can find invaluable insights into the spatial practices of refuge. These dynamic and adaptable practices, borne from necessity and the indomitable human spirit, speak to the resilient potential of communities. In order to better address the unique challenges faced by these communities in trauma-ridden geographies, we must fundamentally re-evaluate our conventional modes of architectural and spatial practices. Instead of imposing top-down, one-size-fits-all solutions, the spatial justice championed within this book is dedicated to recognizing the challenges people face, foregrounding their needs, validating their lived and felt experiences, and appreciating the creativity expressed in their capacity to adapt.

This manifesto therefore proposes a radical shift in our approach to spatiality, embracing uncertainty and dynamism as key aspects of our built environment, rather than viewing them as anomalies. We must acknowledge the architecture of rupture and refuge and integrate it into mainstream spatial planning and design practices. A justice-centred approach seeks to bridge the gap between the professional expertise of architects, designers and planners, and the lived experiences and needs of the communities they serve. Architects and policymakers must commit to fostering and supporting a spatial justice that embraces change, and that recognizes and validates different spatial practices of refuge as valuable forms of knowledge and world-making. This commitment requires an openness and willingness to learn from, and engage with, communities who are intimately familiar with the spatial impacts of war, conflict and displacement. A just spatiality recognizes the value of everyday practices of refuge in creating a sense of home, community and sense of belonging amid chaos and change. A justice-centred approach must account for these refuge spaces and seek to integrate them into different forms of homing and more-than-inhabitation practices. By so doing, we can create environments that are more responsive, resilient and reflective of the communities they serve. In volatile geographies, a fixed lens will not suffice. We require a framework of knowledge that, while fragmented and nonlinear, remains both performative and imaginative. Only then can we truly address the ever-shifting spatial needs of those navigating the aftermath of trauma.

REFERENCES

Abdelmonem, M. G. (2017), *The Architecture of Home in Cairo: Socio-Spatial Practice of the Hawari's Everyday Life*, Abingdon: Routledge.

Abujidi, N. (2019), *Urbicide in Palestine: Spaces of Oppression and Resilience*, Abingdon: Routledge.

Adams-Hutcheson, G. (2017), 'Spatialising Skin: Pushing the Boundaries of Trauma Geographies', *Emotion, Space and Society*, 24: 105–12.

Ahmed, S. (2018), 'Fifteen Years of Blast Barriers in Iraq with a Kurdish Twist', *RUDAW*, 15 December. Available online: https://www.rudaw.net/english/business/15122018 (accessed 3 June 2023).

Aksamija, A., R. Majzoub and M. Philippou, eds (2021), *Design to Live: Everyday Inventions from a Refugee Camp*, Cambridge, MA: MIT Press.

Al-Ali, N. S. and D. Al-Najjar (2013), 'Introduction: Writing Trauma, Memory, and Materiality', in Al-Ali, N. S. and D. Al-Najjar (eds), *We Are Iraqis: Aesthetics and Politics in a Time of War*, xxv–xiii, Syracuse, NY: Syracuse University Press.

Al-Ali, Z. (2014), *The Struggle for Iraq's Future: How Corruption, Incompetence and Sectarianism Have Undermined Democracy*, New Haven, CT: Yale University Press.

Al-Azzawi, B. (2022), Interview with S. Murrani.

Al-Baroodi, A. (2022), Interview with S. Murrani.

Al-Harithy, H., ed. (2010), *Lessons in Post-War Reconstruction: Case Studies from Lebanon in the Aftermath of the 2006 War*, London and New York: Routledge.

Al-Hassani, R. A. (2021), 'Storytelling: Restorative Approaches to Post-2003 Iraq Peacebuilding', *Journal of Intervention and Statebuilding*, 15 (4): 510–27.

Al-Jaffal, O. (2022), 'Informal Settlements in Baghdad: Home Is Everywhere', *Assafir Al-Arabi*, 6 June. Available online: https://assafirarabi.com/en/45495/2022/06/06/informal-settlements-in-baghdad-home-is-everywhere/ (accessed 19 April 2023).

Al-Jawari, S. M., S. K. Al-Mosawy, A. A. Al-Jabari and A. N. Al-Baghdadi (2020), 'Strategic Analysis of New Cities (Case Study Basmaya City - Republic of Iraq): An Analytical Study of Strength, Weakness, Opportunity, and Threat', *IOP Conference Series: Earth and Environmental Science*, 459 (6): 062108. https://doi.org/10.1088/1755-1315/459/6/062108.

Al-Kaabi, M. (2019), 'Applied Solutions to Tackle Random Housing in the City of Basra', *Arab Gulf*, 47 (3–4): 362–411.

Al-Mamouri, A. A. (2020), 'Serious Housing Crisis Creeps up on Iraq', *Al-Monitor*, 23 July. Available online: https://www.al-monitor.com/originals/2020/07/iraq-economy-housing.html#:~:text=The%20housing%20sector%20is%20directly,work%20for%20other%20major%20sectors.&text=Member%20of%20parliament%20Hazim%20al,need%20of%20250%2C000%20housing%20units (accessed 10 February 2022).

Al-Naimi, S. (2020), 'Intensities, Part 1: In Search of Baghdad', *Platform: Provocative Timely Diverse*, 23 August. Available online: https://www.platformspace.net/home/intensities-part-1-in-search-of-baghdad-1?rq=baghdad (accessed 23 August 2023).

Al-Sabouni, M. (2016), *The Battle for Home: The Vision of a Young Architect in Syria*. Foreword by Roger Scruton, London: Thames and Hudson.

Al-Ta'ai, A. F. A. and S. S. M. Al-Ali (2022), 'The Impact of Symbolic Values in Regaining Lost Heritage Buildings After War: A Case Study from the Modernist Architectural Heritage in Mosul', in A. Versaci, H. Bougdah, N. Akagawa and N. Cavalagli (eds), *Conservation of Architectural Heritage*, 367–77. https://doi.org/10.1007/978-3-030-74482-3_29.

Ali, Z. (2018), *Women and Gender in Iraq: Between Nation-Building and Fragmentation*, Cambridge: Cambridge University Press. Available online: https://www.cambridge.org/core/product/identifier/9781108120517/type/book (accessed 22 March 2022).

Ali, Z. (2021), 'From Recognition to Redistribution? Protest Movements in Iraq in the Age of "New Civil Society"', *Journal of Intervention and Statebuilding*, 15 (4): 528–42.

Ali, Z. (2023), 'Theorising Uprisings: Iraq's Thawra Teshreen', *Third World Quarterly*, 17 January. https://doi.org/10.1080/01436597.2022.2161359.

Alkhudary, T. (2022), '"We Want a Country': The Urban Politics of the October Revolution in Baghdad's Tahrir Square', *Third World Quarterly*, 2 December 2022. https://doi.org/10.1080/01436597.2022.2141219.

Alkhudary, T. (2023), *Changing the System from Within? The Role of Opposition Parties in Consolidating Democracy in Iraqi Post-2019*, London: LSE Middle East Centre Paper Series (64). Available online: https://eprints.lse.ac.uk/118474/ (accessed 30 May 2023).

Alnsour, J. A. (2016), 'Managing Urban Growth in the City of Amman, Jordan', *Cities*, 50: 93–9.

Alobaydi, D. (2022), Interview with S. Murrani.

Alslik, G. (2008), 'Baghdad: Images and Memories', *Journal of Architectural Criticism and Theory*, 1: 49–72. Available online: https://dialnet-unirioja-es.translate.goog/servlet/articulo?codigo=4020472&_x_tr_sl=es&_x_tr_tl=en&_x_tr_hl=en&_x_tr_pto=sc (accessed 2 March 2022).

Alslik, G. (2022), Interview with S. Murrani.

Amin, A. (2016), 'On Urban Failure', *Social Research: An International Quarterly*, 83 (3): 777–98.

Amnesty International (2008), *Carnage and Dispair: Iraq Five Years On*, 17 March. Available online: https://www.amnesty.org/en/documents/mde14/001/2008/en/ (accessed 12 June 2023).

Anderson, J. L. (2006), *The Fall of Baghdad*, London: Abacus.

Andraos, A. and N. Akawi, eds (2015), *The Arab City: Architecture & Representation*, New York: Columbia Books on Architecture and the City.

Antoon, S. (2023), 'Al-Amiriyya: Once upon a Bombing in Iraq', *AlJazeera*, 13 February. Available online: https://www.aljazeera.com/opinions/2018/2/13/al-amiriyya-once-upon-a-bombing-in-iraq/ (accessed 18 February 2023).

Aprim, F. (2022), 'Northern Iraq and the Kurdistani Disputed Territories', *Modern Displomacy*, 20 November. Available online: https://moderndiplomacy.eu/2022/11/20/northern-iraq-and-the-kurdistani-disputed-territories/#_edn13 (accessed 21 November 2022).

Asquith, L. and M. Vellinga, eds (2006), *Vernacular Architecture in the Twenty-First Century: Theory, Education and Practice*, London: Taylor & Francis.
Atalay, S. (2019), 'Braiding Strands of Wellness', *Public Historian*, 41 (1): 78–89.
Atalay, S. (2020), 'Indigenous Science for a World in Crisis', *Public Archaeology*, 19 (1–4): 37–52.
Atomic Heritage Foundation (2017), 'Survivors of Hiroshima and Nagasaki', *Atomic Heritage Foundation in Partnership with National Museum of Nuclear Science & History*, 27 July. Available online: https://www.atomicheritage.org/history/survivors-hiroshima-and-nagasaki (accessed 31 May 2022).
Auslander, L. and T. Zahra, eds (2018), *Objects of War: The Material Culture of Conflict and Displacement*, Ithaca, NY: Cornell University Press.
Awan, N., T. Schneider and J. Till (2011), *Spatial Agency: Other Ways of Doing Architecture*, Abingdon: Routledge.
Azzouz, A. (2020), 'Re-Imagining Syria: Destructive Reconstruction and the Exclusive Rebuilding of Cities', *City*, 24 (5–6): 721–40.
Azzouz, A. (2022), Interview with S. Murrani.
Azzouz, A. (2023), *Domicide: Architecture, War and the Destruction of Home in Syria*, London and New York: Bloomsbury.
Bădescu, G. (2022), 'Architects as Memory Actors: Ruins, Reconstructions, and Memorials in Belgrade', *Contemporary Southeastern Europe*, 8 (2): 51–82.
Bahrani, Z. (2008), *Rituals of War: The Body and Violence in Mesopotamia*, Princeton, NJ: Princeton University Press.
Baldwin, B. (2019), 'Rifat Chadirji Archive Includes Drawings of His 1966 Building Destroyed in January 2019', *Aga Khan Documentation Centre, MIT Libraries*, 7 October. Available online: https://libraries.mit.edu/akdc/2019/10/07/rifat-chadirji-archive-includes-drawings-of-his-1966-building-destroyed-in-january-2019/ (accessed 28 February 2023).
Barad, K. (2003), 'Posthumanist Performativity: Toward an Understanding of How Matter Comes to Matter', *Signs: Journal of Women in Culture and Society*, 28 (3): 801–31.
Barad, K. (2007), *Meeting the Universe Halfway: Quantum Physics and the Entanglement of Matter and Meaning*, Durham, NC: Duke University Press.
Barakat, S., and S. Milton (2020), 'Localisation Across the Humanitarian-Development-Peace Nexus', *Journal of Peacebuilding & Development*, 15 (2): 147–63.
Barr, J. (2011), *A Line in the Sand: Britain, France and the Struggle That Shaped the Middle East*, London: Simon & Schuster.
Beirut Urban Lab (n.d.), 'About'. Available online: https://beiruturbanlab.com/en/About (accessed 3 April 2022).
Bennesved, P. (2020), 'Sheltered Society: Civilian Air Raid Shelters in Sweden – From Idea to Materiality, 1918–,1940 and Beyond', PhD Thesis, Umeå University, Malmö.
Bergson, H. (1988), *Matter and Memory*, trans. N. M. Paul, W. S. Palmer, New York: Zone Books.
Bergson, H. (1992), *The Creative Mind: An Introduction to Metaphysics*, New York: Carol Publishing Group.
Bet-Shlimon, A. (2019), *City of Black Gold: Oil, Ethnicity, and the Making of Modern Kirkuk*, Stanford, CA: Stanford University Press.
Bevan, R. (2016), *The Destruction of Memory: Architecture at War*, 2nd edn, London: Reaktion Books.
Bhabha, H. K. (1994), *The Location of Culture*, Abingdon and New York: Routledge.

Blum, V. L. and A. Secor (2014), 'Mapping Trauma: Topography to Topology', in P. Kingsbury and S. Pile (eds), *Psychoanalytic Geographies*, 103–16, London and New York: Routledge. Available online: https://www.taylorfrancis.com/books/e/9781315602806 (accessed 7 March 2022).

Blunt, A. and R. M. Dowling (2006), *Home*, London: Routledge.

Blunt, A. and A. Varley (2004), 'Geographies of Home', *Cultural Geographies*, 11 (1): 3–6.

Boano, C. (2011), "'Violent Spaces': Production and Reproduction of Security and Vulnerabilities', *Journal of Architecture*, 16 (1): 37–55.

Boano, C. (2022), Interview with S. Murrani.

Boano, C. and G. Astolfo (2020), 'Inhabitation as More-than-Dwelling. Notes for a Renewed Grammar', *International Journal of Housing Policy*, 20 (4): 555–77.

Boccagni, P. (2022), 'Homing: A Category for Research on Space Appropriation and "Home-Oriented" Mobilities', *Mobilities*, 17 (4): 1–17.

Bodenhamer, D. J., J., Corrigan and T. M. Harris, eds (2015), *Deep Maps and Spatial Narratives*, Bloomington: Indiana University Press.

Bou Akar, H. (2018), *For the War Yet to Come: Planning Beirut's Frontiers*, Stanford, CA: Stanford University Press.

Boyer, M. C. (2001), *The City of Collective Memory: Its Historical Imagery and Architectural Entertainments*, Cambridge, MA: MIT Press.

Breen, L. J. (2007), 'The Researcher "in the Middle": Negotiating the Insider/Outsider Dichotomy', *Australian Community Psychologist*, 19 (1): 163–74.

Brickell, K. (2012), 'Geopolitics of Home', *Geography Compass*, 6 (10): 575–88.

Brown, S. D. and P. Reavey (2015), 'Turning around on Experience: The 'Expanded View' of Memory within Psychology', *Memory Studies*, 8 (2): 131–50.

Brownlee, J., T. Masoud and A. Reynolds (2013), 'Tracking the "Arab Spring": Why the Modest Harvest?', *Journal of Democracy*, 24 (4): 29–44.

Bsheer, R. (2017), 'Heritage as War', *International Journal of Middle East Studies*, 49 (4): 729–34.

Butler, J. (2009), *Frames of War: When is Life Grievable?*, London and New York: Verso.

Byron, K., S. Khazanchi and D. Nazarian (2010), 'The Relationship Between Stressors and Creativity: A Meta-Analysis Examining Competing Theoretical Models', *Journal of Applied Psychology*, 95 (1): 201–12.

Cairns, S. (2004), 'Drifting: Architecture/Migrancy', in S. Cairns (ed.), *Drifting: Architecture and Migrancy*, 17–47, London and New York: Routledge.

Campos-Delgado, A. (2018), 'Counter-Mapping Migration: Irregular Migrants' Stories through Cognitive Mapping', *Mobilities*, 13 (4): 488–504.

Campus in Camps (2012), 'Collective Dictionary'. Available online: http://www.campusincamps.ps/about/ (accessed 20 July 2022).

Caruth, C., ed. (1995), *Trauma: Explorations in Memory* Baltimore, MD: Johns Hopkins University Press.

Cetorelli, V., I. Sasson, N. Shabila and G. Burnham (2017), 'Mortality and Kidnapping Estimates for the Yazidi Population in the Area of Mount Sinjar, Iraq, in August 2014: A Retrospective Household Survey', *PLOS Medicine*, 14 (5): e1002297. https://doi.org/10.1371/journal.pmed.1002297.

Chadirji, R. (1986), *Concepts and Influences: Towards a Regionalized International Architecture, 1952–1978*, London: Routledge.

Chandrasekaran, R. (2008), *Imperial Life in the Emerald City: Inside Baghdad's Green Zone*, London: Bloomsbury.

Charlesworth, E. R. (2014), *Humanitarian Architecture: 15 Stories of Architects Working after Disaster*, London and New York: Routledge.
Chatty, D. (2010), *Displacement and Dispossession in the Modern Middle East*, New York: Cambridge University Press.
Chatty, D. and N. Mansour (2011), 'Unlocking Protracted Displacement: An Iraqi Case Study', *Refugee Survey Quarterly*, 30 (4) 50–83.
Chilmeran, Y. and J. Hedström (2021), 'Reflexivity and Fieldwork in Feminist Peace Research', in O. Richmond and G. Visoka (eds), *The Palgrave Encyclopedia of Peace and Conflict Studies*, 1–7, London: Palgrave Macmillan. http://doi.org/10.1007/978-3-030-11795-5_181-1.
Cigar, N. (2014), 'Did Iraq Expect a Nuclear Desert Storm? Deterrence, Paradigms, and Operational Culture in a Weapons of Mass Destruction Environment', *War in History*, 21 (3): 274–301.
Coddington, K. and J. Micieli-Voutsinas (2017), 'On Trauma, Geography, and Mobility: Towards Geographies of Trauma', *Emotion, Space and Society*, 24: 52–6.
Cole, G. (2021), 'Pluralising Geographies of Refuge', *Progress in Human Geography*, 45 (1): 88–110.
Cole, T. (2015), '(Re)Placing the Past: Spatial Strategies of Retelling Difficult Stories', *Oral History Review*, 42 (1): 30–49.
Colomina, B. (2007), *Domesticity at War*, Cambridge, MA: MIT Press.
Corner, J. (1999), 'The Agency of Mapping: Speculation, Critique and Invention', in D. Cosgrove (ed.), *Mappings*, 213–52, London: Reaktion Books.
Coward, M. (2009), *Urbicide: The Politics of Urban Destruction*, London: Routledge.
Craps, S., B. Cheyette, A. Gibbs, S. Andermahr and L. Allwork (2015), 'Decolonizing Trauma Studies Round-Table Discussion', *Humanities*, 4 (4): 905–23.
Culcasi, K. (2010), 'Constructing and Naturalizing the Middle East', *Geographical Review*, 100 (4): 583–97.
Daiute, C. (2017), 'Narrating Refuge', *Europe's Journal of Psychology*, 13 (1): 1–15.
Damluji, M. (2010), '"Securing Democracy in Iraq": Sectarian Politics and Segregation in Baghdad, 2003-2007', *Traditional Dwellings and Settlements Review*, 21 (2): 71–87.
Das, V. (2007), *Life and Words: Violence and the Descent into the Ordinary*, Berkeley: University of California Press.
Davis, M. (2007), *Planet of Slums*, London and New York: Verso.
Davoudi, S., J. Crawford, R. Raynor, B. Reid, O. Sykes and D. Shaw (2018), 'Policy and Practice Spatial Imaginaries: Tyrannies or Transformations?', *Town Planning Review*, 89 (2): 97–124.
de Certeau, M. (1988), *The Practice of Everyday Life*, trans. S. Rendall, Berkeley and Los Angeles: University of California Press.
De Nardi, S. (2021), *Visualising Place, Memory and the Imagined*, Abingdon and New York: Routledge.
Della Dora, V. (2009), 'Performative Atlases: Memory, Materiality, and (Co-)Authorship', *Cartographica: The International Journal for Geographic Information and Geovisualization*, 44 (4): 240–55.
Dillon, S. (2007), *The Palimpsest: Literature, Criticism, Theory*, London: Bloomsbury.
Dodd, M., ed. (2019), *Spatial Practices: Modes of Action and Engagement with the City*, London and New York: Taylor & Francis.
Dodge, T. (2014), 'Can Iraq Be Saved?', *Survival*, 56 (5): 7–20.
Douglas, M. (1991), 'The Idea of a Home: A Kind of Space', *Social Research*, 58 (1): 287–307.

Drozdzewski, D., S. De Nardi and E. Waterton (2016), 'Geographies of Memory, Place and Identity: Intersections in Remembering War and Conflict: Geographies of Memory, Place and Identity', *Geography Compass*, 10 (11): 447–56.
Dyregrov, A., R. Gjestad and M. Raundalen (2002), 'Children Exposed to Warfare: A Longitudinal Study', *Journal of Traumatic Stress*, 15 (1): 59–68.
Elden, S. (2013), 'Secure the Volume: Vertical Geopolitics and the Depth of Power', *Political Geography*, 34: 35–51.
Elfversson, E., I. Gusic and K. Höglund (2019), 'The Spatiality of Violence in Post-War Cities', *Third World Thematics: A TWQ Journal*, 4 (2–3): 81–93.
Emerson, R. M., R. I. Fretz and L. L. Shaw (2011), *Writing Ethnographic Fieldnotes*, 2nd edn, Chicago, IL: University of Chicago Press.
Fanon, F. (2001), *The Wretched of the Earth*, trans. C. Farrington, London and New York: Penguin Classics.
Fathy, H. (2000), *Architecture for the Poor: An Experiment in Rural Egypt*, Chicago, IL and London: University of Chicago Press.
Feng, Z., S. Logan, G. Cupchik, U. Ritterfeld and D. Gaffin (2017), 'A Cross-Cultural Exploration of Imagination as a Process-Based Concept', *Imagination, Cognition and Personality*, 37 (1): 69–94.
Fiddian-Qasmiyeh, E., ed. (2020), *Refuge in a Moving World: Tracing Refugee and Migrant Journeys Across Disciplines*, London: UCL Press. https://doi.org/10.14324/111.9781787353176.
Fiddian-Qasmiyeh, E. and M. L. Berg (2018), 'Inaugural Editorial', *Migration and Society*, 1 (1): v–vii.
Flusser, V. (2003), *The Freedom of the Migrant: Objections to Nationalism*, ed. A. K. Finger, trans. K. Kronenberg, Urbana and Chicago: University of Illinois Press.
Frechette, J., V. Bitzas, M. Aubry, K. Kilpatrick and M. Lavoie-Tremblay (2020), 'Capturing Lived Experience: Methodological Considerations for Interpretive Phenomenological Inquiry', *International Journal of Qualitative Methods*, 19. https://doi.org/10.1177/1609406920907254.
Fromkin, D. (2001), *A Peace to End All Peace: The Fall of the Ottoman Empire and the Creation of the Modern Middle East*, New York: Henry Holt.
Gieryn, T. F. (2000), 'A Space for Place in Sociology', *Annual Review of Sociology*, 26: 463–96.
Goodman, N. (1978), *Ways of Worldmaking*, Indianapolis, IN: Hackett.
Gordon, J. (2010), *Invisible War: The United States and the Iraq Sanctions*, Cambridge, MA: Harvard University Press.
Graham, S. (2004), 'Vertical Geopolitics: Baghdad and After', *Antipode*, 36 (1): 12–23.
Graham, S. (2007), 'War and the City', *New Left Review*, 44: 121–32.
Graham, S. (2018), *Vertical: The City from Satellites to Bunkers*, London and New York: Verso.
Graham, S. and P. Healey (1999), 'Relational Concepts of Space and Place: Issues for Planning Theory and Practice', *European Planning Studies*, 7 (5): 623–46.
Graham, S. and L. Hewitt (2013), 'Getting off the Ground: On the Politics of Urban Verticality', *Progress in Human Geography*, 37 (1): 72–92.
Greene, M. J. (2014), 'On the Inside Looking In: Methodological Insights and Challenges in Conducting Qualitative Insider Research', *Qualitative Report*, 19 (29): 1–13. Available online: https://nsuworks.nova.edu/tqr/vol19/iss29/3/ (accessed 16 February 2022).

Gulick, J. (1967), 'Baghdad: Portrait of a City in Physical and Cultural Change', *Journal of the American Institute of Planners*, 33 (4): 246–55.
Gyger, H. (2019), *Improvised Cities: Architecture, Urbanization & Innovation in Peru*, Pittsburgh, PA: University of Pittsburgh Press.
Hadad, H. (2022), 'Path to Government Formation in Iraq: How Violence and Elite Sectarianism Lead to Consensus Governments', *Foundation Office Iraq*, 7 January. Available online: https://www.kas.de/en/web/syrien-irak/single-title/-/content/path-to-government-formation-in-iraq (accessed 24 April 2023).
Hadad, H. (2023), 'From Shock and Awe to Stability and Flaws: Iraq's Post-Invasion Journey', *European Council on Foreign Relations*, 25 May. Available online: https://ecfr.eu/publication/from-shock-and-awe-to-stability-and-flaws-iraqs-post-invasion-journey/#climate-change (accessed 29 May 2023).
Halbwachs, M. (1992), *On Collective Memory*, ed., trans. and intro. L. A. Coser, Chicago, IL: University of Chicago Press.
Hamdi, N. (1995), *Housing Without Houses: Participation, Flexibility, Enablement*, London: Practical Action.
Hamdi, N. (2004), *Small Change: About the Art of Practice and the Limits of Planning in Cities*, London and Sterling: Earthscan.
Hasan, S. (2022), Interview with S. Murrani.
Haught, C. (2015), 'The Role of Constraints in Creative Sentence Production', *Creativity Research Journal*, 27 (2): 160–6.
Hay, F. M. (2017), *Post-Conflict Issues of Housing, Land and Property in Iraq 2017*, Baghdad: International Organization for Migration. Available online: https://www.humanitarianlibrary.org/resource/post-conflict-issues-housing-land-and-property-iraq (accessed 7 April 2023).
Hay, F. M. (2019), *Everyday Sites of Violence and Conflict: Exploring Memories in Mosul and Tal Afar*, Baghdad: International Organization for Migration. Available online: https://iraq.iom.int/resources/everyday-sites-violence-and-conflict-exploring-memories-mosul-and-tel-afar (accessed 7 April 2023).
Heidegger, M. (1992), 'Building, Dwelling, Thinking', in D. F. Krell (ed.), *Martin Heidegger: Basic Writings*, 344–63, London and New York: Routledge.
Henson, C., D. Truchot and A. Canevello (2021), 'What Promotes Post Traumatic Growth? A Systematic Review', *European Journal of Trauma & Dissociation*, 5 (4): 1–9. https://doi.org/10.1016/j.ejtd.2020.100195.
Herranen, T. (2012), *Hundred Years of Experience: YIT 1912*, Helsinki: Edita. Available online: https://www.slideshare.net/YIT_Home/yit-englanti-taittolow1 (accessed 23 February 2023).
Herscher, A. and A. I. Siddiqi (2014), 'Spatial Violence', *Architectural Theory Review*, 19 (3): 269–77.
Hewitt, K. (1983), 'Place Annihilation: Area Bombing and the Fate of Urban Places', *Annals of the Association of American Geographers*, 73 (2): 257–84.
Heynen, H. and G. Baydar, eds (2005), *Negotiating Domesticity: Spatial Productions of Gender in Modern Architecture*, London and New York: Routledge.
Hilal, S. and A. Petti (2021), *Refugee Heritage*, Stockholm: Art and Theory.
Hilal, S. and A. Petti (2022), Interview with S. Murrani.
Hoelscher, S. and D. H. Alderman (2004), 'Memory and Place: Geographies of a Critical Relationship', *Social & Cultural Geography*, 5 (3): 347–55.

Holbraad, M., B. Kapferer and J. F. Sauma, eds (2019), *Ruptures: Anthropologies of Discontinuity in Times of Turmoil*, London: UCL Press.
hooks, b. (1990), 'Homeplace: A Site of Resistance', in *Yearning: Race, Gender, and Cultural Politics*, 41–9, Boston, MA: South End Press.
hooks, b. (2004), 'Lasting Trauma', in *Rock My Soul: Black People and Self-Esteem*, 21–34, New York: Washington Square Press.
hooks, b. (2009), *Belonging: A Culture of Place*, New York: Routledge.
Hornstein, S. (2011), *Losing Site: Architecture, Memory and Place*, Farnham: Ashgate.
Human Rights Watch (1991), 'Needless Deaths in the Gulf War: Civilian Casualties During the Air Campaign and Violations of the Laws of War', *Human Rights Watch*, 1 June. Available online: https://www.hrw.org/report/1991/06/01/needless-deaths-gulf-war/civilian-casualties-during-air-campaign-and-violations (accessed 20 June 2023).
Huyssen, A., ed. (2008), *Other Cities, Other Worlds: Urban Imaginaries in a Globalizing Age*, Durham, NC: Duke University Press.
Ibrahim, A. (2022), Interview with S. Murrani.
Ibrahim, H. (2022), 'Mega Projects Do Little to Calm Iraq's Housing Crisis', *Al-Monitor*, 19 July. Available online: https://www.al-monitor.com/originals/2022/07/mega-projects-do-little-calm-iraqs-housing-crisis (accessed 24 April 2023).
Ingold, T. (2000), 'Building, Dwelling, Living: How Animals and People Make Themselves at Home in the World', in *The Perception of the Environment: Essays on Livelihood, Dwelling and Skill*, 172–88, London: Routledge.
IOM in Iraq (2022), *IOM: UN Migration*. Available online: https://iraq.iom.int/iom-iraq (accessed 9 December 2022).
IRIN News (2005), 'Housing Problems Increase as Conflict Hits Hearth and Home', *The New Humanitarian*, 4 August. Available online: https://www.thenewhumanitarian.org/fr/node/194386 (accessed 23 February 2022).
Ismael, M. (2022), Interview with S. Murrani.
Jackson, I. (2016), 'The Architecture of the British Mandate in Iraq: Nation-Building and State Creation', *Journal of Architecture*, 21 (3): 375–417.
Jarah, S., B. Zhou, R. Abdullah, Y. Lu and W. Yu (2019), 'Urbanization and Urban Sprawl Issues in City Structure: A Case of the Sulaymaniah Iraqi Kurdistan Region', *Sustainability*, 11 (485): 1–22.
Jones, O. (2011), 'Geography, Memory and Non-Representational Geographies: Geography, Memory and Non-Representational Geographies', *Geography Compass*, 5 (12): 875–85.
Jotheri, J. (2022), Interview with S. Murrani.
Kadhum, O. (2023), 'Nation-Destroying, Emigration and Iraqi Nationhood after the 2003 Intervention', *International Affairs*, 99 (2): 587–604.
Kanekar, A. (2010), 'Between drawing and building', *The Journal of Architecture*, 15 (6): 771–94.
Karimi, P. and N. Rabbat (2016), 'The Demise and Afterlife of Artifacts', in P. Karimi and N. Rabbat (eds), *The Destruction of Cultural Heritage: From Napoléon to ISIS*, 1–24, Aggregate Architectural History Collaborative. Available online: https://www.librarystack.org/the-destruction-of-cultural-heritage-from-napoleon-to-isis/ (accessed 5 May 2022).
Kearney, A. (2016), *Violence in Place, Cultural and Environmental Wounding*, London: Routledge. Available online: https://www.taylorfrancis.com/books/9781317415763 (accessed 1 March 2023).

Khan, T., S. Abimbola, C. C. Kyobutungi and M. Pai (2022), 'How We Classify Countries and People—and Why It Matters'. *BMJ Global Health* 7(6): e009704. https://doi.org/10.1136/bmjgh-2022-009704.

Kiddey, R. (2020), 'Reluctant Refuge: An Activist Archaeological Approach to Alternative Refugee Shelter in Athens (Greece)', *Journal of Refugee Studies* 33 (3): 599–621. https://doi.org/10.1093/jrs/fey061.

Kingsmith, A. T. (2017), 'On Rupture: An Intervention into Epistemological Disruptions of Machiavelli, Hobbes, and Hume', *Journal of Speculative Philosophy*, 31 (4): 594–608.

Kitchin, R., J. Gleeson and M. Dodge (2013), 'Unfolding Mapping Practices: A New Epistemology for Cartography', *Transactions of the Institute of British Geographers*, 38 (3): 480–96.

Kostovicova, D. and E. Knott (2022), 'Harm, Change and Unpredictability: The Ethics of Interviews in Conflict Research', *Qualitative Research*, 22 (1): 56–73.

Kumaraswamy, P. R. (2006), 'Who Am I? The Identity Crisis in the Middle East', *Middle East Review of International Affairs*, 10 (1): 63–73.

Lahoud, A. (2010), 'Post-Traumatic Urbanism', *Architectural Design*, 80 (5): 14–23.

Lane, B. M., ed. (2007), *Housing and Dwelling: Perspectives on Modern Domestic Architecture*, London and New York: Routledge.

Larkin, C. (2010), 'Remaking Beirut: Contesting Memory, Space, and the Urban Imaginary of Lebanese Youth', *City & Community*, 9 (4): 414–42.

Lefebvre, H. (1991), *The Production of Space*, trans. D. Nicholson-Smith, Oxford: Blackwell.

Lichtman, S. A. (2006), 'Do-It-Yourself Security: Safety, Gender, and the Home Fallout Shelter in Cold War America', *Journal of Design History*, 19 (1): 39–55.

Liggett, H. and D. C. Perry, eds (1995), *Spatial Practices: Critical Explorations in Social/Spatial Theory*, Thousand Oaks, CA: SAGE.

Loveday, C. (2018), *The Brain: What it Does, How it Works and How it Affects Behavior*, London: Welbeck Publishing.

Makdisi, U. S. and P. A. Silverstein, eds (2006), *Memory and Violence in the Middle East and North Africa*, Bloomington: Indiana University Press.

Makiya, K. (1998), *Republic of Fear: The Politics of Modern Iraq*, updated edn, Berkeley: University of California Press.

Malabou, C. (2008), *What Should We Do With Our Brain?* 1st edn, New York: Fordham University Press.

Malabou, C. (2012), *The New Wounded: From Neurosis to Brain Damage*, 1st edn, New York: Fordham University Press.

Malko, H. (2019), 'Heritage Wars: A Cultural Genocide in Iraq', in J. S. Bachman (ed.), *Cultural Genocide: Law, Politics, and Global Manifestations*, 207–26, Abingdon and New York: Routledge.

Marston, S. A. and S. De leeuw (2013), 'Creativity and Geography: Toward A Politicized Intervention', *Geographical Review*, 103 (2): iii–xxvi.

Massey, D. B. (1993), 'Power-Geometry and a Progressive Sense of Place', in J. Bird, B. Curtis, T. Putnam and L. Tickner (eds), *Mapping the Futures: Local Cultures, Global Change*, 59–69, London: Routledge.

Massey, D. B. (1994), 'A Place Called Home?', in D. B. Massey, *Space, Place, and Gender*, 157–74, Minneapolis: University of Minnesota Press.

Massey, D. B. (2005), *For Space*, London and Thousand Oaks, CA: SAGE.

Merie, U. (2022), Interview with S. Murrani.

Merie, U. A. K. (2021), 'Heritage, Architecture and the Establishment of National Identity', Conference Paper, University of Al-Qadisiyah. http://rgdoi.net/10.13140/RG.2.2.19677.54241.

Merkel, B., S. W. Al-Muqdadi, N. S. Abdalwahab, and Z. R. Abdulla (2021), 'A Green and Sustainable Vision for Basra', in F. Sharefeddine (ed.), *Water Is Life: Perspectives on Water in the Land of Two Streams*, 138–65. Berlin: Elbarlament. https://elbarlament.org/wp-content/uploads/2022/03/WaterIsLife_2.pdf (accessed 3 July 2023).

Middleton, D. and S. D. Brown (2005), *The Social Psychology of Experience: Studies in Remembering and Forgetting*, London and Thousand Oaks, CA: SAGE.

Mohammed-Amin, R. K. (2022), Interview with S. Murrani.

Monteyne, D. (2011), *Fallout Shelter: Designing for Civil Defense in the Cold War*, Minneapolis: University of Minnesota Press.

Moshenska, G. (2015), 'Spaces for Children: School Gas Chambers and Air Raid Shelters in Second World War Britain', in H. Orange (ed.), *Reanimating Industrial Spaces: Conducting Memory Work in Post-Industrial Societies*, 125–37, Walnut Creek, CA: Left Coast.

'Mosul Destroys Iconic Building Used by ISIS for Gruesome Killings' (2019), *The National*, 15 January. Available online: https://www.thenationalnews.com/world/mena/mosul-destroys-iconic-building-used-by-isis-for-gruesome-killings-1.813704 (accessed 21 February 2023)

Mousa, S. (2022), 'The Tishreen Museum: A Project to Document an Uprising Ends up Destroyed', *Jummar*, 3 October. Available online: https://jummar.media/en/1799 (accessed 30 May 2023).

Moussa, Z. (2022), 'The Campaign to Demolish Encroachments in Iraq: A Fire That Stung Millions', *Assafir Al-Arabi*, 28 May. Available online: https://assafirarabi.com/en/45344/2022/05/28/the-campaign-to-demolish-encroachments-in-iraq-a-fire-that-stung-millions/ (accessed 19 April 2023).

Mumtaz, B. and I. Thung (2020), *Basra Urban Profile*, October. Available online: https://unhabitat.org/sites/default/files/2021/03/basra_urban_profile_-_english.pdf (accessed 20 April 2023).

Murad, N. (2017), *The Last Girl: My Story of Captivity, and My Fight against the Islamic State*, New York: Tim Duggan Books.

Murrani, F. (2022), Interview with S. Murrani.

Murrani, S. (2016), 'Baghdad's Thirdspace: Between Liminality, Anti-Structures and Territorial Mappings', *Cultural Dynamics*, 28 (2): 189–210.

Murrani, S. (2017), 'Estranged Space Appropriated', in M.-D. Hosale, S. Murrani and A. de Campo (eds), *Worldmaking as Techné: Exploring Worlds of Participatory Art, Architecture, and Music*, 296–319, Cambridge, ONT: Riverside Architectural Press.

Murrani, S. (2019), 'Urban Creativity through Displacement and Spatial Disruption', in M. Edema Leary-Owhin and J. P. McCarthy (eds), *The Routledge Handbook of Henri Lefebvre, the City and Urban Society*, 402–10, London and New York: Routledge.

Murrani, S. (2020), 'Contingency and Plasticity: The Dialectical Re-Construction of the Concept of Home in Forced Displacement', *Culture & Psychology*, 26 (2): 173–86.

Murrani, S. (2023), *Ruptured Domesticity Visual Archive*. Available online: https://rupturedomesticity.org/ (accessed 19 March 2023).

Murrani, S., H. Lloyd and I.-C. Popovici (2023), 'Mapping Home, Memory and Spatial Recovery in Forced Displacement', *Journal of Social and Cultural Geography*, 24 (8): 1305–23. https://doi.org/10.1080/14649365.2022.2055777.

Mustafa, B. (2022), 'All About Iraq: Re-Modifying Older Slogans and Chants in Tishreen [October] Protests', *Journal of Asian and African Studies*, 85(3): 401–20. https://doi.org/10.1177/00219096211069644.

Nilsen, A. G. (2016), 'Power, Resistance and Development in the Global South: Notes Towards a Critical Research Agenda', *International Journal of Politics, Culture, and Society*, 29 (3): 269–87.

Nixon, R. (2011), *Slow Violence and the Environmentalism of the Poor*, Cambridge, MA: Harvard University Press.

OCHA ReliefWeb (2022), 'Iraq: Key Figures'. Available online: https://reliefweb.int/country/irq#maps-infographics (accessed 13 January 2023)

Oliver, P., ed. (1975), *Shelter, Sign & Symbol*, London: Barrie & Jenkins.

Oliver, P. (2003), *Dwellings: The Vernacular House Worldwide*, London and New York: Phaidon.

Page, A. (2016), 'Planning Permanent Air Raid Precautions', *Urban History*, 43 (1): 117–34.

Pain, R. (2015), 'Intimate War', *Political Geography*, 44: 64–73.

Pain, R. (2019), 'Chronic Urban Trauma: The Slow Violence of Housing Dispossession', *Urban Studies*, 56 (2): 385–400.

Pain, R. (2021), 'Geotrauma: Violence, Place and Repossession', *Progress in Human Geography*, 45 (5): 972–89.

Pasquetti, S. and R. Sanyal, eds (2020), 'Introduction: Global Conversations on Refuge'*Displacement: Global Conversations on Refuge*, 1–16, Manchester: Manchester University Press. Available online: https://www.manchesterhive.com/view/9781526123473/9781526123473.00007.xml (accessed 11 May 2022).

Pat-Horenczyk, R. and D. Brom (2007), 'The Multiple Faces of Post-Traumatic Growth', *Applied Psychology*, 56 (3): 379–85.

Petersen, A. (1999), *Dictionary of Islamic Architecture*, London and New York: Routledge.

Petrescu, D., ed. (2007), *Altering Practices: Feminist Politics and Poetics of Space*, London and New York: Routledge.

Pfiffner, J. P. (2010), 'US Blunders in Iraq: De-Baathification and Disbanding the Army', *Intelligence and National Security*, 25 (1): 76–85.

Pilav, A. (2020), '"Architects in War": Wartime Destruction and Architectural Practice during the Siege of Sarajevo', *Journal of Architecture*, 25 (6): 697–716. https://doi.org/10.1080/13602365.2020.1800793.

Porteous, J. D. and S. E. Smith (2001), *Domicide: The Global Destruction of Home*, Montreal: McGill-Queen's University Press.

Powell, K. A. (2008), 'ReMapping the City: Palimpsest, Place, and Identity in Art Education Research', *Studies in Art Education*, 50 (1): 6–21.

Preston Blier, S. (2006), 'Vernacular Architecture', in C. Tilley, W. Keane, S. Küchler, M. Rowlands and P. Spyer (eds), *Handbook of Material Culture*, 230–53, London and Thousand Oaks, CA: SAGE.

Przybylinski, S. (2023), 'Spatial Justice', in J. Ohlsson and S. Przybylinski (eds), T*heorising Justice: A Primer for Social Scientists*, 191–204. Bristol: Bristol University Press.

Pyla, P. (2008), 'Back to the Future: Doxiadis's Plans for Baghdad', *Journal of Planning History*, 7 (1): 3–19.

Qasha, R. (2022), Interview with S. Murrani.

Rabbat, N. (2003), 'Hassan Fathy and the Identity Debate', in G. Tawadros and S. Campbell (eds), *Fault Lines: Contemporary African Art and Shifting Landscapes*, 196–203,

London: Institute of International Visual Arts in collaboration with the Forum for African Arts and the Prince Claus Fund.
Rabbat, N. (2018), 'The Hidden Hand: Edward Said's Orientalism and Architectural History', *Journal of the Society of Architectural Historians*, 77 (4): 388–96.
Rabbat, N. (2022), Interview with S. Murrani.
Rajagopalan, M. (2017), *Building Histories: The Archival and Affective Lives of Five Monuments in Modern Delhi*, Chicago, IL and London: University of Chicago Press.
Rashid, M. and D. Alobaydi (2015), 'Territory, Politics of Power, and Physical Spatial Networks: The Case of Baghdad, Iraq', *Habitat International*, 50: 180–94.
Ratnam, C. and D. Drozdzewski (2020), 'Detour: Bodies, Memories, and Mobilities in and around the Home', *Mobilities*, 15 (6): 757–75.
Reavey, P. (2017), 'Scenic Memory: Experience through Time–Space', *Memory Studies*, 10 (2): 107–11.
Richards, R. (2010), 'Everyday Creativity: Process and Way of Life – Four Key Issues', in J. C. Kaufman and R. J. Sternberg (eds), *The Cambridge Handbook of Creativity*, 189–215, Cambridge: Cambridge University Press. Available online: https://www.cambridge.org/core/product/identifier/9780511763205%23c51366-1633/type/book_part (accessed 14 March 2022).
Roberts, L. (2016), 'Deep Mapping and Spatial Anthropology', *Humanities*, 5 (1): 1–7.
Roccu, R. and S. Salem (2019), 'Making and Unmaking Memories: The Politics of Time in the Contemporary Middle East', *Middle East Critique*, 28 (3): 219–26.
Rose-Redwood, R., N. Blu Barnd, A. H. Lucchesi, A. Hetoevėhotohke'e, S. Dias and W. Patrick (2020), 'Decolonizing the Map: Recentering Indigenous Mappings', *Cartographica: The International Journal for Geographic Information and Geovisualization*, 55 (3): 151–62.
Roy, A. (2001), 'Traditions of the Modern: A Corrupt View', *Traditional Dwellings and Settlements Review*, 12 (2): 7–19.
Roy, A. (2005), 'Urban Informality: Toward an Epistemology of Planning', *Journal of the American Planning Association*, 71 (2): 147–58.
Roy, A. (2011), 'Slumdog Cities: Rethinking Subaltern Urbanism', *International Journal of Urban and Regional Research*, 35 (2): 223–38.
Roy, A. and N. AlSayyad, eds (2004), *Urban Informality: Transnational Perspectives from the Middle East, Latin America, and South Asia*, Lanham, MD: Lexington Books.
Rudofsky, B. (1987), *Architecture Without Architects: A Short Introduction to Non-Pedigreed Architecture*, Albuquerque: University of New Mexico Press.
Rugo, D. (2023), 'The Patch as Method: The Arts' Contribution towards Understandings of Conflict', *International Political Science Review*. https://doi.org/10.1177/01925121231177442.
Rundstrom, R. (2009), 'Counter-Mapping', in R. Kitchen and N. Thrift (eds), *International Encyclopedia of Human Geography*, 314–18, Amsterdam: Elsevier. https://doi.org/10.1016/B978-008044910-4.00017-1.
Saad, M., K. Rady and Y. Zohdi (2019), 'Artists: Creators of Social Change', *Baghdad Tahrir Art*. Available online: https://baghdadtahrirart.net/about/ (accessed 29 May 2023).
Sabah, N. (2022), Interview with S. Murrani.
Sabie, D., S. Sabie, C. Ekmekcioglu, Y. Rohanifar, F. Hashim, S. Easterbrook and S. I. Ahmed (2019), 'Exile Within Borders: Understanding the Limits of the Internally Displaced People (IDPs) in Iraq', *Proceedings of the Fifth Workshop on Computing within Limits*, 1: 1–16. https://doi.org/10.1145/3338103.3338104.

Said, E. (1979), *Orientalism*, New York: Vintage.
Said, E. (1993), *Culture and Imperialism*, London, Vintage Books.
Said, E. (2000), 'Invention, Memory, and Place', *Critical Inquiry*, 26 (2): 175–92.
Said, E. (2004), *From Oslo to Iraq and the Road Map*, New York: Vintage.
Salvia, R., P. Serra, I. Zambon, M. Cecchini and L. Salvati (2018), 'In-Between Sprawl and Neo-Rurality: Sparse Settlements and the Evolution of Socio-Demographic Local Context in a Mediterranean Region', *Sustainability*, 10 (10): 3670.
Sameer, S. A. (2022), Interview with S. Murrani.
Santos, B. de Sousa (2016), *Epistemologies of the South: Justice against Epistemicide*, London and New York: Routledge.
Sassoon, J. (2011), *The Iraqi Refugees: The New Crisis in the Middle East*, London and New York: Bloomsbury.
Schalk, M., R. Mazé, T. Kristiansson and M. Fanni (2017), 'Anticipating Feminist Futures of Spatial Practice', in M. Schalk, T. Kristiansson and R. Mazé (eds), *Feminist Futures of Spatial Practice: Materialisms, Activisms, Dialogues, Pedagogies, Projections*, 13–24, Baunach: AADR.
Scott-Smith, T. (2020), 'Introduction: Places of Partial Protection: Refugee Shelter since 2015', in T. Scott-Smith and M. E. Breeze (eds), *Structures of Protection? Rethinking Refugee Shelter*, 1–15, New York: Berghahn Books.
Scranton, R. (2007), 'Walls and Shadows: The Occupation of Baghdad', *City*, 11 (3): 277–92.
Selim, G. (2016), *Unfinished Places: The Politics of (Re)making Cairo's Old Quarters*, London: Routledge.
Selim, G. (2017), 'Legitimizing Everyday Tradition: The Spatial Narrative of Modernity in Cairene Old Quarters', *Traditional Dwellings and Settlements Review*, 28 (2): 53–69. Available online: https://eprints.whiterose.ac.uk/121729/ (accessed 3 July 2022).
Selim, G. (2022), '(Re)connecting with Wounded Spaces: Encountering Memory, Place and Narrative in Cairo's Historic Landscape', in N. AlSayyad (ed.) R*outledge Handbook on Cairo Histories, Representations and Discourses*, 477–82, London: Routledge.
Shadid, A. (2006), *Night Draws near: Iraq's People in the Shadow of America's War*, New York: Picador.
Shelter Cluster and UN-Habitat (2021), *The Status of Housing Rehabilitation Programs in Iraq in the Post ISIL-Conflict*, *Global Shelter Cluster*, 13 April, Iraq: Aziz Abultimman. Available online: https://sheltercluster.org/iraq/documents/status-housing-rehab-programs-iraq-post-isil-conflict-en (accessed 3 July 2023).
Shields, R. (2013), *Spatial Questions: Cultural Topologies and Social Spatialisations*, Los Angeles, CA: SAGE.
Shuker, Z. (2022), Interview with S. Murrani.
Shuker, Z. (2023), 'The Gender Dimension of the Climate Crisis in Iraq', *1001 Iraqi Thoughts*, 21 May. Available online: https://1001iraqithoughts.com/2023/05/21/the-gender-dimensions-of-the-climate-crisis-in-iraq/ (accessed 30 May 2023).
Siddiqi, A. I. (2017), 'On Humanitarian Architecture: A Story of a Border', *Humanity: An International Journal of Human Rights, Humanitarianism, and Development*, 8 (3): 519–21. https://doi.org/10.1353/hum.2017.0031.
Siddiqi, A. I. (2022), Interview with S. Murrani.
Siddiqi, A. I. and N. X. M. Tadiar (2021), 'Insurgent Domesticities', Center for the Study of Social Difference, Columbia University, New York. Available online: https://www.socialdifference.columbia.edu/projects-/insurgent-domesticities (accessed 5 April 2022).

Singh, A. L., A. Gola, L. Beeckmans and H. Heynen (2020), 'Displacement & Domesticity Since 1945: Refugees, Migrants and Expats Making Homes, Following the EAHN's Sixth Thematic Conference (Brussels, 27–28 March 2019)', *Architectural Histories*, 8 (1): 1–9.

Smith, L. T. (2012), *Decolonizing Methodologies: Research and Indigenous Peoples*, 2nd edn, London: Zed Books.

Soja, E. W. (1996), *Thirdspace: Journeys to Los Angeles and Other Real-and-Imagined Places*, Malden, MA: Blackwell.

Soja, E. W. (2010), *Seeking Spatial Justice*, Minneapolis: University of Minnesota Press.

Sorkin, M. (2011), *All over the Map: Writing on Buildings and Cities*, London and New York: Verso.

Sorkin, M. and D. Sharp, eds (2021), *Open Gaza: Architectures of Hope*, Cairo: American University in Cairo Press.

Springett, S. (2015), 'Going Deeper or Flatter: Connecting Deep Mapping, Flat Ontologies and the Democratizing of Knowledge', *Humanities*, 4: 623–36. Available online: https://www.mdpi.com/2076-0787/4/4/623 (accessed 3 March 2023).

Springett, S. (2019), 'Deep Mapping the River: A Palimpsest', in R. Abeliovich and E. Seroussi (eds), *Borderlines: Essays on Mapping and The Logic of Place*, 91–105, Warsaw: De Gruyter Poland. https://doi.org/10.2478/9783110623758-007.

Stanley, A. (2009), 'Just Space or Spatial Justice? Difference, Discourse, and Environmental Justice'. *Local Environment*, 14 (10): 999–1014. https://doi.org/10.1080/13549830903277417.

Stoppani, T. (2016), 'Architecture and Trauma', in Y. Ataria, D. Gurevitz, H. Pedaya and Y. Neria (eds), *Interdisciplinary Handbook of Trauma and Culture*, 133–49, New York: Springer.

Sultan, R. (2022), Interview with S. Murrani.

Tedeschi, R. G. and L. G. Calhoun (2004), 'Posttraumatic Growth: Conceptual Foundations and Empirical Evidence', *Psychological Inquiry*, 15 (1): 1–18.

Tezcür, G. M. (2022), *Kurds and Yezidis in the Middle East: Shifting Identities, Borders, and Experience of Minority Communities*, London and New York: I. B. Tauris.

The Home Office (2012), *The Protection of Your Home against Air Raids*, (reprinted from 1938 edition), Oxford: Old House Books.

The White House (2003), *Apparatus of Lies: Saddam's Disinformation and Propaganda 1990–2003*, The White House Global Communications. Available online: https://georgewbush-whitehouse.archives.gov/ogc/apparatus/index.html (accessed 20 February 2023).

Thomson, P. and S. V. Jaque (2019), *Creativity, Trauma and Resilience*, Lanham, MD: Lexington Books.

Till, K. E. (2012), 'Wounded Cities: Memory-Work and a Place-Based Ethics of Care', *Political Geography*, 31 (1): 3–14.

Till, K. E., J. Sundberg, W. Pullan, C. Psaltis, C. Makriyianni, R. Zincir Celal, M. O. Samani and L. Dowler (2013), 'Interventions in the Political Geographies of Walls', *Political Geography*, 33: 52–62.

Travers, A. (2021), 'Seven Years in Camps: Life for the Abandoned Victims of IS', *Open Democracy* 13 October. Available online: https://www.opendemocracy.net/en/north-africa-west-asia/seven-years-in-camps-life-for-the-abandoned-victims-of-is/ (accessed 23 March 2023).

Tschumi, B. (1999), *Architecture and Disjunction*, Cambridge, MA: MIT Press.

Tuan, Y. F. (1979), *Landscapes of Fear*, 1st edn, New York: Pantheon.

UN-Habitat (2017), 'New Research Finds 3.2 Million Iraqis Living in Informal Settlements', *UN-Habitat*, 19 September. Available online: https://unhabitat.org/new-research-finds-3-2-million-iraqis-living-in-informal-settlements (accessed 19 April 2023).

UNHCR (2020), 'Iraq: Refugee and IDP Population Map', UNHCR Operational Data Portal, 21 January. Available online: https://data.unhcr.org/en/documents/details/73530 (accessed 22 September 2022).

UNHCR (2021), 'IRAQ: Camp Closure Status', UNHCR Operational Data Portal, 24 January. Available online: https://data.unhcr.org/en/documents/details/84406 (accessed 22 September 2022).

Vigh, H. (2006), 'The Colour of Destruction: On Racialization, Geno-Globality and the Social Imaginary in Bissau', *Anthropological Theory*, 6 (4): 481–500.

Wade, S. (2011), *Air-Raid Shelters of World War II: Family Stories of Survival in the Blitz*, Barnsley: Remember When.

Wadi, A. (2022), Interview with S. Murrani.

Waite, M., ed. (2012), *Oxford English Dictionary*, Oxford: Oxford University Press.

Warren, J. and I. Fethi (1982), *Traditional Houses in Baghdad*, Horsham: Coach Publishing.

Weizman, E. (2017), *Hollow Land: Israel's Architecture of Occupation*, London and New York: Verso.

Weizman, E. and A. Herscher (2011), 'Conversation: Architecture, Violence, Evidence', *Future Anterior: Journal of Historic Preservation, History, Theory, and Criticism*, 8 (1): 111–23.

Wertsch, J. V. and H. L. Roediger (2008), 'Collective Memory: Conceptual Foundations and Theoretical Approaches', *Memory*, 16 (3): 318–26.

Wilson, A. (2012), 'Intimacy', in V. Rosner and G. Pratt (eds), *The Global and the Intimate*, 31–56, New York: Columbia University Press. https://doi.org/10.7312/columbia/9780231154499.003.0001.

Wilson, A. (2016), 'The Infrastructure of Intimacy', *Signs*, 41 (2): 247–80.

Wimmer, A. (2003), 'Democracy and Ethno-Religious Conflict in Iraq', *Survival*, 45 (4): 111–34.

Windhauser, B. (2022), 'Walled in, Out of Sight: The Contested Urban Environment of Baghdad', *Journal of Illicit Economies and Development*, 4 (3): 370–81.

Wing, J. (2023), 'Iraqi Govt Wants To End Displacement In 6 Months', *Musings on Iraq*, 18 April. Available online: http://musingsoniraq.blogspot.com/2023/04/iraqi-govt-wants-to-end-displacement-in.html (accessed 19 April 2023).

Woods, L. (1993), *War and Architecture*, New York: Princeton Architectural Press.

Woods, L. (2015), *Slow Manifesto: Lebbeus Woods Blog*, ed. Clare Jacobson, New York: Princeton Architectural Press.

Wright, P. (2021), *The Village That Died for England: Tyneham and the Legend of Churchill's Pledge*, London: Repeater Books.

Young, I. M. (2011), *Justice and the Politics of Difference*. Princeton, NJ: Princeton University Press.

INDEX